I0831795

DAVID FOSTER

David Foster

The Satirist of Australia

Susan Lever

Youngstown, New York

Printed in the United States of America

Library of Congress Cataloging-in-Publication Data
Lever, Susan, 1950-

David Foster : the satirist of Australia / Susan Lever.
p. cm.
Includes bibliographical references and index.
ISBN 978-1-934043-98-1 (alk. paper)
1. Foster, David, 1944–2. Authors, Australian—20th century—Biography. 3. Australia—In literature. I. Title.
PR9619.3.F6Z75 2008
823—dc22
[B]

2007041667

Cover photograph of David Foster by Loui Seselja on 21/1/1991.
NL36770. Permission from National Library of Australia.

In memory of Geoffrey Dutton (1922–1998)
and Helen Daniel (1946–2000),
great supporters of Australian writing

Table of Contents

Foreword

One dilemma in particular exercised the generation of Australian writers who came into prominence during the 1970s: how to escape from the large shadow cast by Patrick White's fame and achievement. By the middle of the decade, White had emerged as a figure of international literary standing. Almost single-handedly, it seemed, he had led Australian fiction out of the ghetto of colonial, provincial, and regional writing. At the time, the only novelist who might have challenged that preeminence, Christina Stead, was generally overlooked by the reading public and even by most academic and professional critics. Besides, by far the greater part of her creative life had been spent as an expatriate who had turned her back on Australian concerns and preoccupations. White, by contrast, had made the difficult decision of returning to Australia to explore his tormented and paradoxical reactions to Australian life, to a world where he felt increasingly out of place and out of sympathy with the temper of the age. The novels and short stories he in wrote in self-imposed semi-isolation in Castle Hill and later in Centennial Park determined the contours of the landscape of Australian fiction in the latter half of the twentieth century. His influence was all-pervasive; younger writers were inevitably drawn to following in his footsteps, yet all felt the imperative to avoid the stigma of imitation and derivativeness and to find their own individual and characteristic voices.

Of the writers of that generation, David Foster—who was born in 1944, thirty-two years after White—resolved that conundrum with the greatest originality and panache. His outrageous fables chronicle the lives of men and women (though mostly men), and are wholly remote from White's patrician background and inclinations, despite the elder writer's attempts to enter into the minds and souls of outcasts, the flotsam and jetsam of modern Australian society. Foster writes about rock musicians and the exponents of martial arts, and about country postmen and petty criminals; his diction is colloquial, vulgar, and frequently obscene; his prose lacks the high-modernist intricacy and rhetorical elevation of the notorious purple passages scattered throughout White's fiction. For all that, the two writers have much in common, particularly their dismay at the world they inhabit—White by choice, Foster by the accident of birth—and the shadowy and ambiguous possibilities of other worlds and other ways of life that each had glimpsed. Both addressed time and again the same riddle: does this mysterious land, populated by the refuse of the British Empire and by those who had fled Europe's brutality, embody values or ideals worthy of respect and allegiance? The answer for both writers seems to be largely negative: only the landscape and those of the continent's original inhabitants who had not been corrupted by the newcomers—the colonisers or invaders—offer a glimmer of something that might be of value and worthy of preservation. Otherwise, both writers could glimpse only bleakness, corruption, and decadence in the rituals of domestic, cultural, and political Australian life. Inevitably, therefore, both turned to satire in order to articulate their anguish; this satire was tempered by the appeal of a visionary Gnosticism in White's case, and Foster's satire was rendered vicious by a similarly Gnostic inclination, which has led him to explore a bizarre species of quasi-theological mysticism.

Susan Lever's comprehensive study of Foster's work and career rightly emphasises the fundamental source of Foster's satire: not the grace and urbanity of Horace, but Juvenal's fierce diatribes. She is also correct in pointing out that in Foster's work—as in Juvenal's—there is no suggestion, not even a hint, that the purpose of satire is to improve or reform society. Instead, in a series of novels, novellas, short stories, poems, and occasional essays, Foster has raged against the stupidity, folly, venality, and spiritual emptiness of his fellow Australians by exploiting the traditional modes of the most savage kind of satire: invective, hyperbole, obscenity, grotesque (generally inarticulate) characters, and outrageously intricate narrative structures. In short, in most of his works Foster has set out to offend and discomfort; more often than not, he has succeeded in bringing off that not inconsiderable feat.

Pointing the blowtorch at one's compatriots is a risky business. Satirical excess may itself prove excessive. The kind of satire Foster practises is always in danger of dissolving into rant and incoherence. And, above all, offending everyone almost indiscriminately and upsetting all manner of ethical, social, cultural, and political applecarts can have unhappy consequences for a writer's career. Accordingly, Foster has never been a popular or fashionable writer. Even winning the Miles Franklin award (the nation's most prestigious literary prize) for *The Glade Within The Grove* produced only a small and temporary improvement in his fortunes. Such relative lack of success—despite enthusiastic support by some (though by no means all) members of what is sometimes referred to as the literary community—has proved irksome for Foster. In recent years he (along with many others) has been prone to blame the neglect of serious writing on two factors: the decline in cultural literacy among the reading public and the mindless pursuit of easy profits by publishers. Equally—and this may prove just as significant a source of frustration—he has failed to provoke the scandalous notoriety that contemporary exponents of satirical invective have achieved in other parts of the world.

The careers of the French writer Michel Houellebecq and of the Austrian poet, novelist, and playwright Elfriede Jelinek provide a poignant contrast to Foster's. Each of these writers has travelled down what is essentially the same path. Houellebecq has scandalised the French literary establishment, not merely on account of his outrageous subject matter that constantly mocks and pillories the cant and hypocrisy of contemporary social and cultural life in France, but equally through his contempt for the preoccupation with fine style that still dominates most of French literary culture. Like her notorious predecessor Thomas Bernhard, Elfriede Jelinek has, in work after work, poured bucketsful of scorn over her compatriots' refusal to acknowledge their shameful past, their persisting dedication to Nazism, and their cynically sentimental investment in images of Austrian charm and civilisation which mingle adulation for great cultural icons (Mozart and Bruckner for instance) with the saccharine clichés of *The Sound of Music*. Both Houellebecq and Jelinek, like Bernhard before them, have been subjected to vicious attacks by politicians and by the conservative press. They have been hounded and reviled. Whenever a new work by either of these writers appears, a noisy public debate is conducted in the media for weeks, sometimes for months. They are, in short, celebrities, even if their fame is of a negative kind. Besides, both Houellebecq and Jelinek have been awarded some of the world's leading literary awards. Houellebecq won the lucrative international IMPAC literary prize for *Platform*, the novel first published (with ghastly prescience) a few days before 11 September 2001. In 2004 Jelinek was awarded the Nobel Prize for Literature, thus provoking even more outrage and teeth-gnashing among conservative Austrians—the majority, it would seem, of that small nation's population.

Such *succès d'éstime et de scandale* has eluded Foster. For better or worse, literature does not play a central role in Australian public and political life. Literary scandals rarely hit the headlines unless as a matter of fraud, alleged plagiarism, or similar misdemeanours. It is true that Foster has come in for a fair share of adverse criticism from every point of the literary and cultural compass: from conservatives as much as from left-leaning critics and commentators, from feminists and from members of almost every ethnic or religious minority. The debate has been vituperative at times, and Foster has been known to give as good as he received. Yet, by and large, all this has been confined to the academy, to the pages of literary journals, to discussions at writers' festivals, and to late-night radio programs. For the public at large, Foster's work is mostly a source of tedium and irritation. They much prefer the relative simplicities of his more popular contemporaries. Susan Lever records a university student's reaction to *The Glade Within The Grove*: 'It's a beaut book...Why isn't this bloke as famous as Peter Carey?'

The reason for that is the immaturity of Australian cultural life. In this country at least, prophets remain generally unheeded. Gresham's Law holds true in matters literary and cultural. Where Foster is concerned, that is very much our loss. What he says about us may not be palatable. The only glimmer of hope he seems capable of offering, the weird self-castrating theology jokingly embodied in several of his works (anticipating by some years Houellebecq's burlesque admiration for the Raelians), is unlikely to attract many adherents. Yet, in generations to come, his writing will be remembered (if anything is remembered) when other, more fashionable writers will be represented by mouldering, unwanted volumes on the shelves of second-hand bookshops or languishing in supermarket cartons at charity bazaars. Susan Lever's sympathetic study of a difficult but rewarding writer will do much, I trust, to rekindle interest in this most individual and challenging of our contemporaries, Patrick White's worthy successor.

Andrew Riemer

Chief Book Reviewer for the *Sydney Morning Herald*

ACKNOWLEDGMENTS

David Foster's writing has fascinated me ever since I encountered *Moonlite* in the early 1980s, so my first debt is to him for a series of witty, baffling, profound, and always disconcerting novels. Foster has also helped in the preparation of this book by allowing access to his papers in the Australian Defence Force Academy (ADFA) Library, permission to quote from his novels and letters, and providing information about his life and his publishing career. He has read the manuscript and added comments on aspects of his life (indicated in italics in the text), though I am responsible for all the discussion of his texts. I am grateful to the late Geoffrey Dutton whose careful preservation of many letters from Foster has formed the basis for the biographical elements of this book, and to Robin Lucas for permission to quote from Dutton's letters. Andrew Riemer has shared my admiration for these novels and has kindly agreed to write the Foreword for this study.

While researching and writing this book, I have worked at the Australian Defence Force Academy campus of the University of New South Wales, and I have benefited from the University's Special Study Program and a small research grant. Rachel Cunneen assisted with some of the research, and Wilgha Edwards in the Special Collections area of the ADFA Library has been unfailingly helpful with advice about the David Foster manuscript collection. Susan Cowan, in the School of Humanities and Social Sciences, helped prepare the final manuscript for publication.

I have been given information and advice by Colin Steele, Paul Hetherington of the National Library of Australia, and Andrew McLennan of the ABC who provided me with details of Foster's radio plays and their dates of broadcast. Kim Scott allowed me to quote his Blaiklock lecture. The photograph of David Foster on the cover (NL36770) was taken by Loui Seselja on 21 January 1991, and the National Library of Australia granted permission to reproduce it.

In the final stages, friends and colleagues have provided crucial advice on the manuscript, especially Delys Bird, Susan Cowan, Jeff Doyle, Hilary Kent, and Katherine McKernan. I am grateful to them all.

David Foster

INTRODUCTION

David Foster is the most original, challenging, contradictory, risk-taking, and infuriating Australian novelist of his generation. He has written at least three novels—*Moonlite* (1981), *Mates of Mars* (1991) and *The Glade Within the Grove* (1996)—that offer grand and sweeping visions of the state of Australia and its place in the world, and they deserve to be read alongside the finest work of Patrick White, Xavier Herbert, and Joseph Furphy. To date he has published twelve novels, three collections of novellas and short stories, two books of poetry, and a collection of essays, and he has also written several produced radio plays. Four of Foster's novels have won major literary awards in Australia: his first novel, *The Pure Land* (1974), shared the first *Age* Book of the Year award (with volume three of Manning Clark's *A History of Australia*) in 1975; his second novel, *Moonlite* (1981), was the National Book Council Book of the Year for 1981; *The Glade Within the Grove* (1996) won the Miles Franklin award in 1997; and *In the New Country* (1999) was the inaugural Brisbane *Courier-Mail* Book of the Year in 1999. Foster's novels have attracted the admiration of many other writers and critics, including White, Geoffrey Dutton, Randolph Stow, and Annie Proulx, and his contribution to Australian writing has been recognised by several Australia Council grants and a prestigious 'Keating' Creative Fellowship in 1991.

Foster writes in an Australian tradition of idiosyncratic satire and comedy that may be traced through the work of Joseph Furphy, Miles Franklin, Xavier Herbert, and David Ireland. His novels are the most wide-ranging and fearless of the Australian novels that have contributed to the late twentieth-century re-examination of Western ideologies and the literary forms in which they are expressed. *Moonlite*, *Plumbum* (1983), *Mates of Mars*, and *The Glade Within the Grove* offer panoramic considerations of the state of humanity in a world propelled into chaos.

Despite the originality and importance of this fiction, Foster's writing is relatively unknown beyond Australia, and in Australia not much beyond a group of loyal readers. He has never acquired the international following of contemporaries such as Peter Carey or David Malouf, or the Australian readerships of Helen Garner or Elizabeth Jolley. By and large, he has defeated translators.[1] His novels are rarely set on university courses, and never on high school curricula. They do not express respectable social attitudes, and they are difficult to read and to classify.

While a degree of critical neglect may account for part of this situation, there are other clear reasons for Foster's lack of fame. Firstly, he is a satirist; his writing sets itself deliberately against the favourite beliefs of the educated readers who are most likely to read it. His work is opinionated, misanthropic, obsessive, and sometimes tedious. Secondly, he is a committed modernist, pursuing linguistic experiment and convinced that writing remains, at least partly, an improvisatory performance. Thirdly, his writing mixes genres, modes, and language registers; his work combines low humour and high cultural seriousness. Foster is a novelist of ideas rather than of character; readers cannot slip into sympathetic identification with his characters because they exist to express ideas rather than individual psychologies. One could go on to list Foster's toughness of mind and his spiritual obsessions as if they were negatives, but the qualities that make Foster difficult are, of course, also those that make his books rewarding to read.

Foster claims not to consider his readers when he writes; his novels certainly demand persistence and a willingness to enjoy the unexpected. They reward this persistence with a wealth of complex and exciting ideas and the inventive use of language and laughter. Foster's writing is brilliantly witty and often revelatory. It is committed to presenting an Australian perspective on the particular dilemmas of our times. Three of his novels in particular—*Moonlite*, *Mates of Mars*, and *The Glade Within the Grove*—speculate about the place of Australians in history and the prospects for their future. These novels express a complex engagement with the paradoxes of contemporary Australia and with the fundamental ideology and theology behind the assumptions of Australian society. They also engage with the place of Australia in the world, finding absurdity, stupidity, and hilarity in human failing.

This study will attempt to penetrate the mysteries of Foster's fiction, as well as provide some guidance to those readers who are willing to approach them. It will examine the contradictory nature of his commitments and interests as expressed mainly in his novels. Foster is driven by a romantic impulse to seek the creative source within himself; he attributes a sacred and spiritual status to this creativity, and at times his writing proposes that language itself may offer a key to spiritual knowledge. This romanticism emerges in a commitment to improvisation of expression—to the kind of modernism that Foster admires in James Joyce's experimental novels and practised in the improvisatory jazz groups in which Foster once played as drummer.[2] Foster has committed himself to modernist experiment as being essential to the writer's claim to be an artist. None of his novels work to a formula, nor abide by conventions of narrative or style. Each moves in different directions to the previous novel as he seeks out new material and new possibilities for writing.

Though Foster changes genres and subjects frequently, an attentive reader will identify his writing immediately, be it a comic riff on an Australian country town, a burlesque of history, or a fairy story. He has that 'originality of literary style which constitutes the only real honesty of a writer', as Vladimir Nabokov's narrator claims in *Ada* (377). Foster's personality dominates his fiction, and his excessive, sometimes angry, and often hilarious extemporisations create a voice that readers will hear as satirical. Yet Foster's fiction does not conform to the standard expectation of satire: that it mocks folly and vice in order to reform it. He has no stable political or social targets, nor any program for reform. Most often he declares his interests to be spiritual and even lyrical, and it may be that he is a satirist by temperament rather than choice. If the source of his art is a commitment to an individual, unfettered creativity, and an attempt to seek out spiritual enlightenment through this creativity, then satire emerges from the way that this unfettered individual expresses himself. Foster's habit of mind is critical and inclined to seek the alternative or contrary view to any assumption; he sees himself as 'the sceptical chymist' of the celebrated work by the Anglo-Irish physical chemist, Robert Boyle. In his novels he creates a writing persona that questions, subverts, or turns over the subject of his attention. This persona is also inclined to pursue ideas to their limits.

Readers may enjoy the sharpness of Foster's social observations and value his novels for asking questions about the state of Australian life at the turn of the twenty-first century. They may admire the disrespect for colonial history in *Moonlite*, the derision of popular music culture in *Plumbum*, the affectionate small-town comedy of the Dog Rock novels, the mockery of masculinity and feminism in *Mates of Mars*, and the comic observation of the MacAnaspie family in *The Glade Within the Grove*. But it is difficult to ignore the author's interest in spiritual enlightenment and religion. This interest is apparent in his accounts of the pagan lives of the islanders of *Moonlite*, of life on the Calcutta streets in *Plumbum*, and, most of all, of the experiences of the hippie communards and the accompanying poem of *The Glade*. Spirituality and religion are central to *The Adventures of Christian Rosy Cross* (1986) and *The Land Where*

Stories End (2001). His readers may respond most enthusiastically to his satiric commentaries on contemporary Australia, but Foster writes in the interest of his own 'immortal soul';[3] 'Readers? Fellow writers? For the most part, I wish them well, but in the end, it is to my god, the god of the literary novel, that I offer up my literary art' ('Like Spinoza' 74).

Any disjunction between the interests of author and readers may be exacerbated by the divisions in the author's own allegiances. Foster's training as a scientist provided him with a careful eye for detail and a sense of the complexity of the observed world. At the same time, he seeks an understanding beyond the limits of the rational; he moves from the order of the known world to the chaos beyond. In his fiction, the rational logic and critical habit of the scientist meets a quest for spiritual enlightenment. His satirical savagery confronts a lyrical impulse that sometimes emerges in poetry. This struggle for enlightenment through a tough and unsentimental vision of the world gives his work a depth and complexity beyond the conventional expectations of social satire.

Foster's personality and his experience of the world directly inform his fiction, so some understanding of his background helps in the appreciation of his work. His interest in a range of philosophical traditions (particularly those outside Christianity), his training as a scientist, and his artistic commitment to improvisation are not only elements of his idiosyncratic approach to fiction, but they are also part of the main intellectual debates of his times. While committing himself to his own peculiar path to art, Foster has absorbed many of Western society's fundamental concerns about the damage caused by technology and progress, and about the possibility for a human future.

In the following chapters I discuss each of his works of fiction and poetry in the order of publication (except for *The Adventures of Christian Rosy Cross* and *The Pale Blue Crochet Coathanger Cover*, which are discussed alongside similar novels), and I pursue the development of Foster's philosophical ideas and technique as a novelist over the thirty-five years of his writing life to date. Foster's letters to Geoffrey Dutton early in his career and his interviews and essays provide some of the background to these novels, and my study attempts to give a sense of the Australian context for his work. In order to do this, I will begin with a brief biography of Foster's early life and a discussion of his approach to satire, before discussing the novels in detail.

Endnotes

1. *The Glade Within the Grove* has been translated into German (Stuttgart: Klett Cotta, 2000) and Mandarin (Honan: Honan Publishing, 1998).
2. Foster tells me he has worked professionally with Australian jazz pianists as diverse as Graham Coyle and Serge Ermoll—usually in trios or quartets, although he was a member, during his doctoral years, of Greg Gibson's seven-piece 'New Capital City Jazz Band'. At the same time as he was working with Gibson and Coyle in their quartet 'Mood Indigo,' he was jamming with a fellow doctoral student, the Swedish alto saxophonist/physicist Jan Hellström, who had worked with the great American pianist, Cecil Taylor, in Stockholm. Foster describes Hellström as 'totally free: he couldn't find work in Canberra'.
3. Letter accompanying revised MS of *The Glade Within the Grove,* David Foster to Annie Proulx, August 1995: 'The shadowy presence of the goddess Brigid—treated fully in the Poem—indicates that D'Arcy—and indeed I—must tread lightly in certain areas. I, too, have the welfare of my immortal soul to consider.' David Foster papers (FP, Series 2.10, Folder 12)

Chapter 1

Scientist, Artist, Satirist

The Making of a Manichee[1]

David Manning Foster was born on 15 May 1944 to Hazel (née Manning) and George Foster, and spent his early childhood in Katoomba, the largest town in the Blue Mountains west of Sydney. George Foster, a well-known vaudeville and radio star of the time, left Hazel before David's birth. Hazel had been a talented actress and, as a young woman, won a scholarship to the Royal Academy of Dramatic Art in London—according to her son, her foster-parents would never have allowed her to take this up (Frost 18, 20). Foster comments, *George Foster reconfigured his convent-educated virgin first wife (in a total of four) as the vaudeville soubrette "Miss McGerkhinsquirter".*

For the first years of David's life, she and David lived in an apartment in Katoomba near his maternal grandparents, while she worked as an announcer for the local radio station. Foster remembers 'my mother's voice coming out of the radio whilst I did my utmost to make her respond to me' (Frost 20). David was an adult by the time he met George for the first (and only) time, but he also heard his unknown father's voice through this medium, feeding straight lines to the gags he had written for other comedians. Though he began his career as a dancer and worked in Sorlie's travelling burlesque troupe, George's fame in the world of Australian vaudeville, radio, and later television, lay in his prolific joke writing. During the 1950s he was a joke writer and straight man for the more famous comedian George Wallace, and in the early days of television he hosted a quiz show called *Tell the Truth.* Jacqueline Kent describes him as 'a man with mad eyes and the dapper moustache of a used-car salesman' (30). In a reflection on his own work, David later commented: 'I've become a low farceur. I never intended to be one when I started but my father was a low farceur and so there exists a schism between what I write and what I would like to write, what I would be and what I am' ('Red band' 8).

When he was six years old, David developed poliomyelitis, which left him crippled for some years. He spent months in the Katoomba hospital, racing through correspondence lessons and reading prodigiously. He believes that this experience of enforced reading and reflection turned him into a writer ('Aggression' 9–10). As a child, he believed himself to be a special boy, doted on by the women of his mother's family: 'Even at a young age, I was served with the same generosity and concern that the women of the household lavished on Pop, and I took it as my due' (Frost 20).

When Foster's mother married again, the family moved to Sydney where he attended Eastwood primary school and the selective Fort Street Boys' High. In his last two years of high school, Foster's stepfather was posted as a bank officer in the northern tablelands of New South Wales, and he attended Armidale High, then Orange High School ('Quod' 300–304). Foster, already an accomplished Scots marching band snare drummer, learnt to play kit drums while the family was staying at a hotel during one of their moves. He played professionally while in high school, travelling around the Tableland country towns with various dance bands. At Armidale High, he played in the same 'atrocious' school band as the singer-songwriter Peter Allen. *As an altar boy at Armidale Cathedral, Foster recalls that his first ambition in life was to take Holy Orders. He also recalls, some years later, being sexually abused by a Catholic priest.*

Before he was seventeen, Foster had enrolled in a classics-based Arts degree at the University of Sydney. He soon abandoned it to 'roam Australia, working at the usual variety of unskilled jobs' ('Aggression' 10). A year later he returned 'in a more sober mood' and enrolled in Science, though this degree, too, was interrupted for a year while he worked as a foreman on Marrickville Council. He married his Orange High School girlfriend Robin Bowers in 1964, and over the next ten years they had three children. Robin, an anthropologist, for many years ran the Katherine Aboriginal Language Centre in the Northern Territory, and her son with Foster, Seth, became an initiated man of an Aboriginal people.

Eventually Foster's work for a Chemistry honours degree won him the University Medal for Inorganic Chemistry in 1967. Foster moved straight from his undergraduate degree to a doctorate in the Institute for Advanced Studies at the Australian National University (ANU) in the national capital city, Canberra. Once again he was exceptional, gaining a Fellowship to the Department of Biophysics at the Institute for Cancer Research of the University of Pennsylvania, for 1970. (*Dean of the Research School of Chemistry during Foster's stay was A. J. Birch, one of the co-developers of the contraceptive pill.*)

In 1970 Foster was twenty-six years old, married with two children, a bright PhD graduate, co-author of six papers in the *Journal of the American Chemical Society*, and set for a promising career as a research scientist. In Philadelphia, however, his doubts came to a crisis. He felt that he could never match the enthusiasm and commitment of the Jewish-American scientists at the Ivy League University of Pennsylvania and did not relish the prospect of a second-rate career in science. Suffering from a duodenal ulcer, he began to write fiction partly as a way of working through his difficulties. In 1999, he told the Friends of the ANU Library that 'I was a clumsy experimentalist, an indolent theoretician and I actually spent my postdoctoral year in the States writing the novellas of *North South West*, which was to become my first published work of fiction in 1973, the year in which my last research paper was published' ('Books' 1). In 1971 he returned to Sydney to work as senior research officer in the Department of Medicine at the University of Sydney, but within a year he had made the decision to leave science for writing.

During this time, Foster, his wife, and his two elder daughters—Samantha, now a grazier, and Natalie, a ceramic artist—lived at Hazelbrook in the Blue Mountains and he travelled by train to Sydney each working day. He claims that one day he saw an advertisement for an assistant manager at Penrith pool, and decided to leave science and commit himself to writing. From this time, he worked in a variety of jobs, including postman and truck driver—always, he stresses, as a writer in the guise of other occupations ('Like Spinoza' 78).

At the end of 1972, the family moved back to Canberra where Foster worked as a postman during the day and a drummer by night, giving as much time to writing as possible. He sent the manuscript of *North South West* to Sun Books, where Geoffrey Dutton responded enthusiastically; Macmillan Sun published it in 1973. The Whitlam government won the election at the end of 1972, increasing support for the arts through the Australia Council. The next year Foster was awarded a new writer's fellowship by the Council's literature board.

By early 1974, though, Foster had left his wife and family. He wrote to Geoffrey Dutton:

> My writing has been strangely cramped and withered, my personal life full of restless frustration, and my physical health poor, with two hospitalizations for duodenal haemorrhages in the last few years. For the past four months since taking up my fellowship I have been doing nothing but reading hermeticism (this in preparation for my current book), looking at friends, playing music and smoking hashish. (Dutton, *Southerly* 25)

Foster's letters to Dutton during the following months give an account of a metaphysical and physical struggle for enlightenment and peace. The poems written during this time to Gerda Busch, the singer in his band (*a notorious Canberra beauty, debarred from several local venues*), were later published as *The Fleeing Atalanta* (1975); they give some sense of Foster's quest for a kind of spiritual resolution through alchemical reading, drugs, and sexual love. Later that year he moved in with Gerda, whom he married in 1975.

Since 1975 Foster and Gerda have lived in Bundanoon in the Southern Highlands of New South Wales, raising their three children and (from time to time) Foster's three and Gerda's two children from their first marriages. The three youngest of Foster's children include two high profile daughters: *London-based dance music diva Antigone, Sydney-based 'chick-lit' novelist and beauty director for* Harper's Bazaar *Zöe, and Sydney DJ Levi, of 'La Fiesta Sound System.'* To support his writing, Foster has worked in a range of occupations that have provided material for his novels, including as a musician (*Plumbum*), postman (*Dog Rock*), truck driver, taxi driver, martial arts instructor (*Mates of Mars*), and trawler fisherman (*Mates of Mars*).

Though Foster is, in formal terms, one of the most educated novelists in Australian literary history, the specialised nature of his education in science left him to teach himself about literature, art, and history. Foster has developed as an autodidact, in the tradition of other idiosyncratic Australian writers such as Joseph Furphy, Xavier Herbert, and David Ireland. Andrew Field sees a strong likeness to Ireland in particular as another 'true Aussie autodidact': 'Both Ireland and Foster are frequently dismissed as being too eccentric. The charge is both true and absurd. What the people who say such things really mean is that they cut too close to the bone' (10).

Foster has remained distant from other writers and the literary establishment in the universities. *He says he sees this as providing hostile critics with a 'free kick': meaning, they know they will never have to encounter him at dinner parties.* His reading moves beyond the orderly structures and clear directions that a professional education in the arts brings to bear on literature and history. In his various accounts of his movement towards writing, Foster describes discovering the essays of William Hazlitt on the shelves of the Fisher Library at the University of Sydney, or reading his way through Samuel Beckett and William Burroughs while he was an undergraduate. All three offered models for aspects of his own writing. He later attributed more influence to the discovery of the alchemical texts, shelved near the books on chemistry. As we shall see in the discussion of *The Fleeing Atalanta* and *The Adventures of Christian Rosy Cross* (1985), his discovery of Michael Maier's writing and of Mattheus Merian's woodcuts of alchemical emblems sparked an interest in alchemical analogies that has sustained him as a writer. He told the Friends of the ANU Library:

> The first time I saw these woodcuts, accompanied by the dog Latin epigrams of Maier, I knew I'd come full circle, as a scholar. I was like the dragon biting his own tail in emblem 14 ...I was flung into a world more congenial to the poet than the chemist, a world in which I belonged all along, a world in which spiritual meaning exists because coincidence does not. ('Books' 2)

Foster has relished new reading projects, such as Arnold Toynbee's *The Study of History,* or revising his Latin to read the Roman satirist Juvenal before writing *The Glade Within the Grove*. The self-directed nature of this reading means that it proceeds without the kind of intellectual structures that place such learning in a particular context in, say, a philosophy or classics course in a university. Foster offers original readings of these texts, unperturbed by intellectual fashion or accepted interpretation.

While this account of Foster's life and intellectual development emphasises his individuality and idiosyncrasy, we should not lose sight of the wider social and intellectual context for his work. Foster belongs to the generation of writers and artists who came to national attention in the early 1970s, in the wake of the international social and intellectual upheavals of 1968 and, in Australia, after the federal election victory of the Whitlam Labor government in 1972. Though he may be unusual among the writers, in some ways he is representative of that generation as a whole—the first in Australia to have ready access to tertiary education. In the 1960s, science was promoted to students (by men like Professor Harry Messel) as a heroic intellectual path on which vital discoveries might be made, and the brightest students, like Foster, chose this path. While he felt his crisis of the early 1970s as personal and individual, he was also part of a generation that was questioning the assumptions of Western democracy and its commitment to scientific and technological progress.

In the 1970s, Foster was far from alone in seeking out alternative spiritualities to mainstream Christianity, or in questioning the efficacy of science in solving human problems. His interest in contemporary music, his experiments with marihuana, and his reading of alternative philosophies were shared with thousands of other young Australians at the time. *Indeed, marihuana use in Australia began among the jazz musicians of Sydney in the early 1960s.* Foster's crisis of 1973 coincided with the Aquarius Festival at Nimbin (in northern New South Wales) which led groups of young people to abandon their lives in the city to try communal subsistence in the country. Foster's enthusiasm for New Age philosophies, experimental music, alternative lifestyles, drugs, and sex as a source of enlightenment may be seen as part of a whole generational shift in attitudes and beliefs in the early 1970s. He and Gerda still pursue a version of the pastoral dream of the hippie, living in a country town and growing most of the family's food.

For many young Australians, the government's involvement in the Vietnam War and its decision to conscript young men to fight it gave an immediate political dimension to this critique of national conformity and conservatism. Released from the threat of conscription by his university career, Foster remained apart from this political movement. While many of his writing contemporaries (such as David Williamson) were galvanised into opposition to the War, Foster's only reference to the student protest movement appears to be the narrator's call, in 'North South West', to keep politics off the campus, and his satiric treatment of the draft dodgers in *The Glade Within the Grove*.

While Foster was struggling to become a writer in Philadelphia, Hazelbrook and Canberra a group of writers that included Jack Hibberd, David Williamson and John Romeril were learning how to become dramatists in Melbourne. In Sydney, Frank Moorhouse and Michael Wilding were publishing fiction that defied prevailing literary notions of form and taste. Peter Carey was vacillating between his job in advertising and hippie communes in Yandina and Bellingen. All over the country, poets were challenging the aesthetic models—the poetry of Judith Wright, James McAuley and A. D. Hope—that they read in high school in the 1950s and 1960s. Foster's attitudes probably align most clearly with the poets, with the romanticism of Michael Dransfield, and with John Tranter's and John Forbes's commitment to experiment—though Foster's writing practice differs greatly. These poets acknowledged the influence of the Beats and other American experimental writers, as well as the literate rock songs of Bob Dylan and others (Tranter xv–xxvi). They saw Australian writers' rejection of modernism in the earlier part of the century as a sign of the backward-looking conservatism of the national culture. While some of these novelists looked to Jack Kerouac or even Jorge Luis Borges as models, the dramatists read Samuel Beckett and Bertolt Brecht, and the poets Alan Ginsberg, or Frank O'Hara, and John Ashbery—Foster found William Burroughs.

At the time, this surge in literary experiment was criticised vehemently by conservatives, particularly by members of the anti-communist group around *Quadrant* (edited by James McAuley) on the grounds that it endangered liberal democracy.[2] While most of the writers attacked in this way might find such a charge overblown and ridiculous (as it has proved to be), Foster's development as a writer supports a view of the modernist aesthetic as anti-liberal. Just as the modernism of the early twentieth century emerged partly in protest of the failures of the Enlightenment order of the late nineteenth century, the reinvigorated modernism of 1970s Australia formed part at a protest against the conformity and complacency of the immediate postwar period. It was radical in this sense, but its commitment to individual expression challenged the communal values of the times. Later liberation movements, such as gay liberation or women's liberation, called for an extension of communal freedoms, rather than privileging the individual—usually masculine and heterosexual—consciousness.

Foster's writing always privileges this consciousness, and he repeatedly mocks the liberation enthusiasms of the 1980s and 1990s. His assumption of masculine privilege and his commitment to art as a source of enlightenment leads to both radical and conservative positions. While Foster might be called radical in his interest in alternative philosophies and in his commitment to experimental writing, he appears conservative in his lack of patience with liberation movements and his resistance to any communal politics. At a time when ideology has become a major criterion for critical responses to literary work, this has proved an obstacle to sympathetic reading of his work. Simplistic feminist and postcolonial approaches to the novel find little solace in Foster's commitment to a white, male, individualist art.

While the generation of the 1970s reinvigorated Australian writing across the major genres of fiction, poetry, and drama, satire has not been a dominant mode in the novel. Patrick White certainly has a strong satirical voice, especially in his later novels, and a range of other contemporary writers—especially David Ireland, Frank Moorhouse, and Peter Mathers—write in satiric mode. Nevertheless, satire in novels published after 1980 is more likely to be perceived as a form of postmodernism, as in the fiction of Peter Carey, Rodney Hall, or Murray Bail.

It is impossible to mistake the satire in Foster's fiction. He writes with a consistent determination to disturb readers' complacency. His satire comes not only from a sense of the ridiculous nature of trivial human obsessions, but also from a deliberate critique of our fundamental assumptions about ourselves. Foster's satire expresses a crisis experienced across his generation of Western intellectuals who had lost faith in the efficacy of rational order and sought its alternatives.

The Satirist

Though Foster may not have set out on his literary career with the intention to become a satirist, the satirical voice sounds clearly from the first lines of his first published novella, 'North South West' (1973). It appears intermittently in his first novel, *The Pure Land* (1974), and retreats in his collection of poetry, *The Fleeing Atalanta* (1975); but Foster's first unquestionable success, *Moonlite* (1981), established that a satiric voice would dominate his work. By 1987, Foster had come to terms with this situation sufficiently to do his own research on the genre, published in the *Phoenix Review* as 'Satire' (*Studs and Nogs S&N*, 76–97). This article—as witty as any of Foster's fiction—offers his own interpretation of satire.

In the article, he surveyed some of the major commentaries on satire, approving Gilbert Highet's definition of Roman satire—with the exception of its statement of intention: 'improving society by exposing its vices and follies' (*S&N* 78). Foster supported all the other qualities listed by Highet, and indeed his novels display them all: 'the free use of conversational language, the frequent intrusion of the author's personality, a predilection for wit, humour and irony, great vividness and concreteness of description, shocking obscenity in theme and language, an improvisatory tone, topical subjects' (78). Foster speculates, with some foundation, that the high-minded notion of the satirist as reformer is merely a defensive ploy by satirists to give themselves some respectability. He argues that the satirist has a particularly aggressive personality that must express itself in satire: he is 'an angry response looking for something to respond to' (85).

Foster, following Highet, adopts the classification of satires by Joseph Hall (1574–1656) as 'toothless' satires, in the entertaining and relatively gentle mode of Horace, and 'biting' satires modelled on Juvenal. 'Toothless satire uses wordplay, parody, humour and many of the other rhetorical devices developed by the Greek street orators, but it steers well clear of philosophy and obscenity', while biting satire 'is filled with an often egotistical sense of moral outrage and indignation; it is violent; and it is unashamedly cruel' (81). Of course, Foster sees himself as Juvenalian rather than Horatian. Taking Juvenal as a model, he argues that satire belongs to a civilisation in decline:

> The satirist alone can give a full overview of society in decline. He observes and laments his own destructive impulses. Society in decline is his premise and his only subject, and I use

> the word 'he' with absolutely no apologies to any feminists present: satire is a uniquely masculine form. In Juvenal's nostalgia for the Golden Age, in his superb poetic technique, we sense the legacy of Greek high culture. But in his vulgarity and cruelty he makes us feel the barbarian at the gate. (85)

In this way, Foster calls on Juvenal to support the qualities of his own writing: the panoramic vision of society, the destructive and self-hating narrative persona, the aggressive masculinity, the mix of refined thought and expression with coarseness and brutality. He goes on to quote at length from William Burroughs as a twentieth-century exponent of this kind of self-loathing satire, asserting that Burroughs shows the moral side of satire by writing his way out of his own depravity. At the same time, he presents Burroughs as evidence for the modernist and experimental nature of satire, admiring Burroughs' technical skill and experiments with cut-up prose.

Foster ends with his own list of the 'immutable features' of satire:

> A satire must offend; it must be crude; it must be humorous; it must be philosophical. But above all, it must be written with consummate skill. Satire is intrinsically modernistic. A satire is not something that's so bad it's good: that is a postmodernist category. Nor is it something that's so good it's irrelevant: that is a classical category. Satire is a form expressly developed to describe the complexity of civilisation in decline, by a man who has felt it in his own personality. (97)

While this article may seem like an idiosyncratic or distorted account of satire to any reader nurtured on the 'reform of folly and vice' formula, Foster's argument finds support among a range of critical writers. In their introduction to *Theorizing Satire*, Brian Connery and Kirk Combe argue that satire may be seen as a spirit that 'inhabits' a text, rather than as a consistent literary genre (1–15). One can take this further to see the persona of the satirist 'inhabiting' the text, so that satire takes on the mode of performance with the personality of the author intruding (as noted by Highet) to improvise extravagant digressions. This also accords with Foster's vision of himself as 'an angry response' seeking a subject. Without reading the text as a simple function of the author's personality, it allows us to understand the satirist as performing a role within the text.

Steven Weisenburger's introduction to his study of the American novel, *Fables of Subversion: Satire and the American Novel, 1930–1980*, provides a succinct survey of critical writing on satire that challenges the formal definition of satire as didactic. He makes a distinction between 'generative' and 'degenerative' satire: generative satire may be seen as reformist in intention while degenerative satire is 'delegitimizing…it functions to subvert hierarchies of value and to reflect suspiciously on all ways of making meaning, including its own' (3). While Weisenburger's idea of 'generative' satire may be equated to the Horatian satire of Foster's essay, he argues that 'degenerative' satire forms part of the postmodernist challenge to meaning. His discussion of American novels places degenerative satire not as a revivification of Juvenalian satire so much as a twentieth-century attack on the structures of meaning and representation, a challenge that came to be termed postmodernism.

In his essay, Foster dismisses postmodernism as facetious and morally evasive. He prefers to see himself as a modernist who looks to the classical model of Juvenal than as a participant in a contemporary attack on the assumptions behind the structures of art. As I will argue in later chapters of this book, his novels and poetry seek to explore the possibilities of language as a source of ineffable meaning; at the same time, the frequent shifts in style and language register, and the ready abandonment of conventions of narrative suggest a more postmodernist challenge to the very ways in which meaning is created. His fiction participates in a postmodernist critique of narrative structures, while maintaining a modernist faith in language.

For the purposes of this study, Weisenburger's argument on the basis of the American novel is most useful in emphasising the irrelevance of the formalist 'folly and vice' definition of satire for understanding contemporary work. Such a definition has led to the dismissal of some important contemporary writing, and to a failure even to acknowledge the satirical qualities of much recent fiction, especially when the term 'postmodernist' can be applied. Weisenburger surveys the American novel from Nathanael West to Thomas Pynchon, arguing that satire, far from being a 'stale' genre that cannot contribute to the 'oppositional, subversive work of much twentieth-century art,' forms a major strand in that art (2). Weisenburger aligns this satire with the postmodernist project of questioning representation and (what Jean-Francois Lyotard calls) the 'master narratives'.

Placing Foster's fiction alongside that of contemporary American satirists such as William Gaddis, Thomas Pynchon, Robert Coover, or Don DeLillo immediately suggests that he is part of a major development in the late-twentieth-century novel—the most prominent Australian participant. We could add Salman Rushdie, Thomas Bernhard, Georges Perec, and others to this list of international writers producing major works of satire in the closing decades of the twentieth century. Yet, the postmodernist epithet does not fit neatly with Foster's work. While his fiction does frustrate 'the desire for a stable and objective meaning', and although it mixes high culture and popular culture, voice registers and genres, behind it remains a drive to discover meaning through the representational system of language. Foster's commitment to language and analogy as a source of some immanent meaning aligns, as he suggests, with a modernist sensibility. His novels examine and depend on the dualities that Weisenburger describes as common to modernism: male/female, nature/culture, mind/body (4).

At the same time, Foster's playfulness with form, the intrusion of the satirist's voice in his fiction, the deliberate inclusion of material likely to be excluded from a place in high culture, and the very waywardness of his art invites a postmodernist label. Foster's novels may depend on the dualities listed by Weisenburger, but they also seek their limits—the woman in man, the interdependence of culture and nature, the way that spiritualism must emerge from the physical senses. Foster proposes that there is more than one way to find the answers: 'Gotta hold two views at once. The Tlute is not this is not that—is a combination', as Ar Wat says in *Moonlite* (198). *Mates of Mars* insists on the recognition of feminine as well as masculine principles, of both the yin and the yang. In *Testostero*, Foster plays with dualities, using a set of English and Australian twins to mock high and low culture, science, and poetry. He gives several pages to a description of the filter system at a municipal pool in Sydney, inserts a pastiche of a drawing-room play, and finally reveals a third sibling (a triplet and a transsexual) in the carnival scene at its end. In *The Glade Within the Grove* his narrator dies before the novel can end—surely a postmodernist conceit—while the accompanying poem, *The Ballad of Erinungarah*, adopts a modernist lyricism that is permeated with satirical elements.

The distinctions between modernism and postmodernism are never clear-cut in a writer's practice, but the terms are useful in providing a critical marker for the broad intellectual shifts in late twentieth-century writing. Brian McHale has traced a development from modernist to postmodernist consciousness in a range of writers, such as William Faulkner and Vladimir Nabokov, seeing a transitional stage in which a postmodernist interest in ontology (with an emphasis on what McHale calls 'problems of *modes of being*' [10]) begins to dominate the modernist focus on epistemology (McHale's 'problems of *knowing*'(10)). Foster's fiction never really abandons the quest for meaning, though he shares the postmodernist consciousness of the failure of the fundamental philosophies (or master narratives) that guide Western civilisation. Perhaps a novel like *The Glade Within the Grove* has moved beyond postmodernism in its lament for the lost possibilities of human endeavour. We should not, however, fall into the fallacy of seeing the history of literature as progress, or even the development of a writer's œuvre through a career as improvement over time. This idea of progress is one of the fallacies that Foster attacks in his fiction.

While Weisenburger's summary of critical theories of satire and his resounding rebuttal of the reformist claims of satire provide support for my study of David Foster's work, several earlier critics also offer perspectives that illuminate elements of his satirical approach. Among these, Wyndham Lewis argues that great satire is not moral, but has as its aim a kind of intellectual stiffening 'to correct our soft conceit' (76). He also links satire with a scientific approach: 'That objective, non emotional truth of the scientific intelligence sometimes takes on the exuberant sensuous quality of creative art: then it is very apt to be called "satire", for it has been bent not so much upon pleasing as upon being true' (76).

Foster approves this last phrase, and would perhaps endorse Lewis's idea that satire represents a creative form of the scientist's commitment to uncover truth. Although the exuberant pursuit of scientific paradox drives *Moonlite* as it works its way from primitive spiritualism to quantum physics, Foster's ambivalence towards science is further evident in the attacks on statistical method in *Testostero* and on the generalising tendency of science in *Mates of Mars*. Most of all Foster's scientific training shows in his carefully detailed descriptions of aspects of life normally beyond the novel—subsistence practices in the Outer Hebrides, the daily routine of a baker in a country town, the rituals of a doorman in a Western suburbs club.

Northrop Frye also provides some important historical context for Foster's work when he argues that in modern times the Menippean satire might be more properly called the anatomy (312). By reference to Richard Burton's *Anatomy of Melancholy*, Laurence Sterne's *Tristram Shandy*, Herman Melville's *Moby Dick*, and James Joyce's *Ulysses*, Frye proposes that the novel has combined with the anatomy to emerge in encyclopedic forms that often baffle critics. While several of Foster's early works are clearly Menippean satires in the 'short form', *The Glade Within the Grove* belongs to a hybrid form of novel and anatomy, as described by Frye in reference to *Tristram Shandy*: 'the digressing narrative, the catalogues, the stylizing of character along "humor" lines, the marvellous journey of the great nose, the symposium discussions, and the constant ridicule of philosophers and pedantic critics are all features that belong to the anatomy' (312). Foster's writing moves from the short Menippean satires of his early career to satirical novels that have elements of the anatomy, and he has declared that he would prefer his work to be seen as one single creative effort, as we do the work of Burton and Sterne.

Frye's comment about the critical reception of the anatomy may also be applied to Foster's work: 'there is hardly any fiction writer deeply influenced by it who has not been accused of disorderly conduct' (313).

Various critics have emphasised the pagan origins of satire, most significantly Robert Elliott in *The Power of Satire: Magic, Ritual, Art*, in which he traces the origins of satire to ancient, pre-Christian beliefs in the efficacy of cursing. In ancient ritual, the role of the poet who cast out the evil spirits was as important as that of the priest who praised the good in prayer. Elliott's description of the satirist's role in pre-Islamic Arabia recalls the ritual practices of the cultists in *The Glade Within the Grove*: 'The poet-satirist led his warriors into battle, uttering his wild imprecations, shod with one sandal, his hair anointed on one side only, his mantle hanging loose' (15).

Christianity, with its emphasis on loving-kindness, has attempted to negate this darker side of human creativity. Elliott tells us that a range of ancient cultures from Greece to Ireland believed in the magical powers of cursing, and satire developed such cursing into art. Christianity, then, is the suppressor of satire and its links with magic and pagan religion. *Under the sixth century Irish monastic rule of Cummean, 'satirizing'—along with murder, perjury, heresy, adultery, brigandage, incest and druidism—was an irremissible sin* (Foster refers readers to Catherine Thom's PhD thesis for further information). It is appropriate that Foster should write satire when his fiction consistently seeks alternatives to the Christian master narrative. His major novels *Moonlite* and *The Glade Within the Grove* criticise the Christian assumptions behind modern Western societies, including the pervasive optimism of Christianity, with its belief in the human progression to a millennial salvation. By contrast, pre-Christian Roman writers such as Juvenal looked to a past Golden Age and saw the passage of time as a process of decline. Foster's references to Juvenal in his 1987 essay, and his subsequent reading of Juvenal's work in Latin, suggest that he enjoys seeing himself, like Juvenal, as the critic of a civilisation in decline; as early as *Moonlite* he had challenged the notion of History as progress, and Christianity as ameliorating. He calls himself a pagan, even a barbarian, in his 'Satire' essay. *More recently, he has returned to the Church, and worships in the High Church Anglican Cathedral at Goulburn, while still describing himself as a Gnostic of Manichean tendency, who must fall silent during the creed.*

Elliott's study offers several other features of satire that help to place Foster's work. He points to the tradition of satirists from Aristophanes to Swift as 'rationally anti-intellectual', though Foster might be seen as 'intellectually anti-rational' in his stance. Using Jonathan Swift as an example, Elliott argues that the satirist's claims of conservatism are undermined by the radical and disruptive nature of the form: 'The pressure of [Swift's] art works directly against the ostensibly conservative function which it is said to serve. Instead of shoring up foundations, it tears them down. It is revolutionary' (274). So we may see satire as a revolutionary, radically disruptive, even subversive literary form that often takes an apparently conservative political stance. But these simple notions of 'conservative' and 'radical' seem inadequate to encapsulate the complexity of Foster's novels, which consistently turn over ideas to examine their underside.

Elliott also argues that satire can only flourish in a society that tolerates a high level of freedom of speech (possibly the same society in decline that the satirists like to attack). The satirist's offensiveness tests the limits of the freedoms in society, no matter how conservative that satire may claim to be. At the same time, satire also threatens the boundaries between art and life, between the author and the society in which he writes, and between the author and the persona or voice in the text. Rather than reaching beyond time to speak of universal truths, satire participates in a particular society in a particular place and time. The author refuses to die into the text, but insists on being acknowledged as a living voice. The intrusive voice of the satirist cannot be detached from the author, as satire insists on the acknowledgment that its author lives with the reader in a world worthy of mockery and abuse.

Foster's writing, as well as his public persona, meets the expectation of the satirist as a misanthropic, dark, and disruptive figure. He performs the role of the satirist whether in novels, essays, or in public appearances where he often deliberately chooses to offend his audience. He acts as a discomfiting, sometimes appalling, dissenter against the civilised aspiration to tolerance and humanity.

CRITICAL APPROACHES

Such an unstable notion of satire presents difficulties to the critic. Once we accept that satire need have no moral intention—or, more correctly, that its morality lies in the satirist's commitment to his own version of truth no matter how unpleasant or offensive—any critical paradigm that seeks a moral program proves useless. Analyses that seek the politics of representation, such as some unsophisticated feminist and postcolonial approaches, are likely to end only in frustration and condemnation.

At the same time, satire's disruption of form dissolves any critique that takes unity of structure as a criterion. The traditional notion of satire as a medley of styles and subjects, of excessive digression and extravagant imagination, defeats the tasteful limits of the 'well-wrought urn'—one of the reasons for its fall from critical favour in the 1950s and 1960s. Satire may challenge conventional criticism because the critic can call on no formal model as a standard. The satirist's answer to any criticism that his work appears uncontrolled and chaotic might be: 'that is the nature of satire'. Critics must respond to the very energy with which traditional structures are broken. They must look to the rhetorical skills of the satirist: to the brilliance of invention, the wit, the humour, the range of poetic imagery, and the sharp accuracy of observation. They must adapt some of the approaches they apply to poetry, appreciating the rhythm, language shifts, and sheer imagination of the text.

While such satire asks critics to judge it on aesthetic grounds, in practice most of Foster's critics have responded to the ideas behind his fiction, and to the way he stimulates intellectual reflection by reference to a broad range of historical, scientific, and social thought. Again we face the paradox of the writer who attacks fundamental intellectual assumptions by means of a stream of intellectual ideas. Those who enjoy Foster's writing usually appreciate the complexity of his ideas and the expression of them in a mix of vulgar comedy and erudition.

Reviewers have taken Foster's writing seriously since the publication in 1973 of his first book, the collection of novellas, *North South West*, but there has also been a consistent pattern of resistance, confusion, and sometimes distaste for his fiction. From the first, critics found Foster's prose style difficult and awkward, but thought his ideas 'savage' (Sage 1978), 'potentially damaging' (Stow), or 'slightly alarming' (Bawden), and some thought that only his energy and originality overcame the awkwardness of his style (Grant). Reviewers repeatedly warned readers about the indigestibility of his prose and the nastiness of his vision, and many noted the bleakness that pervades his early novels. These early works are sometimes clumsy, sometimes overblown, and full of attempts at something beyond the author's grasp, yet intelligent readers immediately saw that the ambition was worth pursuing. Many readers shared Peter Corris's intimation of 'a major writer in the making' (1977).

The success of *Moonlite* in 1981 meant more extended critical attention for his later work. In 1985, I published a review article in the *Age Monthly Review* considering the achievement of *Moonlite* and arguing that *Plumbum* broke the 'reasonable' boundaries of conventional satire with an excess of imagination approaching lunacy (McKernan). After the publication of *Testostero* in 1987, Andrew Riemer wrote an appreciative article in *Southerly*, grappling with the mix of low humour and high intellect in all of Foster's novels, and finding that *Testostero* was 'in many ways [his] most successful and accessible book' (140). This article was the first lengthy consideration of Foster's work as a whole and accorded him the status of a 'major figure' while finding it difficult to state the precise reasons for this claim:

> Foster's eclectic scientific-literary 'machinery' is beyond the capacity of most 'literary' people, especially as he avoids entirely the type of rhetorical afflatus that many writers use

> to signal their 'elevated' concerns. Moreover his novels and stories do not chart the familiar territory of modern Australian writing: there is little compassion, perhaps no caring evident, at least on the surface of his work. The fashionable causes of the seventies and eighties are either ignored or mercilessly lampooned. Clearly Foster is not concerned with the twin preoccupations with personal fulfilment and social conscience that characterize so much recent writing. Nor does he display any penchant toward the alternative possibility: a social, 'cultural' even at times religious politesse that one encounters from time to time in 'conservative' writing. As these pages have insisted time and time again, his writing is raucous, impolite and entirely lacking in fine feeling. (Riemer 143)

Endorsing Riemer's assessment of Foster's importance as a novelist, Helen Daniel included him alongside Peter Mathers, Peter Carey, David Ireland, Murray Bail, Nicholas Hasluck, Gerald Murnane, and Elizabeth Jolley in *Liars: Australian New Novelists*, her 1988 study of what she called the New Novel in Australia. Daniel also recognised *Moonlite* as 'one of the most important novels ever written in Australia' (86) and she used Foster's interest in alchemy to extricate the paradox and contradiction that she saw in a range of Australian novels by her chosen writers. Rather than use the term 'postmodernist', Daniel linked this writing with South American fabulism and a growing international trend for double-storytelling. Her chapter on Foster's novels (77–104) gave detailed attention to *Moonlite*, *Christian Rosy Cross*, and *Dog Rock*, exploring the way in which his fiction always insists on a more complex world—with alternate meanings and possibilities—than their surface can contain.

Since 1990 Narelle Shaw has published a series of articles extricating many of the mythical references and hidden structures in Foster's work, insisting on his control and direction in what may appear 'chaotic' novels. She has given close attention to the novels from *Moonlite* to *The Glade Within the Grove*, carefully tracing the development of Foster's 'poetics'. Shaw places Foster's work within longstanding traditions of literary art, tracing connections and allusions to classical texts, and emphasising his conformity with existing, if forgotten, comic modes. Though this may sometimes appear to be an attempt to keep Foster's waywardness under critical control, Shaw reminds us of the diverse heritage of literature upon which he draws.

Until the publication of *The Glade Within the Grove*, *Moonlite* attracted more critical attention than any of Foster's other novels. In 1992 D. R. Burns contrasted it with the 'Visionary Monster' novels of Australia in the years since the 1960s—White's *Riders in the Chariot* (1961) and *The Eye of the Storm* (1973), Xavier Herbert's *Poor Fellow My Country* (1975), and David Ireland's *A Woman of the Future* (1979)—and saw it as a landmark novel in the history of Australian fiction, particularly in its 'export-quality bullshit' rendering of the life in the outer Hebrides in its first part. Stephen Harris later read *Moonlite* as a postcolonial critique of imperial claims to history as progress. Harris compared *Moonlite* to Peter Carey's and David Malouf's revisions of Australian history, arguing that satire gave Foster an 'inherently political and oppositional mode' with which to demolish imperial history (72).

Since the award of the Miles Franklin prize to *The Glade Within the Grove*, a larger range of critics has given Foster attention. In 1997, Marilla North wrote an appreciative article on the D'Arcy D'Oliveres novels, *Dog Rock*, *The Pale Blue Crochet Coathanger Cover*, and *The Glade Within the Grove*, noting the influence of Konrad Lorenz on Foster's theories of population control, and remarking that Foster shared Miles Franklin's satirical attitude, her hatred of the establishment, her 'intense national chauvinism', and even her concern about 'unregulated fecundity' (696). Kerryn Goldsworthy published a sympathetic reading of *The Glade* and its poem *The Ballad of Erinungarah* that gave due consideration to Foster's commentary on his work, and she overcame her feminist misgivings to recognise the 'hypnotic quality' of *The Ballad*'s images and rhythms. She wrote:

> Foster must be the only writer in Australia who can produce a novel that both laments the loss of religious coherence and spiritual direction in late 20th-century Western culture and, at the same time, mercilessly satirises the artefacts of religious culture, the notion of the sacred text, and the random,

> arbitrary and polyvocal origins and narrative transformations of religious cults and myths. (12)

All of these critical responses emphasise the patterns of paradox and self-contradiction in both the subject matter and the form of Foster's novels. While claiming one thing, Foster enacts its opposite. His characters represent one aspect of existence (corruption, cynicism, aggression) then shift to its opposite (purity, enthusiastic belief, meditative spiritualism). At the same time, the satirical voice seems to invoke the antithesis of what it presents. In *Moonlite* the critics found a novel driven by anger at the destructive nature of progress; but it was a novel that also refused nostalgia for the misguided beliefs of the past. In *The Glade* and its *Ballad*, critics could attribute the apparent misogyny and the disconcerting advocacy of castration to the vagaries of the narrators, D'Arcy D'Oliveres and 'Orion'—at least, until the publication of 'On Castration' under Foster's own name in *Heat* magazine in 1997.

The award of the Miles Franklin prize brought Foster attention from outside the world of literary critics and academics. At the reception to announce the award, Foster made a speech deploring the marketing culture of literary festivals and prizes, in particular the promotion of foreign writers (his rivals) in Australia. His 'ungraciousness' drew comment from several journalists covering the event. A few weeks later he wrote an editorial feature for the *Sydney Morning Herald* under the headline, 'Race Debate Is Skin Deep,' arguing that all people born in Australia of mixed race should be regarded as Australian 'pure and simple' rather than as Aborigines or Asians, except for 'those initiated few who retain a tribal culture' who might be called Aboriginal (*S&N* 17). No matter how innocent Foster's intentions, the appearance of this article soon after the release of the *Bringing Them Home* report, the result of a government enquiry into the official practice of taking mixed race Aboriginal children from their parents, meant that his comments were read as an intervention in the debate about white responsibility (Wootten).

The disguise of the reclusive satirist could no longer be maintained. The journalist Paul Sheehan became an enthusiastic promoter of Foster, and he devoted a chapter of his polemical book *Among the Barbarians* to quoting Foster's opinions (some from the novels) on a range of matters (279–293). Sheehan described the criticism of Foster's article on race in the language commonly used to close down intellectual engagement in Australia: 'For his frankness Foster was given a head-kicking by the Thought Police in Sydney' (288). The Miles Franklin award also drew the attention of the feminist writer, Anne Summers, who objected to the absence of women in Foster's notion of Australia and the bush. *For his part, Foster claims his reluctance to create female characters is a token of his incapacity to understand women and hence, a mark of respect.* In 1997, David Matthews's review of *The Ballad* pointed to the way in which Foster had moved beyond a 'persona' confined to his fiction to become 'a kind of hyper-Foster himself.' Matthews concluded that *The Glade* and its accompanying works asked 'to be read as a political intervention'.

In a sense, Foster created an impasse in the critical response to his work. He has been taken up by journalists (such as Paul Sheehan and Michael Duffy) who like to take positions oppositional to what they see as those of the left-leaning intelligentsia. In the past few years, he has published essays in *Quadrant*, a journal that has supported attacks on revisionist history and postmodernist theory. This suggests his alignment with the vocal group of right-wing 'stirrers', who contribute to the daily newspapers or 'talkback' radio in Australia, upholding conservative social attitudes. While some of Foster's essays may support this alignment, his extravagant and brilliant fiction never leaves readers with such clear-cut positions.

Foster's fiction is so ambitious and wide-ranging that it is difficult to do justice to it in a single critical work. Each of the major works is sufficiently complex to warrant an individual study. The novels not only argue for multiple philosophical positions to be held simultaneously, but they also demand to be read in a multitude of ways.

Foster's distrust of single systems of belief mocks any reductive or monolithic reading that earns the 'critic's hat: that's the big pointy one with "dunce" written on it' (*S&N* 166). Clearly, there are many ways to approach these novels: in terms of their place in the development of the novel in the late twentieth century and their contribution to a more local tradition in Australia; from poststructuralist feminist or masculinist perspectives; as integrations of scientific philosophy and art; as comic performances; as commentaries on Australian life. To choose one mode of criticism that can encompass the many complexities of these novels is not only impossible but also out of keeping with the spirit of the fiction.

One of the most recurrent concerns in the fiction is the sense of Australia as an outpost of civilisation, a colony that did not manage to shake off its mimic British culture before it embraced further colonisation by a homogenised global culture. Clearly, this book could trace Foster's analysis of the postcolonial (or colonial, as Foster would insist) condition of Australia. Such a reading might give fuller consideration to Foster's more recent comments about the state of Australia's Aborigines and their relationship to white settler society. It might also attend more to Foster's commitment to Australian vernacular language and humour and his resistance to more 'international' and cosmopolitan styles of writing.

I have been attracted by the possibilities of reading Foster's novels as satires that contribute to the development of the novel as a postmodernist art form. Clearly, the relationship between satire and postmodernism has been neglected by a critical practice that is often dispersed into interest groups along national, international, ideological, or historical lines. This book comments on the experimental nature of individual novels, and notes that Foster has a postmodern awareness of the failures of a range of belief systems from religions and scientific theories to the narrative forms of literature. Yet he does not adopt a postmodernist cynicism about belief, as he continues to pursue spiritual answers in the analogies of language. His determination to hold contradictory ideas simultaneously gives Foster's novels their satiric and comic sharpness.

Rather than pursue one of these strands of argument exclusively, I have chosen to present a chronological account of Foster's career, discussing almost all his published fiction in the order of publication. This provides a narrative structure for the book and allows readers to understand some of the relationships between and among Foster's novels. In proceeding in this way, I do not mean to suggest a simple progressive development of Foster's art alongside his life, nor do I wish to present the novels as merely a function of his personality. But the idea of satire as a performance in which the author's satirical persona 'inhabits' the text suggests that the living place of the satirist needs to be acknowledged in discussion of his work. Foster's writing insists on the presence of a writer behind the text, a living, struggling human being intent on creating art that is necessarily incomplete and provisional.

ENDNOTES

1. This heading was suggested by David Foster. Foster has made annotations to this and later chapters. Factual information has been incorporated into the text, but Foster's annotations are indicated by italics.
2. For further discussion, see Susan Lever, 'The Question of Literary Independence: *Quadrant* and Australian Writing'. *Outside the Book: Contemporary Essays on Literary Periodicals*. Ed. David Carter. Sydney: Local Consumption, 1991.165–176.

Chapter 2

'Hey Listen Australia! Wake Up to Yourself Will You!' Early Works

North South West

> There is no doubt about these goddam Students for a Democratic Society. You have to hand it to them. They'll bash your head in for you if you don't! I am against the politicization of the campus. Too much is at stake. (*North South West* 3)

So begins the ranting narrator of David Foster's first novella in his first published work, *North South West* (1973). He is a young married man, a former primary schoolteacher who failed Chemistry at the University of Sydney, now training to become a television producer-director for the Australian Broadcasting Commission (ABC). His historical moment is precise: 1968. John Gorton is Prime Minister, the Vietnam War rages, and university campuses are full of middle-class protesters. He scorns these comfortable radicals, but he is not some right-wing conservative. He rages against the mediocrity and mimicry in Australia's response to America:

> Let's be the kind of capitalists Americans will hate! Let's be capitalists who won't let the USA exploit us. Let's kick the USA ass once and for all off of our territories! What sort of a country must we be if the USA like us? And they do like us, they love us you know, they think we may be their only real friend left, ever since that time disgusting Harold Holt made our sycophantic intentions plain. Good old Australia Americans think as with doors locked against the SDS and Black Militia they watch on the television Tony Roche from outback Tarcutta play Rod Laver from outback Rockhampton. It is the last frontier, they say to their wives, I should buy a piece of it at the going market price. I should immigrate. Let's take their one last friend away! Let's show the bastards they don't have a friend in the world! (31)

As he raves against the cultural backwardness, the decadence, and hypocrisy of Australia, he wanders the Sydney western suburbs line between Redfern and Strathfield. His pregnant wife, Angela, returns to the suburb of her childhood home, Strathfield, while the narrator struggles back towards Redfern, renting flats and units in Stanmore, The Warren, Croydon Park, Strawberry Hill. The narrator provides obsessive and absurd detail about the railway stations on the line between Redfern and Strathfield. He details the bus routes necessary to cross the city beyond the railway, and he mocks the culture of Angela's family:

> All the furnishings on the way made me want to throw up. The chandeliers, the plush sofas, the carpetings, the correct darkwood furniture where the plates and ornamental knives were kept. All *tasteless*, uncomfortable, not very splendid at last, typically Strathfield quack. I could furnish a house in Strathfield quack, things that you hate fasten on to you, oh, oh, if only one could learn to *ignore*! (38–39)

The narrator is unstable, irresponsible, concerned about his masculine status, and caught in mental processes that move between thesis and antithesis: 'Not merely can I *see* both sides of the story—I favour both impartially!' (51).

So, while the narrator rails against the comforts and complacency of Australian life, his unreliability and instability bounce back to satirise him. He wants to be an artist, but he is confined by the sheer ordinariness of Australian life, even his own ordinariness, and the overwhelming cultural heritage from Britain and America. The running script for the film he is writing depicts Australianness, not in the city scenes of the rest of the novella, but in the gibber deserts of the interior. The narrator's idea for a film falls back on stereotypes of the outback, despite the city boundaries of his life. The narrator of his script finds himself lost in the desert with the companionship of Salty Sands, an Aboriginal boxer, and in a moment of 'chagrin' knocks him out with a rock. When he returns to their truck and is rescued, he assumes Salty 'met up with some of his own people and went off to live with them' (72).

North South West has the hallmarks of satire—its rancorous, digressive narrative voice floods us with excessive detail about the narrator's world as well as his own imaginings. Its humour builds on our recognition of the accuracy of the absurdities it notes—the masses of official reading matter on the walls of the waiting room at Stanmore station, the view from The Warren View Hotel, the bleak nature of suburban home units. Now it reads like a time capsule of inner Sydney life in the late 1960s; Foster's observation almost invites nostalgia for the homely customs of the past.

The novella runs for seventy-six pages—about the limit for its excursion into one man's comic anger and despair. It is a version of Patrick White's rave against Australian cultural mediocrity, 'The Prodigal Son', though delivered to a new generation fifteen years later, as White seemed to recognise (337).[1] Foster invites us to laugh at the impossibilities of the Australian situation. We're too comfortable to have a revolution, yet we do American things so ineptly: '*As Australians, we're going to miss out on having a culture of our own*! That's a national tragedy' (20). This attitude, too, was a feature of the moment of his writing; indeed, such sentiments formed part of the movement for change that brought the Whitlam Labor government to power in 1972.

Foster had declared his interests and his abilities. He was embroiled in contradiction, struggling with masculine irresponsibility and domestic duty, angry at the complacent culture in which he found himself, and anxious that he too might be mediocre. His eye for detail would be the basis for his comic writing and for his digressive excesses. As his narrator stares out of the train window on the Western suburbs line, he claims that 'as the future cinematographic poet of all these stations (Sydney in general) it was of the utmost necessity that I be familiar with *all* the people of Sydney, as my subjects' (34). This desire to encompass all the diversity and variety of experience and possibility drives Foster's fiction. He later objected to the social science practice of generalising from a few particular cases, but when he applies his scientist's training to observing everything, the detail overwhelms us.

The contradiction between the multiplicity of the observed world and the selectiveness of fiction pushes Foster's voice towards satire. It is as if a postmodernist consciousness of the partiality of narrative demands a satiric response. Foster appears to be finding his own way towards a kind of satire emerging in 1970s and 1980s fiction that came to be called postmodernist. Of course, we may call it postmodernist now, but this kind of satiric response to multiple possibilities also appears in Furphy's *Such Is Life* (1903) and the pre-modernist *Tristram Shandy* (1767).

The other stories in the book, 'Mobil Medley' and 'Time's Arrow', do not have the same driving energy as does the title story, but they also sound out areas that Foster would develop in later work. 'Mobil Medley' consists of a series of anecdotes told by three young men as they walk along a country road on their way to a town called Mobil. Keith, a musician, talks about sharing a compartment with an unemployed beekeeper on a train trip home, how he was surprised at the man's tender care for him, before overhearing him describe Keith as a 'poof with hair down to his arse' (98). John, described by the frame narrator as the 'country narrator', talks about his relationship with his brother, Shane, and the way in which they gradually exchange roles. The frame narrator tells a city story about his girlfriend and their journey to the Blue Mountains. Then John and Keith return to stories about their relationship with the town of Mobil, and the story ends with yet another storyteller, Seamus Kakaclyptos, talking to an unidentified speaker.

The narrative voices are undifferentiated and they all express a masculine sense of loneliness and unease. Domestic life fills them with disgust and fear:

> I awoke being grimly shaken and unaccustomed and resentful at being thus awakened, fearful for the conduct of my weekend, heard the declamation, disgusting, left in a disgusting condition! What, what I cried, what is this? For by this time my head had been cuffed and my blankets torn from about me. The bathroom has been left in a disgusting condition, whereupon a cloth smelling most overpoweringly of disinfectant was thrust in my face, and in confusion I was shoved into the bathroom where, as far as I could discover, my mission was to soak up one frightened globule of liquid from the toilet seat. (176–177)

The three storytellers all yearn for a life beyond the confines of the family house and the country town, but their experiences of the city are squalid and hopeless. While they are repelled by the domesticity represented by women, each of the men seeks some meaning from spiritualism, drugs, or the bush. The frame narrator, the city boy, finds nature to be the answer:

> Since I was a little boy happily ripping paper bark off Melaleuca species in the National Park, I have had a sensuous respect for bushland. To go amongst it blinded would be to die wise. Now a thorn pierces the sole of the foot, now a blackboy's salicaceous or whatever leaf rips the leg. Now dark mosses and cold clammy round grey-feeling stones, now the cold trunk of an angophora, smoother than a child's thigh. Now, bumbling down amongst hakea, now clambering higher, witnessed by the mountain devils. Eventually to fall over some precipice or other, to die wise or at any rate wiser, of a cracked head. (131–132)

These narrators and their stories fold into each other, leaving us uncertain of their status and of whether there is one narrator or three—though we know, of course, that there is only one author writing the three voices. The frame narrator tells us at the beginning that 'after a time, I forgot I had never been to Mobil at all, but began to think I had perhaps lived there, perhaps as a child' (79), inviting us to see the stories of Keith and John as fictions of his own invention. All this is offered in a high style in contrast to the catalogue of domestic trivia and absurdity. The tales of masculine frustration and failure come to us through a detached, educated voice. They detail aspects of life too minor for the attention of literary authors—except that William Burroughs, Jack Kerouac, and later Charles Bukowski were travelling this path. The stories appear to be structureless improvisations on the theme of escape from domesticity, but we can see some of Foster's later preoccupations beginning to emerge. Even the fall from the precipice recurs in *Moonlite* and *The Land Where Stories End*.

'Time's Arrow' takes scientific enquiry as the basis for philosophical doubt about any possible future for the universe. The narrator discovers the concept of entropy in Nathanael West's satiric novel, *Miss Lonelyhearts* (1933), and commits himself to understanding it through scientific research. He takes the thermodynamic theory of entropy as a prediction of future chaos: the Second Law of Thermodynamics, as announced in 1850 by the German scientist Rudolf Clausius, states, 'the entropy of an isolated system not in equilibrium will tend to increase over time, approaching a maximum value at equilibrium', or more sensationally, 'the entropy of the universe tends to a maximum'. The title of the story refers to the irreversibility of time, and appears to reference Ludwig Boltzmann's theories about probability and molecular chaos.

With his scientist drinking companions at the ANU's University House, the narrator develops theories about the imminent end of the world. His friend, Fargo, argues that the solution would be for the human life span to be reduced to thirty years, making room for variety in the species, combating pollution, and preventing 'the boredom and spiritual malaise liable to descend around age twenty nine' (216). As Fargo approaches his thirtieth birthday, the narrator plans to act on this theory by taking all of them up to the Brindabella hills outside Canberra and shooting them all. At the last minute, he baulks and we are left with the slightest moment of optimism: 'a sudden flash of inexpressible lust for life—negentropy triumphing in the instinct of self forever' (239).

Here Foster makes his first attempt to apply scientific concepts and theories to his fiction. The increased entropy of the universe presents the prospect of total destruction, which makes much of the scientific research conducted at the Research School needless. It also confronts literary notions of narrative and faith in the movement towards a future. Despite its absurdities, the story also sets out some of the ideas that Foster would develop in major novels, such as *Moonlite* and *Mates of Mars*. It demonstrates that he could seek out the underlying philosophy of science and explore some of its implications in fiction. This seems like an alternative universe to the conventional Australian fiction of the early 1970s.

In 1976, Foster recommended that Geoffrey Dutton read *The Eight Deadly Sins of Civilized Man* by the Austrian zoologist and Nobel Prize winner Konrad Lorenz, as an accessible and enlightening scientific account of the imminent collapse of society—including the risks of entropy and overpopulation (11 Mar 1976 DP Series 2/ Box 13/ Folder 86). Elements of Lorenz's argument about the way that civilisation is causing the destruction of the natural world appear in Foster's novels and essays throughout his career—especially the human abuse of domesticated animals, and our voracious consumption. Lorenz saw the gradual triumph over the obstacles to human biological success through technology and medical advance as creating a 'positive feedback' cycle that would lead to entropy, in the form of the destruction of the rest of the natural world.

In summary, his 'sins' are overpopulation, the devastation of the natural environment, the dependence on technology and consequent loss of human values, the human self-indulgence and weakness that follows loss of any serious challenges to survival, genetic decay, the loss of tradition and respect for elders, the de-individualising effects of mass media, and nuclear weapons. Lorenz predicted that '[e]ventually Western peoples will no longer be able to compete with the less pampered and more healthy peoples of the East' (21). In his view, technological progress was creating a spiritual crisis—not just through the devastation of the natural world, but through the loss of the human capacity for 'emotion and awe'. Clearly, these ideas, with their prediction of an inevitable human decline as a result of human success, drew a response from a satirist/scientist who was alert to paradox. Foster's writing in the 1970s puts these ideas into a scientific perspective, though he would elaborate them in poetic and religious terms in later novels, such as *Mates of Mars* and *The Glade Within the Grove*.

The novellas of *North South West*, particularly 'Time's Arrow' with its explanations of the various definitions of entropy (and lack of capitals), require considerable commitment by the reader. They are most interesting now as experiments with voice, in the case of 'Mobil Medley', and with the possibilities of adapting scientific concepts to literary art in 'Time's Arrow'. While all three novellas are peculiar, 'North South West' remains memorable simply because it is so funny, turning the commonplaces of Sydney life over to uncover every aspect of incongruity and absurdity. Foster asked how such a mimic city could possibly take itself seriously, how Australians could even pretend to participate in the political, intellectual, and cultural struggles of the world. He wanted to participate in these struggles and to address serious issues, though satire might prove the only appropriate mode.

One of the interesting aspects of 'Time's Arrow' is its reference to Nathanael West's *Miss Lonelyhearts*, a novel that figures in literary histories of contemporary satire as one of the central Menippean satires of the twentieth century. Weisenburger sees it as the precursor to the American postmodernist satires of William Gaddis, Thomas Pynchon, Robert Coover, and others, because of its exposure of various levels of fiction-making. West's novel insists on the bleakness of a secular world as it follows the myths that sustain its characters. In his novellas, Foster shares some of West's critical observations of the emptiness of the modern world, and his awareness of the fictions that give us faith in any future, or any belief system.

West wrote novellas rather than novels (only three were published before he died in a car accident), and it is difficult to see how his bleak view of the world could be sustained over the length of a novel. *North South West* consists of three similarly short canters in the direction of misanthropy and despair. Foster explores ambitious ideas that he would pursue in his later fiction, but he had not yet found a form that could lead him out of a single satiric voice into the more complex characterisation and narrative of a novel. Just as Peter Carey's stories, published around the same time, provide the necessary limit to his fantastic ideas, Foster's novellas could bear ideas rather better than characters. Nevertheless, these ideas opened up a storehouse of material that would support a range of novels.

The Pure Land

With the support of Geoffrey Dutton and a grant from Whitlam's Australia Council, Foster pushed on to write the full-length novel, *The Pure Land* (1974). Like many first novels, this relies heavily on the author's autobiography, even assigning a variation of his mother's family name, Manning, for the errant grandfather of his young scientist, Danny Harris, and a version of his father's name for Wee Georgie Harris, Danny's absent vaudevillian father.

Apart from family similarities, Danny's dilemma as a scientist and spiritualist expressed Foster's own crisis at the time. Danny, driving himself towards a career in biochemistry, is appalled by the emptiness and hypocrisy of scientific culture, with its dependence on rational logic, and he abandons it to seek a more creative and spiritual existence.

The novel begins in the Blue Mountains of New South Wales in the 1930s, where Albert Manwaring conducts a photographic business, taking photographs of mountain scenery that express his own sentimental attitude to nature. Manwaring's photographs suggest that 'a European principality had somehow been broken up and concealed in valleys and behind ferns, and the tourist game lay partly in guessing where' (40). A chance moment of voyeurism leads Manwaring to embark for America to pursue a career as a pornographer. He takes his daughter Janet with him, deliberately separating her from her mother, who remains in Bondi. Janet, as Jean, marries the vaudeville and radio star, George Harris, and gives birth to Danny, before marrying again (this time to an academic doctor) and finding herself in the 'death in life' of the American intellectual middle class. Manwaring, on the other hand, abandons his sleazy calling to seek spirituality in an ashram in Los Angeles.

Danny represents the hope for stability of his mother and grandfather, and his stepfather nurtures him in the intellectual life. He diligently pursues biochemistry through degrees at MIT and subsequently Berkeley, before facing a crisis of belief as a postdoc at Foster's own postdoctoral campus in Philadelphia. The permissive society of the late 1960s begins to rage around him but, apart from smoking marihuana, Danny has kept an unswerving devotion to the intellectual discipline of science. In Philadelphia, he can no longer keep up with the 'East Coast Jews intent upon Nobel Prizes and other secrets of the universe [who] literally ran from bench to desk and back again' (138). Danny and his stepsister, Sylvia, become lovers before he finally abandons science in a public scene at a conference in Los Angeles.

From this point, the novel follows Danny's search for a philosophical answer; he visits his grandfather for advice and drives up the West Coast of America with various dropouts, while pondering the limitations of Scientific Method. The logically trained mind, though, cannot easily adopt the fashionable philosophies of the West Coast. Danny rejects Zen (as Foster has done) as 'too practical'. In the campus bookshop, he buys Daisetz Teitaro Suzuki's essays on the Pure Land, a sect of the Mahayana, as a starting point. His grandfather suggests that Australia may be this Land for Danny, but warns him that it will be a step down to 'a less advanced culture'. So Danny makes his way to Australia, in the hope that it is his Land of Purity.

Through his American eyes, Danny sees Sydney as simple and backward. He wanders through the same parts of the city that

Manwaring had rejected as secondhand British. Where Manwaring tramped through the Domain area of Sydney scorning:

> The mock buildings, the library with its cavernous and portentous air as though no one should shout out in it for fear of dislodging the colony's naked dust and cobwebs and musty mock scholarship, more than one century old and undisturbed...He trod venomously all around and over Australia on the tiled foyer mosaic, thinking how little he cared for or admired Bass and Flinders and their confreres and schoolboy exploits. It was a pubescent dream, all this a dream, this colony, a dream of the accursed British, another fluttering of their dusty, blood-encrusted gonfalon. (77)

By contrast, Danny enjoys the Library, and he finds the Australian art in the State Gallery marvellously derivative—seeing Chagall in Arthur Boyd, and Rousseau and Klee in Sidney Nolan (208).

In the last few chapters, Danny's voice takes over the novel in a stream of letters to Sylvia describing his reactions to Katoomba and the traces of his grandfather's and mother's lives there. We leave him as he tries to interpret Manwaring's nostalgic photographs of Blue Mountains life before the war. The novel has returned to its beginning. Australia is the Pure Land only in the sense that it is backward, sentimental, conformist, comfortable, mimicking other civilisations, and simple-minded. Compared to Philadelphia, it is uncorrupted, not so much through inherent purity and innocence as through ignorance and distance. Jean breaks into tears over 'The Sick Stockrider' and 'Clancy of the Overflow', and the contrast between those simple ballads and the despairing novel we are reading could not be more striking.

Despite its occasional humour and sharp critique of Australian and American life, the novel creates an unrelieved sense of bleakness. Manwaring's life in Katoomba is circumscribed and dull; he has failed as a husband and proves an insensitive and selfish father. Janet/Jean struggles through adult life in the United States, deceived by Danny's father and bored by her second husband. Her life as a housewife consists of a sterile routine that leaves her distant and on the edges of sanity. After years of docile submission to logical reasoning,

Danny, at least, responds energetically to his enlightenment, surrendering himself to the experience of a new/old land.

When the novel comes close to Danny's consciousness, its pace increases, as Danny gives Foster the opportunity to rant about the slums of Philadelphia, or the New Age philosophies of California, or the somnolent backwardness of Australia. At its most exuberant, the novel bursts into long sentences, full of digressions and parentheses that go on for pages. It is also packed with bits of learning, misspellings, and arcane words (e.g., 'obtund,' 'saprophyte'), including the jargon of biochemistry.

The Pure Land offers a critique of contemporary scientific culture in which the bench scientist devotes himself to the routines of testing, unaware of developments outside his own narrow field. The discoveries of particle physics imply the demise of all such single-minded certainties, but the scientist in the laboratory is in no position to speculate about alternatives. As a result, Foster suggests, modern science denies creativity to the most highly trained intellects in society. In Australia, the situation is exacerbated by the small scale of research activity—the Australian conference delegates tell Danny that Australian biochemistry is: 'Full of bacterial cultures, plants in greenhouses, you wouldn't believe it. Also a great many local products overseas stranded on postdocs trying to get back home. Small country overproducing in the field of pure science for reasons best known to itself, no national science policy…' (160).

This is, of course, also the dilemma of Danny, and of David Foster at the time of writing. Western society offers science as the highest form of intellectual striving, yet in practice it is routine and unimaginative. On the other hand, the creative arts appear divorced from any reference to scientific truth. Danny's quest moves him towards the life of intuition and art, even to the writing of the novel we are reading. Nevertheless, the novel measures what he has lost.

Ken Gelder has argued that *The Pure Land* offers a self-contradictory movement, with the characters becoming their own opposites. Danny's nostalgia for purity is dismantled by the way his journey to Australia is also a movement backwards to the past.

Gelder compares this pattern with Paul de Man's reading of Derrida on Jean-Jacques Rousseau, in which Rousseau's mythology of innocent beginnings is self-contradictory so that his idea of history is 'a simultaneous movement towards progress and retrogression' (153). This kind of continuous undermining of ostensible commitment reappears in Foster's fiction.

In a letter to Dutton before its publication, Foster made it clear that the sense of regression in the novel was intentional:

> It is more or less intended that the book become capable of a wholly new interpretation after having been read through. The pattern in section 4, where 'fiction' is increasingly taking over from 'fact', should serve to jolt the reader into a feeling that the book is perhaps not a simple chronology. Danny is obviously beginning to fantasize his experiences—with his disaffection towards logic and causality adumbrating this—and the book can be now seen as beginning with his arrival in Australia. It then should be obvious that the first 3 sections, which read at first as conventional storyline, are capable of being reinterpreted as having been written by Danny *after* the end of section 4. You will note, for example, that there are no incidents in section 1 that are not recapitulated in section 4, more or less in reverse order. In other words, I suggest an identification between myself and Danny, and put him in the position of having invented himself. The effect should be that he arises naturally out of the novel, but once he has appeared the novel becomes apparent as the product of his own mind. This is intended as, partially, comment upon the attitude of a person of his makeup is obliged to adopt in the circumstances he places himself in. It also forecasts the effects of refuting logic and causality, both good and bad—He has opted for 'fiction' over 'fact' and the book should slide the same way… I would like it to confound analysis, but oblige the reader to reconsider the whole book. (1 Jun 1973 DP 2/12/81)

The rejection of logic and causality leads to fiction and self-invention. *The Pure Land*, then, invites us to question its reliability as a chronology and as a representation of anything beyond the author's own invention. This is the kind of undermining of fiction that we now might see as postmodernist. Foster divides fact from fiction, science from the imagination, and logic and causality from intuition, though the divisions cannot be clear-cut. His novel folds into itself to suggest the blurring of boundaries. Just as Foster questions the basis of science and finds it wanting, he also questions the premises of fiction.

Whenever Danny ponders the hopelessness of suburban America or the narrow-mindedness of science or the imitative Australian culture, *The Pure Land* plunges into satire, but unlike the earlier novellas it has too much commitment to its characters to maintain a detached satirical position. Manwaring, Janet/Jean, and Danny are more than the embodiment of particular ideas; they are lonely, despairing individuals and, at least for a time, the novel appears to care about how they reached this predicament. Nevertheless, the novel ruthlessly leaves Manwaring and Jean behind (Danny has no idea what has happened to his mother) as Danny pursues spiritual enlightenment.

Foster clearly was developing a form that could encompass the conventions of the novel at the same time that it questioned them. He had moved beyond the obsessive male narrators of *North South West* to try a third person voice approximating that of the conventional novel, at least at the beginning of the work. But Danny's ambivalent relationship to that voice allows him to disturb the reader's confidence in knowing precisely who is speaking.

While it is sharp and savage, *The Pure Land* only occasionally incites laughter. Its characters retain our sympathy enough for us to feel appalled at their discontent and the impossibility of their escape. When it was republished in 1985, reviewers advised readers that it posed difficulties of comprehension, but it also seemed to belong to an earlier time (Leonard). In 1974, though, it appeared as a brilliant addition to the fiction of a new generation that was changing Australian culture.

THE FLEEING ATALANTA

In the wake of the success of *The Pure Land*, Foster published his first book of poems, *The Fleeing Atalanta* (1975). Together the two books give some insight into the crisis that Foster was undergoing during 1973 and 1974. Though they do not form a clear narrative, the poems follow a lover's journey towards reconciliation and spiritual understanding through love. None are titled; they are simply numbered in consecutive order from 1 to 110.

Foster described them as 'an honest account of the battle to achieve enlightenment through love' (17 Sep 1974 DP 2/12/86). They are love poems, dedicated to Gerda Busch (but also to Frank Dwyer, a professor of Chemistry at ANU who was revered by Foster, and to the Alchemical writer Michael Maier). Nevertheless, they depict love as dangerous, savage, and difficult, shrouded by lust and requiring an exhausting struggle with the self. There is no sweetness or seductive bravado here; the achievement of a pure and beautiful love demands confrontation of the ugliness, jealousy, and despair within the lover.

While Foster's love poetry may seem surprisingly distant from the bleak cynicism and wit of *The Pure Land*, it is possible to feel that in *The Fleeing Atalanta* we are sharing the struggle for purity that Danny sought at the end of the novel. Purity is not to be found in sweet innocence, but through the 'sewers of experience', the recognition of one's weaknesses and the endurance of despair.

Gerda has admitted her surprise on receiving some of these poems during the first months of their relationship (Lacey 14); they do not offer any soft or flattering approach to love. The poet's feelings of guilt at abandoning his wife and children for a new love fill many of them, and he does not preserve his lover from his jealousy of her past. The question of how to achieve rebirth, in order to maintain a pure new relationship, dominates many of the poems. Alchemy, with its theory of achieving gold through the various black states of purification, provides an allegory for this progress to purity.

Images from alchemy, chemistry, and medieval and ancient mythology mingle with references to the more familiar life of Australian cities and country towns. There are passages of autobiography, such as the account of working in the train sheds at Darling Harbour (later to be developed in *Mates of Mars*), and scenes from the nightclubs where Foster played drums in the band while Gerda sang. Canberra's Haig Park with its cockatoos, or the lake where the lovers take their children, figure in individual poems.

Foster finds unusual images to depict the lover's mental state: his lover can describe his life as 'like a droplet poised in a pipette' (10), or himself like the toad of alchemic imagery that becomes an eagle '[b]y admitting its toad-like qualities' (88). Some familiar irony intrudes towards the end, as in 107:

> Those who climb the mountain by its difficult east face
> Find at the summit a kiosk a picnic spot
> And a government bus. The mountain is nonetheless theirs
> They dedicate it to all travellers. Who
> Walk without feet and climb without rope
> They allow to be other men travelling

Foster clearly saw the poem as a form in which he could confront emotion and express it, without the multiple layers of irony of his prose writing. These poems are deeply personal, and transparently about Foster's experience of investing in love, despite the pain and failures of the past. They express his particular private emotional journey at the beginning of his second marriage. Yet, by virtue of their refusal to sentimentalise emotion, they explore a more universal experience of adult love, with its accompanying lust and guilt.

There is evidence, too, of self-regarding male ego and misogyny. One wonders what is to be made of poems 102 or 103, where the poet states:

> A woman is a mirror, to be judged
> On her capacity to reflect
> Nothing more
> Easily debased
> Easily inspired (102)

Or:

> If you want a virgin for a wife
> Take a brazen, foul-mouthed slut
> And offer her respect…

> ...A woman
> Introduced to sex through rape
> Stays virginal and is very easy to find... (103)

At the very least, these attempt to express an unswerving account of a man's response to sexual love, including a fear of dispossession and an ambivalent attitude toward the physical sexual attractiveness of women. If the lover is self-centred, and projecting his own fears and imaginings onto 'woman', then that, too, may be an accurate account of the emotional and psychological response to love of some men. So, while the attitudes in the poems appear more savage and nasty than affectionate, they express an emotional turmoil that appears to be deeply felt.

Though these poems might have been well regarded among readers who admired Michael Dransfield's drug images or John Tranter's postmodern ironies, they were both too personal, and possibly too painfully direct, to meet the fashions of the mid-1970s. They do not follow the symbolist discipline taught in Australian universities as the mark of good poetry; there is no careful delineation of resonant sensual imagery. Like all of Foster's work, however, they are striking in their originality and willingness to address difficult subjects. Les Murray, who declares a preference for idiosyncrasy over the 'effortful originalities of modernism' included numbers 98, 104, and 109 in his *New Oxford Book of Australian Verse* (xxiii, 325–326).

These strange and disturbing poems also provide evidence for the sources of Foster's creative energy. He is not a romantic in the manner of Dransfield, seeking a source of imagery through hallucinatory drug experience. Nor is he romantic in the sense of seeking a higher and more beautiful creative world. His poems have some of the wit and experimental drive we expect from Tranter and John Forbes, but there seems to be no awareness of a public audience here, no shaping of the poetry to please friends or fellow poets. Yet Foster believes in seeking inner truths, and he has faith in his own creative powers as the source of this truth. He believes in inspiration and in the individual aesthetic urge that comes from it.

Foster has spoken and written many times of his desire to write lyric poetry rather than satire; for him, both kinds of writing come from the same source. He is as willing in his later novels to allow himself to improvise on a satirical theme as he is here to trust in an inner emotional journey as a source for poetry. Foster's later book of poetry, *The Ballad of Erinungarah*, has striking similarities to *The Fleeing Atalanta*, both in its structure and its use of mythology. *The Ballad* includes some nature lyrics that sit within a recognisable tradition. In his first book of poetry, Foster created his own.

ESCAPE TO REALITY

In 1977 a collection of short stories edited by Brian Kiernan, *The Most Beautiful Lies*, announced the arrival of a new generation of Australian men writers, represented by Murray Bail, Peter Carey, Morris Lurie, Frank Moorhouse, and Michael Wilding. Kiernan made no claims for his chosen writers constituting a movement, but saw their work as evidence of a new, less conventional approach to fiction, and he had no qualms about calling them 'major' writers (ix). Foster's collection of stories, *Escape to Reality*, appeared in the same year, and it was sometimes reviewed with it. He seems to have had no contact with more sociable writers such as Moorhouse, and he never published stories in journals, so he was outside the networks of critics like Kiernan and Wilding in the university English departments.

Foster's stories share some of the experimental concerns of Kiernan's selection, though he gives himself greater length to digress than in the short pieces in the anthology. Randolph Stow reviewed the two books together with Sumner Locke Elliott's *Water Under the Bridge* in the *Times Literary Supplement*, commenting that Foster wrote about 'aspects of life which could not have been mentioned in *The Most Beautiful Lies* without a jarring note', and he was therefore the writer 'most likely to say something acute, and possibly damaging, about Australia now'. While other writers of the 'new generation' played with self-conscious adaptations of fabulist or postmodernist styles, Foster distinguished himself by pursuing possibilities to the point of discomfort.

Escape to Reality has no currency in recent discussions of the Australian short story—Foster is not even mentioned in Bruce Bennett's 2002 survey. At the time of publication, though, it was greeted with respect by a range of critics both in the British Isles and in Australia. All of them found the collection disturbing: Nina Bawden found Foster 'an unusual and slightly alarming talent', and John Redmond speculated that Foster's cynical and despairing view of things might 'well cause some trouble back home in Australia'. Tom Paulin thought Foster had a 'powerful talent which can seize dreams as subjects and not be duped by them'; Lorna Sage found the book 'splendidly, not to say hermetically Australian: seven very funny, fast-talking, deadpan pieces, polished on the surface and savage in the interior' (1978).

Several admirers of *The Pure Land* saw *Escape to Reality* as confirmation of their trust in Foster's talent. Jamie Grant, reviewing it for the ABC's *Books and Writing* program, thought that Foster was 'frankly a bad writer', but he conceded admiration for 'The Job', in which 'the clumsiness of the writing, and the way the narrator often contradicts himself or misinterprets other people's actions...gives the story its humaneness'.

'The Job' is the strongest story in the collection, cleverly structured and blackly funny. The narrator of the story has just left jail when he is picked up by Brian, who is looking for an accomplice to rob the local RSL (Returned Servicemen's League—a social clubhouse, common in Australian towns). The two men spend months in the shed at Brian's farm, indulging in variations of masculine indolence, before a ludicrous practice robbery attempt at the local golf club. When they finally succeed in robbing the RSL, Brian disappears with the money, leaving the narrator with Brian's pregnant wife and several children. The narrator gradually takes over Brian's life, which includes his mistress from the local pub, and after a year with her in the city, he returns to prepare for another robbery of the RSL. The story ends with him waiting outside the jail in the hopes of picking up a young accomplice.

The narrator's mixture of learned vocabulary (aetiological, vermiculate, sudorific), passivity and stupidity, and the ploddingly deliberate style of his account create a constantly ironic narrative. At the same time, the narrator reflects philosophically on his condition—his passivity is a deliberate behavioural choice and one of the options of masculinity. Readers may recognise Brian's and the narrator's experiences with motor bikes, beer and life in the shed, and their attitude toward women and children as authentic to one form of Australian men's behaviour. The story does not simply mock this condition; it explores it as a valid approach to life.

Indeed, all of the stories in *Escape to Reality* reflect on the nature of masculinity, particularly its self-destructive and self-absorbed tendencies. 'Green Changes' gives an account of a drug-taking musician, neglectful of his young wife and child, who gradually destroys himself in Canberra. In 'The Salt Man' a young man visits his grandmother's sister and her husband. This gives Foster an opportunity to observe the domestication and feminising of old men, who spend their lives at the bowling club and sleep in feminine bedrooms. 'Going About' begins with a narrator who reflects that 'the sort of life most men lead today doesn't let them exercise their manhood. Most men today I think you'll find would still like to be hunters or fishermen' (55–56). 'The Hat' follows the life of jazz musicians in Sydney and details the absurdities of the Hat's day job in Inward Parcels at Central Railway Station. 'Murray River Breakdown' comes closest to the kind of stories written by Carey or Bail, in its development of an atmosphere of imminent action and threat. 'Escape to Reality' developed a more complicated story of artists in country towns.

Foster was apparently working through his ideas and techniques in these stories. Most have first person narrators, as in *North South West*, always men with a philosophical approach to their lives. Only 'Escape to Reality' adopts a more distant narrative position to handle its various points of view. This story addresses the problem of art and its relationship to Australian life, not to mention the way in which drugs can prevent the achievement of art while inciting aspirations to it. This suggests that after his defection from science, Foster now had doubts about the efficacy of art as an intellectual response to contemporary life.

The four main characters in 'Escape to Reality' are a migrant artist, an art teacher, an art critic, and a hypnotist, their lives linked only by the wife of the artist (taking the minor role typical for Foster's women). At one point in the story, the artist starts to write a novel on the premise that 'novels were causing the decline of civilised man' (178), and the story as a whole suspects art as an activity. The critic hates every artwork he sees; the art teacher is so addled by drugs that everything appeals to him. The hypnotist wants to abandon the entertainment part of his show to speculate about the imaginative world evident in his subjects. This is the 'escape to reality' of the story's title, where the hypnotist proposes that subjects enrich their fantasies 'by presenting reality as the *ultimate fantasy*!' (176).

It may be that Foster is proposing that the creation of art is less important than the intellectual and imaginative processes behind it. Art may be a retreat from life into fantasy—or life may be apprehended as fantastic through art. Certainly, he seems already jaded by the world of critics, teachers, and promoters that surround the making of art. Josef, painting with blood on sheets of iron and then destroying his own work, offers a kind of model for a pure artist. Maybe the journey of the mind mattered more than the work it created.

In 1977 Foster replied to a questionnaire from *Australian Literary Studies*, saying that he felt he was contributing to 'an already vast literature on twentieth century disaffection', and he described the qualities of his fiction as 'ambivalence, flippancy, obscurity, wit, gnosticism, guilt, schizophrenia, monomania, disgust, and the struggle to emerge from all this ratiocination grown tired towards something better' (196–197). The stories of *Escape to Reality* retain the bleakness of vision that marked *The Pure Land*, and it is clear that Foster was trying to find a style that could release him to explore his own particular obsessions. Though these stories offer deadpan delivery of ludicrous material, their humour is understated and black, rather than the exaggerated and excessive comedy of some of Foster's later work. Elements of satire intrude from time to time, particularly when the stories observe the detail of Australian domestic life, but Foster had not yet found the exuberant inventiveness of his later satiric voice.

The Empathy Experiment

In 1977, the same year that *Escape to Reality* appeared, the independent publishers Wild & Woolley published a strange little book, co-written by D. M. Foster and a fellow scientist, 'D. K. Lyall'. *The Empathy Experiment* was as much a scientific experiment as science fiction, in that it appears to have been written as an exercise in empathy by its two authors. In 1975 Foster told Dutton that he and Des Kirk, a scientist friend, had planned the book together but that he had written it (17 May 1975 DP2//13/90). In 1986 he told Candida Baker that Des was having a nervous breakdown at the time and 'we thought it was too good an opportunity to miss': 'It was a real collaboration in so far as he did some of the writing and I contributed some of the scientific ideas to it' (116). The proposition is absurd enough—it portrays the experiences of F. X. Galton, a dope-addicted empathic psychologist in a scientific institute in a town like Canberra, as he conducts experiments on fellow scientists and animals and becomes increasingly deviant himself.

In some respects, *The Empathy Experiment* is a drug novel, seemingly fired by dope as well as describing the paranoid drug fantasies of F. X. Nowadays, the most entertaining aspect of *The Empathy Experiment* is the photo of the two profusely bearded young authors dressed in duffle coats, jeans, and strange headgear, peering out of the back cover. The novel is an artefact of the 1970s, and a sign that Foster could not take himself too seriously as a high literary writer. Despite its silliness, it also has lots of the wit that marks Foster as a writer: 'Because of research he had lost his marriage, but thanks to research he could tolerate the loss' (9).

When it appeared, Damien Broderick understood *The Empathy Experiment* as a 'Spenserian allegory with slapstick and farce' and he could see that the authors were 'concerned with subjectivity versus objectivity in science, and the general truth of Heisenberg's Uncertainty (that experimenter and experiment are mutually interactive)'(62). But most reviewers, even those who admired Foster's earlier work, found it impenetrable and overwritten. This 'backwater of eccentricity' (18 Dec 1977 FP Series 9/Folder 1), as the ABC radio reviewer called it, gave warning of the unpredictability of Foster's talent, and his willingness to try anything.

Foster later tried science fiction, writing a radio play called 'The Elixir Operon' (produced on ABC Radio in 1980) that was then published as a story in Damien Broderick's *Strange Attractors: Original Australian Speculative Fiction* (1985). This story, narrated by a cell on the bronchial wall, follows the cell's conversion to a cancer and eventual destruction of the whole body. While this sounds educational—Hobart Medical School put it on a student reading list (letter from G. W. Boyd 11 Sep 1991 FP 1/29)—the story plays off the totalitarian nature of the functioning body (with cells never questioning their role) and the cheeky rebellion of the narrator. An invading virus promises the cell an elixir of understanding—entangling Christian, alchemical, and sci-fi mythology in a new dimension. Surprisingly, the story has a political element; the rebellious cell, once enlightened by knowledge gives up working: 'I'd become a thinker, free to dwell on social problems' (140). She preaches freedom to the other cells, with the encouragement '[r]ealise your full potential'. This is futile, however, and the cell goes on to an individual (and multiple) destiny, dividing itself to massive and destructive proportions.

The story is an amusing projection of contemporary ideas onto the biological system of the body, particularly enjoyable for its dialogues between cells:

> Above the raucous jeering of the police, I heard another sound. 'Leave those kids alone,' said a voice. 'Yeah, leave those kids alone,' said another voice. 'pick on someone your own age!'

> The cells of the channel wall were speaking! They hardly ever spoke. What was I doing to attract their attention? Was it my crying? It was! I made myself as infantile as possible. 'Goo goo goo,' I said to the police. The channel wall went ga-ga.
>
> 'Steady on, girls,' said the chief of police, 'you're not going to fall for the oldest trick in the book! Show some discrimination! This is no baby, this is a tumour. Can't you tell the difference?'
>
> 'Leave that kid alone.' Came the answer.
>
> 'She was invaded by a virus,' said the chief. 'Many moons ago, of course, but…'
>
> 'Poor little darling,' retorted a wall cell. 'Imagine what she's been through! If we can't provide for those less fortunate than ourselves, what kind of a society are we? It's not her fault she can't get a job. And you want her thrown on the scrapheap—for shame.' (146)

Foster later claimed that he was disappointed in science fiction as a mode; it 'had nothing to do with science, much less to do with fiction' (av 1987). In practice, this little story came closer to satire, using the crisis of the cancerous cell as another version of the rebellious seeker for hidden knowledge, and as a mockery of the complacent attitudes of the society in which he or she festered.

By the late 1970s, then, Foster was recognised not only as a writer of talent, but also (more importantly) as one who had the courage to address ambitious ideas. Few critics doubted his capacities, but he was clearly eccentric and wayward. In Australia, of course, there is always the hope that a new writer may produce a major work that will define the nation. There were signs, though, that he would go his own way, and that he resisted the accepted notions of high literary art. He might play around with farce, experiment with drugs for inspiration, try some science fiction, or write strange poetry. He might well have shone for a decade like others of his generation before settling down to an academic career or being overwhelmed by drugs. In 1981, however, he published *Moonlite*, a novel that fulfilled the expectations of his admirers. The next chapter will explore Foster's emergence as a novelist of account.

Endnote

1. Geoffrey Dutton quotes White's comment: 'I suppose one reason why I like Foster's novels is that he isn't afraid of sour milk and what's repulsive in life' in 'David Foster: The Early Years'.

Chapter 3

Satirical Histories: *Moonlite* and *The Adventures of Christian Rosy Cross*

Until 1981, Foster's career as a writer appeared to follow a familiar path for the beginning author, despite the peculiarities of his writing. He had published a novella and short stories, then a mainly autobiographical novel. On the strength of *The Pure Land*, he was able to indulge himself in the eccentricities of *The Empathy Experiment*, and to publish a collection of personal poetry.

Then he published *Moonlite* (1981), a novel that would establish his reputation and which continues to be rediscovered and acclaimed by critics. While *North South West*, *The Pure Land*, and *Escape to Reality* revealed Foster's brilliant potential as a writer, *Moonlite* confirmed that potential by offering a sustained, ambitious, and passionate novel of ideas. Helen Daniel, D. R. Burns, Stephen Harris, and Kerryn Goldsworthy all refer to it as an important or 'landmark' Australian novel, and Geoffrey Dutton felt confident enough of its merits to make it the last book in his *The Australian Collection: Australia's Greatest Books*. Dutton called it 'perhaps the most original of all Australian novels' and compared it to *Tristram Shandy* as a novel that 'could survive on the style alone' (395, 398).

Moonlite offers a satiric interpretation of the history of Australian settlement by considering the intellectual forces behind colonialism. It imagines the pre-Christian religious beliefs of a group of Scottish islanders, and it delineates the way that nineteenth-century positivist thinking prepared the path for Australian materialism and greed. The novel explores the philosophical encounter between Western civilisation and the natural religions that preceded it, and it contrasts the timeless outlook of pre-industrial societies with the swiftly passing time of the modern world. *Moonlite* mimics this collision of time by devoting half its length to the unchanging patterns of life on a remote Scottish island, then by accelerating as its protagonist encounters life at an English university, and finally by reaching high speed as he rises to prominence in the New West Highlands. It was a surprising shift to large and expansive matters from the rather self-absorbed individual focus of Foster's earlier short stories and novel. After the brittle pessimism of his earlier work, *Moonlite* offered a more humane and comic understanding.

Behind this extraordinary achievement lies another novel, *The Adventures of Christian Rosy Cross*, which Foster began writing in 1973. This novel had been completed as a trilogy by 1976, but did not reach the public until 1986, after the publication of *Moonlite* and *Plumbum*. Writing it turned Foster into a novelist capable of taking on subjects well beyond the range of personal experience and it provided the testing ground for his satirical approach. It was also a spiritual journey, a means for Foster to explore alternatives to the Christian tradition, and a way to discover the nature of his own creativity. This spiritual and creative journey accompanied his emergence from a personal crisis.

At the end of May 1973, Foster and his family moved from Hazelbrook in the lower Blue Mountains to suburban Canberra where he worked as a postman in the mornings and played drums at night. In August he heard that he had been granted an Australia Council fellowship for the next two years, and he became 'a full time cultural bludger' in September (21 Sep 1973 DP 2/12/86). He began to immerse himself in alchemical reading and he experimented with drugs. In February 1974 he left Robin and the children and moved into University House at ANU. He wrote to Dutton that he felt he had been reborn through his reading of alchemical and hermetic texts, and through a new love for 'a woman who makes meaningful all the seemingly meaningless factors I have hitherto attempted to suppress' (14 Feb 1974 DP 2/12/84). This enlightenment would surely have an effect on his writing:

> All the sour misanthropy, confusion, suspicion, misogyny, cynicism, of my work up till now feels to have been swept totally away. I know now that if you seek long enough, & hard enough, you find. I am at the usual age for this type of realization (death is after all only metamorphosis) and I see now a kind of sense in the work I have written up till now. It may have been bad, but it was the truth as I saw it, and that is the only prospect for a work of art. (14 Feb 1974 DP 2/12/84)

In a postscript to a letter to Dutton, he explained his use of hashish and the enlightenment that he felt this brought him—though he was 'easing off' on the drugs 'since I feel I don't need them any more (in case you feel worried that my so-called "enlightenment" may be nothing more than a drug-induced psychosis)'. He claimed that drugs like hashish 'teach one the existence of a separate reality':

> If one is prepared enough and preparation, ie years of struggling and reading and thinking over works which describe and events which depict the truth, but which one cannot understand—one immediately or gradually realizes that a separate reality, no less beautiful and a great deal more abiding, may also be obtained by recognizing and living the *truth*; this is a separate reality, and I suppose it offers a paradise on earth—insofar as the symbolism of the enlightenment experience—leaving one's whole life as Joseph his coat in the land of the

> harlot (Emerson)—teaches one the real necessity for death prior to rebirth. (27 Feb 1974 DP 2/12/84)

Foster deplored the abuse of drugs, but:

> I regard them as one of the few ways in which modern man can achieve some insight, and in *this* sense, I am very strongly in their favour. It is quite certain, from hermetic literature and elsewhere, that carefully controlled and rigidly prepared experiences of a similar nature constituted the initiation to the higher mysteries of the ancient religions. (27 Feb 1974 DP 2/12/84)

This was the subject of the novel he was writing, *The Adventures of Christian Rosy Cross*.

By the end of 1974, Foster and Gerda Busch were living together. Foster finished the manuscript of *Christian Rosy Cross* in January 1975 and the next month they moved to the village of Bundanoon on the plateau above the Morton State Forest in New South Wales, roughly equidistant from Sydney and Canberra. They married later that year, and have lived in Bundanoon ever since.

Foster's letters to Dutton over the next ten years reveal the progress of *Christian Rosy Cross*. It came from the same period of immersion in alchemical writing that produced the poems of *The Fleeing Atalanta*; in his letters, Foster mentions Michael Maier's writing, A. E. Waite's translation of the *Fama Fraternitas*, Emerson, Thoreau, Whitman, and even Carlos Castaneda on the teachings of Don Juan. Soon after Foster sent the manuscript for *Christian Rosy Cross* to Dutton, he announced that it would now be a trilogy, and he set about writing the second part.

By March 1976, Foster had nearly finished the second volume of the novel, and, in October, Gerda wrote to Dutton from Bundanoon announcing the completion of the third volume on the same day that their son, Levi, was born. The manuscript then travelled the rounds of literary agents and publishers in Australia, the USA, and the UK, finding some enthusiasts but never sufficient confidence to lead to publication. In the meantime Foster worked on a novel that he called

'Charge your glasses and be upstanding', set in the Outer Hebrides, England, and Australia. This novel was to become *Moonlite*, published by Macmillan in 1981.

Foster's personal crisis, his struggle to understand alchemy, and his work on *The Adventures of Christian Rosy Cross* contributed to his shift from semi-autobiographical fictions and bitter contemplations of the frustrations of Australian life, to considering history and spiritualism in a confident, satirical mode. Nevertheless, Foster struggled personally to achieve this shift. In 1987 he told listeners at the Australian Defence Force Academy Library, 'I laboured until my mind broke to understand alchemy' (av 1987). In grappling with these difficulties, Foster turned himself into a satirist with a wide range, no longer merely the bitter comic voice of his early work.

Moonlite

Foster first mentions *Moonlite* to Dutton in 1978, after his return from ten weeks in the United Kingdom on a Marten Bequest fellowship. He had been researching and planning the novel for a year and knew that it would 'concern the life of a St Kilda man who emigrates to Oz, via England, after the 1850 clearances' (15 Dec 1978 DP 2/14/103). Foster spent two weeks on St Kilda in June 1978 with a party from the Scottish National Trust. He was back in Bundanoon, working as a postman/night exchange operator, when he was offered an immediate contract for the novel: 'I've only written 25 pages...but the book is pretty clear in my mind & I am making a deliberate effort to write for an audience' (15 Dec 1978 DP 2/14/103).

Foster read Charles MacLean's *Island on the Edge of the World: The Story of St Kilda* and recognised the reverberation for Australians of the fate of these Scottish islanders. St Kilda is a tiny island, also known as Hirta, an outlier off the Outer Hebrides—too far northwest to be included in the regular maps of Scotland. Its people had been isolated for hundreds of years, developing their own language and religion, before the arrival of Christian missionaries in the eighteenth and nineteenth centuries. Their encounter with civilisation decimated their population and, in the 1850s, a group of islanders migrated to Australia. After years of struggle, the remaining islanders were finally convinced to abandon the island in 1930.

This story presented Foster with the kind of paradox he could enjoy. The demise of St Kilda offered a clear example of the devastating effects of colonialism and material progress. Obviously, the people of St Kilda had suffered similar depredations to the Australian Aborigines at about the same time, but a further irony lay in the fact that some of them became the gold-seeking colonisers of Australia. Foster's visit to the island heightened his interest; he was impressed by its sheer cliffs, its beautiful bay and beach, and flocks of seabirds. Foster also managed to interview some of the people who had lived on St Kilda before its abandonment—including an old man who displayed his short but massive legs, developed by years of fowling on cliff faces.

MacLean quotes some anecdotes about the islanders' fear of 'the stranger's cough' or the 'boat cold', and their habit of speaking in unison with affectionate address such as 'my dear'. Foster elaborated this material and his own observations to create the world of his imagined island of Hiphoray; its ecology and geography in the novel, and the names of its outriding islands (Boreray and Soay) are those of St Kilda. This landscape also excited Foster's interest in the spiritualism developed by the islanders—the submerged mountains, dramatic cliffs, and isolation in a wild sea suggested proximity to a world beyond the material. Foster's islanders were close to the fairy world, and he gave careful attention to creating their spiritual universe.

Foster begins the novel on an inner island called Mugg, with three pages that test the reader and serve as a kind of caution before proceeding. The first sentence presents a puzzle about the narrative voice and about whose point of view is being 'obscured' by the old woman's hand: 'The livid hand of an old woman, prominently boned, comes to rest against the door of a turf hut, obscuring two seapies on the nearby shore' (1). A funeral is in progress on the island of Mugg, but the novel flips back to events of two days before. The story of Lamech

MacDuffie's vision of a black figure in the mist and his discovery of his dead wife offers an enigmatic sign of the spiritual interests of the novel along with its commitment to the earthy material nature of life and death. It also provides the kind of barrier to reading typical of Foster's opening pages (*Christian Rosy Cross* begins with a similarly grotesque description of childbirth and a woman's death).

By the third page the reader can recognise an exaggerated comic tone and the familiar signs of satire. Foster introduces the MacIshmael, Laird of Mugg, whose debts have bound him to capitalists from the South. The Laird's folly has brought the highland clearances to Mugg, though the local people cannot recognise the threat represented by the men who will clear them from their land in favour of sheep. When Lamech's new bride Flora protests at the eviction, the Laird exiles her with Lamech and her father Donald to the outer island of Hiphoray. Finding that there's no alcohol on the island, Lamech drowns attempting to return to Mugg. Left on Hiphoray, Flora and Donald begin a process of challenging the fairy beliefs of the MacEsaus, the clan that lives there; Flora's outspoken Christianity and Donald's Druidism encounter a tolerant acceptance of multiple belief systems.

Foster describes Hiphoray in sensuous detail, which invokes a dreamlike beauty:

> On a typical summer approach Hiphoray is a blue shape in the distant mist, a submarine mountain with its peaks above water. Sunlight roving through the cloud illuminates hills of tropical greenness. The reason for this fertility is seen at close quarters: This is one of the great breeding grounds of the North Atlantic, a bottleneck in the marine nitrogen cycle. Visible for half a day, so small, so tall, so jagged, so green in a cobalt sea, the island has a reputation for distracting sailors. There is something here that exceeds the imagination. (19)

Throughout the section set on the island, Foster maintains this sense of reverence for the magic of the place. He gives attention to every aspect of the island's plant life and bird life, and to the islanders' domestic arrangements and techniques for subsistence. While the MacEsaus have no understanding of causality and the logic of science, their absurdities are given dignity by Foster's care in presenting their struggle to survive in a wild and inhospitable environment. The people have no sense of individuality; all the men are called Murdo or Gillie, their women Buntata or Mary, and they speak in unison or interchangeably as if the same person.

Time moves slowly on the island, though the people live in constant fear of crop failure and disease. Flora's Christianity gives her the confidence to take action against these fears, for example by harvesting the meagre crop of corn on the one day when it ripens. Foster describes the extreme weather of the island in credible detail, while maintaining a sense of its proximity to an otherworld, where magic impinges on human life:

> The wind is chilly, but Flora works naked to the waist. Cursing her absent father, she starts to wander, pulling a swath that doubles back on itself like an ideogram. By midnight she has cleared maybe an acre, but the corn lies on the ground. To her relief she sees her father picking it up and stuffing it in the nearest cleit. The people too have decided to help, she can see them from the corner of an eye, some harvesting, others carrying corn to shelter. By a trick of the light they seem quite pale and luminescent. The wind is galeforce now, and were it not for Ruaival and Mullach Sgar the whole crop would have blown away. Exhausted Flora stops to wipe some sweat from her eyes, and as she does a flash of lightning exposes the body of a fledgling fulmar ripped from its nest and hurtling into the corn, and beyond that, a spume of spray exploding over Hamalan. Whole sheaves, still with topsoil in their roots, are lifting in the wind. (35)

The MacEsaus live mainly by fowling on the cliffs. This requires dexterity and courage, and they maintain these qualities by a combination of physical training and spiritual faith. Their precarious way of life depends on the balance between humans and nature, on control of the population by infanticide and the abandonment of old women (the men always die fowling), and on isolation from the diseases of the wider world. They live close to death, but their lack of individualism helps them accept death with great courage. Foster may find the simplicity of the islanders amusing, but he gives due respect for their physical courage:

> As Murdo thirteen descends a third time, the men holding the next rope shout and fall over backwards. Donald looks down in time to see a man, still with a bird in his hand, tumbling and crashing down the cliff face. A length of rope flails from his waist dislodging young fledglings one after the other, who set off nervously on their first ever flight in the wake of the falling man. The men holding Murdo thirteen, both Gillies, need all their strength to retain their grip as the silent body becomes a red stain, effaced by the next wave. Without a word they haul up their Murdo, milk his fulmars, tuck them in their belts and head home. Gillie five, a young man of fifteen, has gone over but gone in style: it's the mark of a man he hold his bird and make no sound as he falls. (40)

When Flora expresses her Christianity in her sense of justice and practical care for the future, she comes into conflict with her father's Druidism and the islanders' belief in the fairyworld. The MacEsaus are tolerant and ready to listen to Donald and Flora, but they cannot understand the exclusive nature of their religions. At the winter solstice the men fling themselves into the wind at the top of the cliff in a ritual of propitiation to Bel. When Donald suggests that Bel is not ill but merely visiting the Land of the Fee, the islanders accept his ideas alongside their own: 'Donald's habit of letting one thing exclude another equally likely, puzzles the MacEsaus' (47).

In Act One of the novel, Foster achieves a convincing and sympathetic portrayal of island life while never pretending that it is romantically savage. The MacEsaus' religious beliefs and practices are founded on ignorance, but their sense of proximity to a spiritual world makes their lives fulfilling. Flora's son, Finbar—the 'Moonlite' of the novel's title—enjoys his island childhood, though he is distinguished by being born an albino, with night sight, making him a kind of anti-visionary among the visionary islanders.

When, in Act Two, a form of civilisation reaches Hiphoray with the Sabbatarian Christianity of Reverend Stewart Campbell, Finbar becomes his pupil. Campbell brings rabbits and a blackberry bush—signs that Australians recognise as ominous. He also organises the visits of tourists and scientists to the island, and the narrative voice mocks the battle between Christianity, science, and tourism:

> Within a few short years the island will be irredeemably spoilt, and the islanders, squatting like gulls on a garbage tip, sufficiently greedy and lazy to repel even a steerage class tourist. Thereafter the people will die or dissipate if they are lucky, and if they are not, become the stalking horse of many a fanatic anxious to deprive them of those vices they have come to love with a fervour distasteful to witness. Any attempt, at any point, to reverse or arrest this process, has about as much chance of success as a globe artichoke on the Champs Elysee [sic]. (75–76)

Any doubts Finbar may have about Christianity are dispelled when he ventures out alone at night in an attempt to encounter a fairy spirit, like every other islander does. His night sight allows him to see that the cry of the Spirit Host, so feared by the islanders, is actually the cry of a small night bird, never seen by the others. At dawn he sees a vision of a white cloud, 'and on it the immense figure of a man in a blinding glory of coloured light' (102). Having found that the Host is nothing more than a bird, Finbar believes that he has seen the Holy Spirit and he decides for Christ.

By Act Three, the novel has become a picaresque satire, recalling the novels of Henry Fielding, Laurence Sterne, or Tobias Smollett. Finbar quests for enlightenment through Scotland, the colleges of Newbridge, then across the world to the goldfields of the New West Highlands. At the university in Newbridge, he devotes himself to mathematics and optical physics while enduring the mockery of his upper class English fellow students. He experiences a country house weekend with Lady Virginia Creeper and her cronies at Haughty Manor, and learns the true purpose of the university dinner party, where a man 'learns…all those skills indispensible [sic] to the ruling class, though as the very antithesis of science and religion and banned from universities since the time of Plato, scarcely able to be taught or practised openly' (126).

The episode at Newbridge gives Foster scope to digress on a topic he knows well: the absurdities of university life and the contradictory nature of research. His comments on the two kinds of scholar, 'those who work with the minimum possible accuracy and those who work with the maximum' (130), will ring true for academic readers. His digression on statistics (159–160) sets up a paradox that he later understood as a mystery of the novel, as well as of science—that individual behaviour conforms to statistical probability, despite notions of freedom of the individual. Finbar's study reveals that the 'glory' is an optical phenomenon rather than a Christian vision, and he is confronted by the paradoxes and uncertainties of physics (light behaves like a wave and a particle). Even the rainbow and the glory have 'imaginary components'; science is not as rational as it appears.

In Act Four of the novel, Finbar, banished from Newbridge, emigrates to Australia with another group of islanders who have been cleared from their lands. Foster told Erica Travers that he deliberately turns the emigrant boat over at the equator to signify the inversion that occurs in the final section, where Finbar abandons all his Christian idealism and devotion to science, and gives himself over to the materialism of the New West highlands (Travers 77). Various other characters from Act Three of the novel appear in reverse roles—Finbar's drunkard college friend, Mungo MacQueen, is now a temperance campaigner, and the snobbish Anton Ducksbury now a socialist. Finbar, now known as 'Moonlite', finds his mirror image in the Aborigine known as 'Sunbeam', and he discovers further correspondences when Sunbeam explains the religion of his people: 'What worries Finbar most, are the pointed references to his own childhood in this…The Host, for example, are spirit-familiars, souls in the form of birds. The Wawa from the Hiphoray saga is actually mentioned by name. Finbar retaliates by telling his story, implicating Sunbeam's home as the Land of the Dark Fairy' (192).

Australia is an inversion of Scotland; it is the Land of the Dark Fairy where Bel, according to Donald MacDuffie, spends the northern winter.

In turn, Sunbeam and the Aborigines believe Finbar is a spirit man. They conduct a Rainbow fella ritual that goes wrong when Finbar's soul refuses to return to his ugly body. His soul flies away where 'he sees a boulder slope and hears the whispering sea' (215). Without a soul, Finbar is now qualified to become Premier of the New West Highlands. In the last chapter the 'Son of the Dark Fairy' climbs into a strange horse-drawn vehicle that catapults him to the coast, and the narrative voice steps forward to lecture us on Australian complacency and nostalgia for Europe:

> O New West Highlands! Colour of Jerusalem! Knowest Thou well, Thou art the Last Frontier, and when Thy Gates at last slam shut, then must the malcontent child of Europe sit in his shit-smeared nest till he rot. Thou wast, from Thy beginning, a City of Refuge, victim and instrument of Unjust Law; yet clingest Thou, terrified, to the Old Way, worshipping the Travesty at two removes. Murderer by Nature and Inclination, shrink Thou from The Final Task? Hast Thou confected so strong a devotion to Thine Own Most Bitter Adversary as This? Wilt Thou hang, forever pendent, till Thy Thumbs concresce with the Very Rock?
>
> One awaits, Who cannot be Born, till Thou art content to die. Climb or let Go! Thou has had Time Enough, and the patience of Thy Father is exhausted. (223)

While this narrative voice is restrained—even reticent—as it provides a kind of scientific commentary in the first two Acts of the novel, it intrudes more frequently, often with witty diatribes, in the final two Acts. The novel reflects the timelessness of Hiphoray life by moving at a slow pace in the first part, then by gradually picking up momentum as Moonlite encounters the social life of Newbridge until he becomes part of the modern new world, where the novel moves at a breakneck speed. In this way the novel enacts the explosion, or violation, of time that is its subject. The final Act consists, in the main, of unattributed dialogue and commentary by the unidentified narrator, so that its pace becomes hectic.

Foster's satire may have no program for reform, but there is folly and vice aplenty in *Moonlite*. It attacks the greed of the economic reformers, clearing the highlands of people to replace them with sheep; it mocks the narrow-minded Sabbatarian Christianity of the Reverend Stewart Campbell who begins the destruction of the islanders' way of life; it ridicules the English class system and its perpetuation through its universities; and it deplores the irreligious materialism of Australia. It laughs, as well, at the ignorance of the people on Hiphoray—but it also admires their faith and courage. Because of the care Foster gives to describing Hiphoray, we can share some of Finbar's grief when he hears of his mother's death. The novel acknowledges the loss of island life as a loss of humanity—a rare moment for a Foster novel. *Moonlite* also attacks the greed that informs Australian democracy where 'sheer cupidity is this lot's LCD' (218), and Finbar, true to form as an Australian politician, announces that he has 'one goal and one goal only! To *gain* power, by whatever means necessary—and having *gained* power, to *retain* it! Forever and ever!' (219).

Foster explained to Dutton that Moonlite becomes immortal at the end of the novel, and that he is 'destined (the implication is meant to be) to rule the New West Highlands, in one form or another, to perpetuity' (10 Apr 80 DP 2/15/108). The novel is driven by a moral commitment to the defence of the powerless, as well as to the tolerance of multiple belief systems. Most of all it is outraged by the patterns of human destructiveness—the islanders extinguish bird species, the colonisers of Hiphoray destroy the island life, then the colonisers of the New West Highlands dig their way through the land, displacing its people. Every act of destruction is supported by faith of some kind—whether in fairies, Christianity, science, or capitalism.

Stephen Harris has argued that the novel can be read as a postcolonial critique of imperial history, and its mythologising of history as progress (71–88). *Moonlite* provides a counterview of history in which the bearers of progress actually cause decline and destruction.

In a sense, the novel speaks for the colonised, whether indigenous or displaced, railing against the arrogance of the coloniser, in this case the commercial and aristocratic classes of Britain.

Edward Said and other postcolonial critics have argued that the English novel represents one of the most powerful means of British colonisation, they read classic novels like Charles Dickens's *Great Expectations* as bearers of Empire ideology. *Moonlite* calls on another tradition of the English novel—an oppositional tradition of British satire, practised by Swift, Sterne, Fielding, and Thomas Love Peacock, as a way to mock and curse the coloniser (Lever, *Cheeky Fictions* 107–116). It proposes an ambivalent relationship between the colonised colonisers (like the Scottish highlanders in Australia) and British culture. In the New West Highlands, Finbar grows nostalgic for the England he's lost: 'God how *beautiful* it was! The spires of Newbridge on a summer's evening, seen from the banks of the river, golden barley under grey skies, breeze in wych elm, wigwam of red-flowered runner beans, cry of cock pheasant, smell of wet hay, delphiniums!' Then he pulls back: 'It wasn't all beautiful, in fact it was bloody awful: big-beaked charladies drooling over gaspers, phlegm-flecked sidewalks riddled with dogshit, rising damp, stewed tea, complacent contumely, bad teeth' (194).

Foster wrote most of *Moonlite* while living in London in 1979, where he appears to have been sensitive to English attitudes to colonials and to Scots. He felt an affinity with the Scots poet (and fellow postal worker) Hugh MacDiarmid and with his mix of philosophy and Scottish idiom:

> How heartrending to find, in that Broad Scots, which our English friends have taught us to read with an instinctive smirk, the occasional Latin!...The Scots peasant cannot think philosophically, and the intellectual cannot take seriously anything written in Scots. Well, I wonder if there's anything else I, as an Australian, can learn from MacDiarmid. I suppose that I must learn to hate well, and mould my bitterness into an invective that my own people will understand. (21 Apr 1979 DP 2/14/104)

Foster's sympathies with the people of St Kilda and his recognition of English snobbery towards both Scots and Australians fed his sense of colonial resentment. The anger in *Moonlite* is both principled and personal, directed both at a history of imperial greed and at his immediate experience of English arrogance towards speakers with different accents. Australian readers responded to this anger, though it is in fact directed as much at Australian mimicry of and nostalgia for England as at the English sense of superiority.

Foster's allegiance to Australia is evident in the Australian in-jokes throughout the novel, but more particularly in the language of the final section and its commentary on Australian idiom. By chapter 13, we are aware that the narrative voice is overtly Australian in its riff on the English gentleman:

> The English gentleman in new surroundings will always replace them as quickly as he can with a facsimile of his own ancestral seat, complete to the very vermin, and far from deriving any benefit from his love of nature, foreign species are forced to contend with a ruthless policy of depredatory rape, that must be seen to be believed. But then, not every man will leave a toilet seat as he would wish to find it, and the ideal society would contain no English gentlemen. (138–139)

When Finbar reaches the New West Highlands, he gets a lesson in the local idiom from the coach driver who advises him that '[f]ucking oath dead set' is the appropriate expression of agreement, and in no time he can say '[s]he'll be right mate.' But the last section clamours with accents of all kinds—Dutch, Chinese, European Jewish, Aboriginal—and Finbar's own voice shifts from Australian vulgarity to English pomposity to Scottish credulity and back again. The Australian speech of the novel cuts every idea down to its basic parts, making mockery inevitable. Foster wrote of *Christian Rosy Cross* that he had 'treated alchemy, surely one of the most difficult and sophisticated systems of thought, in the language of the Australian pub', but *Moonlite* exploits that language both to deride colonialism and convey the materialistic vulgarity of the colonists (21 Apr 1979 DP 2/14/104).

Geoffrey Dutton's reaction to the manuscript of the novel was ecstatic; after several pages of detailed analysis of its double time structure he concluded:

> It is really a book about the multiple layers of truth and meaning, science and religion, of the conflicting answers that Christ and Anti-Christ give each other. It is a work of extraordinary originality and power. It haunts the reader. It deliberately breaks the illusions it creates, but its images stay whole. It certainly makes most other contemporary novels read like jam-tin labels! (20 Dec 1979 DP 2/14/105)

The novel is so complex that it invites readings from many perspectives. Helen Daniel analysed in detail the alchemical patterns in it, some of its references to physics, and its parody of other forms (*Liars* 77–104). Narelle Shaw has discussed its patterns of light and use of optical physics as metaphor (1992). D. R. Burns placed it within a tradition of Australian tall stories, in the line that includes Patrick White, Dal Stivens, Alan Marshall, and Frank Hardy (62–67). Andrew Riemer sees Swiftean elements in its depiction of Australian yahoo behaviour, but also echoes of Johnson and Voltaire (*Southerly* 4–5). It parodies some texts, or reminds readers of others—the country house novels of Peacock, the goldfield descriptions of Rolf Boldrewood's *Robbery Under Arms* (Dutton thought of the sketches of S. T. Gill; Burns mentions H. H. Richardson), or Joseph Furphy's philosophical reflections on socialism, gentlemen, Christ, and Buddha of *Such Is Life*. Yet, Foster may not have even been conscious of these echoes (he admitted to ignorance of Gill). He worked from the historical accounts referenced in his acknowledgments to create his own original vision.

While *Moonlite*'s anti-colonial history presents an obvious starting point for reading, its critique of History and Christianity might be read as a postmodernist subversion of the progressive narrative of history and the optimism of Christianity. Foster pushes his way through the rationales of Christian improvement and market profit. But he goes further in finding science riddled with uncertainty.

In *The Pure Land*, Danny Harris rejects the logic and causality of science in search of spiritual answers; in *Moonlite*, Finbar MacDuffie rejects spiritualism for science, only to find science as uncertain and ambivalent as religion. Language itself invites the simplification of ideas and the dependence on generalisations. Moonlite tells himself:

> I know that phenomena are purified by language and that men simplify the world through speech; or rather, that some phenomena are purified by some languages, and that certain men are sometimes, though not always, inclined to simplify what they observe or think they observe, for the sake, among other reasons, of convenience. And why not, when a man who declines to generalize makes enemies of God and the Devil both? Christ and anti-Christ have this in common, neither does the other justice. (194)

Even this understanding is tentative.

The novel probes the failures of each belief system, but it reserves its greatest mockery for the unbelievers of the New West Highlands. At the end of the novel, we have no doubt that the gold seekers of the colony have lost something worth having—the awareness shared by the primitive islanders and the Aborigines that they live in a natural world full of spiritual meaning.

Ken Gelder argues that *Moonlite* shows a 'nostalgia for mystification while simultaneously engaging in a process of demystification' (157). While the novel as a form might be seen as part of the 'civilising' and demystifying forces of progress, *Moonlite* makes the 'imaginary component' central. This valuing of what Gelder calls the 'imaginary component' pulls *Moonlite* away from the cynical ironies we expect from postmodernism. The novel holds up every belief system to mockery; but it finds belief systems worth pursuing. Ar Wat, Finbar's Chinese mate on the goldfields tells him: 'Gotta hold two views at once. The Tlute is not this is not that—is a combination' (198). The novel advocates holding both views at once, like the islanders with their refusal to deny the Spirit Host in order to accept Druidism or Christianity, or physicists accepting that light behaves both like a wave and like a particle.

So in this novel, the undermining of belief systems and the chaotic treatment of narrative conventions, often seen as the marks of postmodernism, refuse to converge in a postmodernist denial of belief. While it transgresses realist conventions with its wonderful exaggerations and deliberately undermines ideas of temporal progress, it also refers to a real world in which indigenous people are destroyed by the ideas of others, and a world in which an angry writer wants to intervene with his opinions. By the end of the novel, we are asked to believe that a man can be both alive and dead, and that the superstitions of illiterate people may provide greater enlightenment than can the logic of science.

Moonlite may not fit neatly into categories of modernism or postmodernism, but it certainly belongs to its period of literary experiment. Daniel places it alongside novels by Peter Mathers, David Ireland, Murray Bail, Peter Carey, and other Australian contemporaries, where it sits comfortably enough in terms of its Australian vulgarity and trajectory from realism, though not so well in the context of their cynical attitudes to spirituality. During the same year, Peter Carey published *Bliss*, a novel that examines the American cultural influences on Australia and deplores the insidious commercialisation of the Australian imagination. Though *Bliss* worried about Australia's colonial status with regard to America, as well as the corruption of family relationships in the materialism of the contemporary world, it was sufficiently realist to be adapted as a successful film a few years later. Anthony Hassall reads *Bliss* in Foster's terms as a satire that is essentially modernist despite its postmodern concern with the fictional status of all stories (71–72). Yet, Carey's satire has a 'corrective' function, and *Bliss* maps Carey's own abandonment of advertising as a morally dubious career. The novel has none of the sweeping philosophical concerns of *Moonlite*. Carey's parodic novel about Australia's nineteenth-century history, *Oscar and Lucinda*, published six years later, has striking similarities to *Moonlite*, but it never entertains the possibility that its nineteenth-century characters might actually hold the religious beliefs that they profess. Foster's novels always take the possibility of belief seriously, even while they mock its effects.

Moonlite's preoccupation with time and a real history of colonial stupidity has much in common with Salman Rushdie's *Midnight's Children*, also published in 1981. Rushdie's mode of satire also invokes the tradition of Sterne (as well as Indian models) and sets a physically odd, picaresque figure on a journey through the chaos of a British colony. The notion of history as a construct of Western European thinking, in opposition to the timeless commitment to faith in god, creates India as an independent nation, partitioned from Pakistan, according to the 'tick-tock' of British clocks. Australia's colonial history as a settler colony differs from India's experience as a colonised civilisation, but the colonial imperatives are the same and contemporary with Rushdie's India. Foster's islanders, though based on real people, provide a metaphor for the process of colonisation and the shifts that can turn them into colonisers, once their capacity for belief is destroyed. Just as Rushdie, in *Midnight's Children* and in later novels, worries about religious belief and its influence on history, Foster worries about its loss.

Midnight's Children has become a model of the postcolonial, postmodernist satire though, like *Moonlite*, it also refers to a history in which real people suffer, and it takes a moral stance on the rights of those real people. Rushdie now appears as a leader in the shift from literary experiment towards a new engagement with contemporary politics in the last decades of the twentieth century. In *Moonlite*, Foster offered Australians a vision of their own journey from a timeless, faith-based culture (and Hiphoray stands in for a range of indigenous cultures) into the historical world of capitalism and 'progress'.

THE ADVENTURES OF CHRISTIAN ROSY CROSS

After the success of *Moonlite*, Foster continued to talk about the unpublished novel *The Adventures of Christian Rosy Cross* as his 'magnum opus', and he persisted in trying to publish it. When *Moonlite* was accepted for publication, Foster told Dutton, '[i]t was far too ambitious of me to attempt a work like that [*Christian Rosy Cross*] when I began it, and I paid the price, but I've learnt a lot through struggling with that book, and I don't regret it' (17 Mar 1981 DP 2/15/112). When publishers proved resistant to the novel's difficulty and length, Foster cut the three-volume manuscript down and rewrote it as the 160-page novel eventually published by Penguin in 1986 (17 Mar 1981 DP 2/15/112).

Foster's letters to Dutton contain several revealing comments about what he was trying to achieve in *Christian Rosy Cross*. In 1974 he wrote that alchemy had opened his 'third eye' and was the 'sole remaining western strand of gnostic thought':

> Basically, I think that hermetic gnosticism—and this includes alchemy, craft masonry, rosicrucianism, the Tarot & great literature—all of which contain 9 parts of bogus rubbish to 1 part of genuine literature—is the remnant of the original gnostic church, which probably inherited the Greek, Egyptian & Judaic mysteries: my hardly revolutionary opinion is that the mysteries are concerned with sex and drugs, to put it bluntly. But it is one thing to say this, another to have experienced, it, in practice. Geoff, I am, I think, a logically inclined man. But I now know that the world is far more complex (=simple) than I imagined. (17 Sep 1974 DP 2/12/86)

Later he wrote from Bundanoon that in the novel 'I have made a smutty comedy out of the most divine secret', and that 'I have attempted to create a sea of confusion and obfuscation, through which the unfortunate Christian is obliged to wade' (n.d. [1975?] DP 2/12/86).

The original manuscript of *The Adventures of Christian Rosy Cross* runs to 528 pages of double-spaced typing (FP 2.5/1). The writing is as sustained as that of the published version, and the mix of Australian idiom, jokes, and serious ideas as unflagging. For the published version, Foster cut detail from Part One, including a scene in which the driver who takes Christian out of the monastery leads his barroom mates in sodomising him (Christian believes this to be an enema). He also cut an episode in a brothel from Part One, and a large section of Christian's experiences in the East from the end of Part Two. In the draft of Part Three, Christian wanders through Spain before his incarceration by one of the two rival popes. Where the published novel ends with Christian tending his garden—a deliberate reference to Voltaire's *Candide*—the draft provides additional historical context behind his adventures. Adam Cadman—the young man who follows Christian, who is identified as the 'young king' of alchemical metaphor—rides off to Bohemia: 'After his 73rd year, Christian never spoke again. With the inevitable defeat of the Czechs—Adam was a little ahead of his time—the Royal Red Order was driven underground, and that's the best place for it. In 1483 or 4 Christian died. In the year of his death, a man was born, son to a German miner. The family arms? A rose and a cross' (FP 2.5/1, 528). Thus, the draft of the novel explicitly notes the continuing Rosicrucian influence through Martin Luther and Protestantism.

While the length of the original draft allows Foster to explore more fully the alchemical metaphor as a way of telling a story, his cuts and the shift to present tense create a tighter and more cryptic novel. When faced with the need to cut, he decided that it would be better as a Voltaire *conte*, and the published novel has more in common with *Candide* than with an epic. The resulting novel is a fast-paced farce, loosely based on the movements of the probably mythological Christian. It is an historical burlesque, full of anachronistic jokes, obscenity, and brutal ironies.

In his Introduction, Foster explains his source as a group of German pamphlets that appeared in the early seventeenth century as the work of the Brotherhood of the Rosy Cross. Foster sees the possibility of the Rosicrucian Brotherhood as evidence for a hidden gnostic tradition in the West 'emerging in the Grail legends, alchemy and ceremonial magic' (ix). The figure of Christian Rosy Cross, then, is a symbol of the discontent within the Catholic Church at the time, and the touchstone for an alternative spiritualism. Foster was delighted to find that *The Chemical Marriage of Christian Rosencreutz* was read as 'a comic romance' by its first English readers. Foster reads it as a 'Sufic satire': 'a work superficially satirical, yet incorporating at a structural level those very esoteric elements it purportedly ridicules' (x). In this way, Foster invites us to read his novel as satire, both supporting and mocking the Rosicrucian tradition.

Within the first few pages of the novel, we encounter its grotesque and jokey approach to history. Christian's birth, with all of its associated fluids and afterbirth, is rapidly followed by his mother's death by haemorrhage after his father has sex with her. His father, the Comte de Rosencreutz, loses his fortune, leaving the family 'poor, but noble'—'better than being rich and working class', jokes the narrative voice (6). Christian is brought up in a Dominican monastery where several monks practise the Art. His casual reference to toads, eagles, goats, and wolves suggests to the monk initiates that he is ready for alchemy. He is accordingly baptised in a bath of mercury that leaves him near death. The novel lets our modern scientific understanding consider the absurdity of the alchemical theories, where toads are assumed to generate from mud, frogs from the clouds, and so on.

Within a few years, the Inquisition arrives at the monastery to destroy the laboratories and burn the prior at the stake. At fifteen years, Christian has his first erection, and it does not subside, so he begins to seek relief outside the monastery. In the course of the novel Christian's body is subject to all kinds of pestilences—from leprosy to cankers—and to their horrific medieval cures. His enormous penis, always erect, is circumcised by accident, then split in two by the action of a gate. This focus on male genital mutilation was to appear again in Foster's novels—most notably in *The Glade Within the Grove*. In *Christian Rosy Cross* the extraordinary penis marks its hero as a chosen one.

Christian leaves the monastery with the heretic Brother Pal, embarking upon picaresque adventures that lead him through Venice to Rhodes then Damascus in search of alchemical wisdom. Christian meets a range of adepts, works in a massage parlour, becomes a slave, and participates in an alchemical pageant where the child playing the 'young king' is severed in two. On his escape he finds a lab where chemists are trained, and he eventually joins the Brotherhood.

Christian realises that he is searching for the Vegetable Stone of the East rather than the Mineral Stone of Europe, and he eventually manages to ingest such large quantities of it that he reaches the mystery of Truth. The experience is, of course, that of hallucinatory drugs. Having found the Stone, Christian sets out to reform the Whole Wide World by sharing his enlightenment. The problem is that he has a limited stash and does not know how to make more. After failures in Jerusalem and Fez, he returns to Europe where he is imprisoned by one of the two reigning popes, until he recants. In the final chapters of the novel, Christian becomes an Inquisitor travelling through Europe seeking out and condemning users of the Stone. The Book he wrote while in prison has travelled before him, so he is attempting to destroy his own followers. Finally, Christian and his band of Inquisitors reach Germany where he retires to the family castle to grow bulbs.

If there is any difficulty in reading this novel, it is in keeping up with the pace of the comic dialogue and understanding events that happen without explanation—often recalled by one of the characters or announced by the narrative voice. For example, this is what we learn of Christian's circumcision:

> The wagon stops and the driver, a man with whom Christian is casually acquainted, gets out. 'Take shelter' he says, and they lay down together between the sheets all fresh and clean. Suddenly it's colder, and the storm hits.
>
> The circumcision of Christian Rosy Cross 1393.
>
> Pulling up later outside the grogshop, the driver rushes in. 'Here drink this' he urges, emerging with a quart pot. 'There's no more potent anaphrodisiac.'
>
> Christian drinks till drunken. The swelling subsides, and the bleeding stops (just as well: just in time). (38)

The smart-talking monks and adepts in the novel drive home the ironies of a corrupt Christian church riven by political disputes and ruthless inquiries into the state of its members' souls. In the East, Christian finds himself in a society administered and ruled by slaves so that the free men can enjoy the privileges of civilisation. In

Damascus, the Gatekeeper tells Christian (now called Mohammad): 'what we have in Damascus is the "twilight system", suitable for empires at their peak, that is, on the way out. The ideas of an empire at its peak, when implemented, bring about its downfall. These are your so-called "enlightened" ideas. What we need to study are the ideas *before* the peak, that lead to that peak when implemented' (110).

Foster returns to this idea about civilisations at their peak (with reference to late twentieth-century Western civilisation) in later novels. In this novel, the conflicting approaches of belief and critique are represented by the master's attitude; he teaches alchemy by day and the 'fraud squad' at night. He takes the modern scientist's rational view of alchemical metaphor:

> I don't deny the Resurrection but see this retort in my hand? It is a retort. It is not the soul of man. It is not the womb of the Virgin Mother. It is not the belly of the Microprosopus. It's a retort and nothing else. You see, when the ancient chemists decided to conceal their nomenclature, the favorite and natural butt for their spleen were their bitter antagonists, the mystics. Out of context it's almost impossible for us to understand their satire. What was meant as parody is often taken for the Real Thing and vice versa. That strike you as paradoxical?
>
> 'Yes and no' says Christian. (59)

As Christian struggles along his path to enlightenment, suffering physical abuse after abuse, the meaning of his enlightenment fades from attention. The patterns of alchemy appear over and over again—the toad and eagle connected by a golden chain, sun and moon embracing, the colours of black and white turning to red, the enclosed rose garden, and so on. Is it parody or the real thing? Clearly, Foster satirises both the authority of the medieval Christian Church implemented by brutal force, and the irrational science of the Rosicrucians. Neither have access to the physics and medicine of our contemporary world. He enjoys the alchemists because they, at least, challenge a repressive Church.

Given the evidence of Foster's commitment to alchemy as a spiritual alternative (if not a scientific one) at the time of writing *Christian*, the challenge to readers is to find this commitment beneath the slapstick of Christian's life. What we read is a contemporary take on alchemy and the history of the Inquisition informed by modern knowledge of science and medicine. Perhaps, the journey is the important thing, and the mystery of Truth cannot be handed over simply by reading about it.

Lyndy Abraham, in the introduction to *A Dictionary of Alchemical Imagery*, argues that the Renaissance enthusiasm for alchemy recognised no division between the material and metaphorical worlds, so that the spiritual component was integral to the alchemical approach to science. 'The alchemist's aim was to explore the inner workings of nature, and this meant delving into the very secret of God's creation' (xvii). In this way, the exploration of correspondences between 'substances, objects and states of mind' could be 'a valid perception of an inner, subtle connection existing between things' (xvii). This obviously speaks to Foster's dual allegiances to science and to spirituality. It may also throw light on Foster's interest in metaphorical systems—in languages—as a source of wisdom. In essence, alchemy is a system of analogies whose metaphors contain hidden truths. The search for meaning among its paradoxes may lead to enlightenment. But it is not an enlightenment that can be readily displayed; it must be achieved through struggle with the language of alchemy. In all of his novels Foster struggles for enlightenment through language.

Christian Rosy Cross does not function as a guidebook to alchemy or Rosicrucian belief. It mocks the absurdities of the pseudo-scientific theories now discredited by modern discovery; the rational understanding of a contemporary intellect finds these ideas laughable. Nevertheless, the novel finds the quest and its paradoxes worthy of our attention. Alchemy provides the novel with its historical material, and with a wealth of ideas and imagery for Foster to play with.

We can read the novel as an elaborate joke at the expense of alchemy and medieval Christianity, but that does not account for its abundance of ideas and paradoxes. The refrain, 'believe that and you'll believe anything', repeated throughout the novel, suggests that a final belief in nothing is not desirable. At the end of the novel, Adam declares that '[r]eligion and heresy are only gimmicks to keep men's minds off the issues!'. However, Christian replies that religion is 'the method of choice when events are out of hand and kicking you up the arse. When you're in control, doing the kicking, you tend to become logical' (160). It sounds like a warning to the Western world of the late twentieth century.

Though *The Adventures of Christian Rosy Cross* shares *Moonlite*'s preoccupation with the influence of belief systems on history, *Moonlite* speaks to a shared colonial experience, immediately recognised by Australian readers. *Moonlite* may be exuberantly inventive, but it also recounts an absurd and ironic history of Australian heritage, confirmed by Don Watson's study of Angus McMillan and the islanders from Skye in his *Caledonia Australis* (1984). It also shows Foster's range as a writer—his ability to write scientific observations so detailed that they become poetry, then shift to broad comedy to digress on learned matters, then adopt the satiric manner of Swift or Peacock. *Christian Rosy Cross* is less varied in style, and it never manages the moments of pathos that give pause to the reader amid the satiric activity of *Moonlite*.

CHAPTER 4

A THOUSAN' MILES FROM NOWHERE: *PLUMBUM* AND *DOG ROCK*

PLUMBUM

If *Moonlite* considers how Australia came to be the way it is, Foster's next published novel, *Plumbum* (1983), grapples with the limitations (particularly for an artist) of trying to engage with the world from an Australian base. The novel follows a rock band—from the protected, small-scale world of Canberra, to Bangkok, Calcutta, and finally to Utrecht. Its trajectory from the parochial, suburban concerns of Australia's capital to the mass power of an internationally successful rock band suggests that Foster wants to imaginatively encompass the universe, starting with every street and house in Canberra and spiralling outwards to include every place and person in the world.

In *Plumbum* Foster explores the possibilities of art through the analogy of music, drawing on his own experiences as a musician. He began his artistic career while a teenager, as a drummer with a dance band touring the New South Wales tableland towns for weekend gigs. But he has never been a rock musician; he instead maintains an allegiance to modern jazz, though during his music career he was often reduced to joining the 'trad' jazz bands favoured by Australian audiences. Modern jazz, with its emphasis on improvisation and the creative skill of the performers, provides the closest musical match for Foster's approach to literary art.

At live performances, modern jazz bands in general adopt the practice of establishing a theme (sometimes a 'standard', sometimes a recent composition), subsequently pursuing variations with each musician taking turns to riff. Most of the time the 'improvised' riffs are pretty well agreed in advance—but there are moments, particularly when an attentive atmosphere has been established, when an audience senses that the musicians are genuinely composing as part of their performance. At the culmination of the modernist movement in art in the 1950s and 1960s, the free jazz movement made completely unrehearsed improvisation its ultimate goal. The artistic task was to invent in the moment of performance, with no opportunity for revision and editing. The free jazz aesthetic privileged experiment, the adventurous journey into new territory, and the process of creation, rather than its product. In the 1950s and 1960s, modernist writing sought to achieve something of this improvised feel, and many American writers attempted to mimic the sounds of jazz or its mode of improvised performance—including Ralph Ellison, Eudora Welty, Jack Kerouac and the Beats, and Alan Ginsberg (Mole). One of Foster's favourite writers, William Burroughs, pushed such improvisation to its limits, even inventing 'cut-up prose' in which he tore sentences apart then pushed the parts together.

By conventional critical standards, free jazz music was bound to be flawed, often incoherent, and always imperfect (Hamilton). The (admittedly tiny) audience for live modern jazz understands that this may be the price for witnessing the moment of creation in the musicians' performance. Literary art, on the other hand, is a textual record of the moment of creation rather than the creation itself (except, perhaps, some performance poetry and theatre sports). Readers expect a degree of refinement in a published book, and they may become impatient when confronted with incoherence and digression. *Plumbum* demands that readers bring to it some of the jazz audience's patience and willingness to enjoy the unexpected. It offers us a literary performance, with the audience close to the author's experience of creativity.

Literary satire is so often associated with eighteenth-century paradigms that any connection between it and modern jazz may seem tenuous. Yet satire also demands a performance by the satiric voice; it must offer an improvisatory element, or at least the appearance of improvisation. The satirist, like the jazz musician, must develop skills that will allow for extravagant digression from a theme, and satiric art depends on a display of energy and inventiveness. It is also an individualist art form and, in the hands of a writer like Foster, an experimental performance.

In *Plumbum* Foster brings a jazz aesthetic, with its commitment to improvisation and experiment, to his writing. But the idea of pursuing a musical group that becomes so powerful and famous that it can change the spiritual state of the world meant that modern jazz could not be its music. So *Plumbum* is about rock musicians, though the author may lament with Pete Blackman that his preferred music is 'an art form already dead as a dodo' (388).

Foster's substantial preparatory notes for the novel include some small spiral-bound notebooks in which he tried out the voices of instruments. It appears that the idea of mimicking the instruments and finding characters to exemplify their qualities was one of the starting points for the novel. So, Felix, the massively strong Maori, plays drums; Roland, the shy, fat man, plays keyboards; Pete, the dark pessimist, plays bass guitar; and Jason, the tall dreamer, sings and plays lead guitar. Sharon, the lead singer, is a red-haired beauty from Glasgow who alternates between sexual and maternal impulses.

The novel begins with the band in a recording studio in the tiny country town of Bungendore, outside Canberra. As the sound engineer asks each band member to give him a sample to work on, they tell us their stories in the mode of their instruments. Pete tunes his guitar and we are plunged into the stories of Blind

Willie Dickinson—'the most authentic blues singer ever to come to Canberra' (4)—and Arthur Blackman, the Dutch immigrant. Through Pete, Foster takes the opportunity 'to praise Canberra, to celebrate her charms' (5):

> This is the man of whom I sing, self-made, a marvel of endurance. Such men have a truth to tell us, and that truth is Canberra. Like it or not, when men have been through Hell, it is Canberra they desire, Canberra they create. If you find this hard to fathom, I guess you never went without. You probably don't remember the Great Depression. I'll bet you never even fought in The War. (7)

At a second call from the engineer, Pete tells his own story of meeting Arthur and Jason, and of his adoption by the Blackman family. In an extended range of comic observations, he tells of the moves away and then back to Canberra, with increasing detail as they slip from suburb to suburb. The third call from the engineer invites Pete to tell us about his life as a jazz musician in Sydney in the 1960s. The bass player is the intellectual, reflective member of the band, who gives Foster the opportunity to theorise about the decline of art in the contemporary world. Throughout the novel, Pete retains an artistic commitment to jazz, though this 'difficult, thoughtful music' can never be popular—'even difficult, thoughtful people like mindless, simple music to relax with' (388).

The keyboardist, Roland Rocca, plays next and the font of the text changes as the novel provides an equivalent to his musical style. Rocca is The Machine, who transforms himself into Platypus Man out on the backroad from Canberra to Bathurst. Then Felix, the drummer, takes over in an obscene riff about his attraction to women and aggression towards men:

> I luv teplay, man, I wood rather play drums than fuck. Partami trakshun wimin no I can takm or leavem. Ilike tageta woman all hot n primed—naked n pantin u no—then walk out. Jus shuthe door gone! Hoo gimme the mos' trubbel? Nothe wimin I haven had yet: the wunz I *hav* had hoo want more! Buthey ony gettit wunce thas my rool. (29)

Sharon starts her riff with a melancholy reflection on domestic life, moving to an aggressive commentary on sex—'[n]o woman ever need be raped, not if she doesn't want to be' (30)—which sounds like a man's projection of a woman's thoughts. Jason tops this with a bizarre romantic account of his love for the teenage Michelle: 'when I take her breasts in my mouth I feel as though I am clearing the snouts of two little sugar gliders' (30). By the end of his solo, Jason has drifted into a fantasy where he's on horseback in a battlefield, falling as he sees a brief vision of 'my Lady' before he finds himself back in the Mawson Hotel. His second solo gives his account of the contradictions of Pete, further establishing him as the satirist figure, with an attitude close to Foster's own:

> He has the meanest, leanest, dirtiest sound you could ever wish you never heard. Pete never got off the ground as a player, but not because he can't play: it's something to do with the personality he had to acquire to get that sound. Unfortunately, personality is not something you can pack away and toss up in the luggage rack. A youthful American jazz giant, on tour with Pete and knocked out by his playing tried to praise him...You know what Pete did? *Spat* in the guy's eye, man, saying, 'Take that from Gough Whitlam!'
>
> Pete, man, who never votes, and when he votes, votes informal. Pete, who thinks Hitler had the right ideas, only didn't go far enough. (35)

As the novel progresses, it becomes evident that while Jason represents the romantic and lyrical elements ('*love* and *understanding*' 44) in the author's personality, Pete carries his satiric and comic energy. Pete dominates the novel, ensuring that its mode is satirical. Pete is the intellect pushing through all the falsity of sentimental and mindless art, though the Blackman Brothers Band will soon become prime purveyors of heavy metal. Pete declares: 'A Canberra Band! That would have to be the end' (45). The novel demonstrates that it is.

Plumbum is a musician's novel in which observations about contemporary music can be applied to literary art. How can an Australian possibly become a first-rate artist? How can anyone from Canberra, that home of suburban comfort and peace, possibly become an artist at all? As Pete puts it, '[a] second-rate culture can still produce a first-rate interpretive artist' (7), but the creative artist needs to experience more than the anodyne life of Canberra. The experience of living a comfortable Australian life in itself presents a barrier to creative art.

Foster confronts the Canberra paradox by devoting the first sections of the novel to accurate, extravagant, and wonderful comic observations on the band's life in 'Mother Canberra'. This is some of the funniest of Foster's writing. He knows the Prussian blue toilet bowls of Spence, the treated pine divider that marks the end of the city, the empty Mercedes buses that patrol it; once he notices it we see how ludicrous it all is. It is not only because this reader has endured domestic life in Groom Street Hughes, dashing over to the Curtin fish and chips shop in emergencies, that the novel elicits laughter. Foster recognises that Canberra is an Australian creation; it represents the aspirations of our culture. Our limitations are manifest in its comforts. As Pete tells Jason: 'The great Canberra *blues*-man! "Nearly died on the weekend, neighbour, don't let that happen to you, when you go out with the family make sure you got coin for yo' barbecue"' (43).

The Blackman Brothers Band provides a vehicle for Foster to record all the absurdities not only of Canberra but also country towns like Captain's Flat and Mittagong, where the band's gigs descend into tedium and disaster. He knows the music scene so well that he presents an encyclopedic account of Sydney jazz venues and players of the 1980s, while lamenting the awful fact that Australian musicians, no matter how brilliant, are destined to play to minimal and undiscerning audiences:

> What's wrong with this universe? Who so designed this cosmos that Christ could die on his Cross? And how come Pete Blackman, a player who, given the right company in his formative years, could have rivalled Ray Brown or Scott La Faro, should be sitting in a panel van outside the Ainslie hotel in this remote corner of the globe, moodily declining the

> neuro-deceptor being passed among his peers, and shortly to take the stand in broad daylight, before an audience of clerks and tyre fitters, in a so-called 'nation' whose musical and literary tastes are formulated by A & R men catering to the lowest level of musical awareness ever registered in hominid stock, as well as advertising copywriters, abetted by some of the deadest wood ever to hold university tenure? (110)

He could be talking about literary writing in Australia.

Foster had never been to Asia, but in 1982, after completing the first sections of the novel, he decided it would need an Asian setting. So he flew to Bangkok, planning to go on to Kathmandu. In Bangkok, he decided to go to Calcutta instead. As he tells the story in 'The Quandary of an India Addict', it was monsoon season and he was the only Westerner to get off at Calcutta airport (*S&N* 149–158). If the account of Calcutta in *Plumbum* left any reader in doubt as to Foster's response to the city, this essay confirms that he was in a state of shock and stress for the six weeks of his stay. He spent the first three days at the Airport Ashok hotel using room service before he ventured into Calcutta itself. There he saw sights and experienced fears that he experienced as demonic. Over six weeks in India he wrote 120 pages of the novel. He hardly spoke to anyone else: 'Of course, I was on the verge of madness' (*S&N* 154).

The two chapters of *Plumbum* set in Calcutta convey an immediate sense of this anxiety, as if the writer is improvising as he experiences the place. They do not reflect on or rationalise the experience, nor do they pretend that the narrative voice has some distant perspective on events. In his heightened state of consciousness, Foster felt 'the existence of God': 'the trouble was that there were so many Gods to choose from' (154). He returned home exhausted and ill, convinced that, for the time of his stay, he 'understood what it was to be fully human' (157).

Writers with Indian backgrounds such as Rushdie, Anita Desai, Amitav Ghosh, or Upumanyu Chatterjee write of the chaos of Indian cities with a degree of affection, but most prefer to write about Mumbai or Delhi rather than Calcutta. Foster's brief experience of

Calcutta during monsoon season struck him with all the force that culture shock brings to most Western travellers in India, and it was exacerbated by the city's contrast with Canberra and his life in Bundanoon. Despite his care to stay in the hotel recommended for 'discriminating travellers' by *Lonely Planet*, Foster had immersed himself in an extreme encounter.

The barrage of impressions of Calcutta that begins the India section of *Plumbum* portrays the overwhelming sense of shock of a Westerner's encounter with an alien city. Chapter 10 begins with a litany of observations of the city exchanged among the band members, with occasional additions from the narrative voice. We share not only the band's response to the city, but also a sense of the extremity of Foster's own feelings as he wrote the novel, holed up in that hotel room near the Maidan. In a virtuoso performance, Foster brings us the absurdity of Calcutta's colonial heritage (Morris Oxford cars, Victorian buildings) and the effects of its crowded street-dwelling population (shit, beggars, and traffic) blended with the horror and fear it strikes in the comfortable Westerner.

This experience of Calcutta takes up a quarter of the final novel, but it constitutes its core. The Faustian character of Nick—who follows the band then, when they are broke and desperate in Bangkok, takes over their management, and changes their name to Plumbum—allows Foster to let them loose in this anti-Canberra (203). Nick finds that the music they record in his Calcutta studio 'lacks balls' (217), so he abandons them on the streets of Calcutta for the necessary suffering. The band discovers that they've sold their immortal souls to Nick in 'a standard rock contract' (220), but the narrator assures us that Nick is no Lord Vishnu, just 'a cheap little demon of the kind that runs advertising agencies everywhere' (202).

In the extremity of Asia, each band member finds a god to match a chosen spiritual path. Pete recognises himself in the angry Buddha in a Bangkok temple, and Jason explains the samrambha yoga as 'the path to enlightenment through *sheer hatred*' (189)—this must be Pete's way. In Calcutta, Sharon becomes possessed by Kali, the goddess of enlightenment through cruelty; she is taken up by the

Ananda Marga. Jason follows Siva, who uses evil and destruction as a form of spiritualism; after walking the streets with a phantom blindness, he is rewarded by the surgical removal of both his eyes as a result of a hospital infection. He hears the Dance of Siva in the noises of the street and understands that 'none of this is random' (244).

Meanwhile, the two more materialistic members of the band embrace Calcutta life—Felix becomes a rickshaw puller, while Roland joins the Indian public service, selling and stealing stamps at the GPO. Felix devotes himself to increasing his bodily strength, developing an addiction to cobra venom. Roland concentrates on amassing as much wealth as possible, pursuing his dream of possessing Coolalie, the great pastoral station near his hometown. Only Pete retains some belief in material progress as a means to salvation. He tries to educate, then minister to, the poor people on the streets; eventually, in desperation, he takes up as an abortionist.

They are all embracing aspects of Kali Yuga, the way of enlightenment through degradation and evil:

> In the age of Kali a revolution is required in the way Man understands himself. His longing for the sight of dead bodies and naked genitalia (death being the biological price he pays for sex), his lust for the transformation of consciousness by the strongest possible means (chemical), must not be seen as wholly evil but as an expression of his need to proceed towards God by what few means remain to him. Man will not conquer these urges by suppression. All he can do is to accept, to dedicate, to sanctify, to understand their purpose and to evaluate their meaning. (246)

This is a religion for a time of complete decadence; it is a preparation for the end of the world. The band has now acquired 'great honesty, great purity, great physical strength, great bodily suffering', and 'great intelligence', the essentials for magic (298). The music that emerges from the band's various devotions proves perfectly suited to the degraded lusts of the whole world, and they rise to spectacular international success.

In the last section of the novel, Foster describes the band before and during their outlandish concert in Utrecht's Musiekcentrum. Each of the musicians has become totally devoted to a particular sensual road to enlightenment, and Jason will reveal Siva's sacred mantra to the tens of thousands who come to the concert. Some of these will pledge to sacrifice their lives in return for a free ticket. This concert will 'usher in the dawning of a New Age' (324). Foster details the decadence of the band as Roland grows ever fatter, Felix becomes addicted to snake venom and sex, Sharon becomes more lewd, Jason devotes himself to the disabled as the elect of Siva, and Nick sells merchandise to profit from their indulgence. Only Pete longs for small-town life and other forms of music—classical concerts and his old love of modern jazz.

At this point, the writing bursts into a broken, excessive, lunatic language, as Foster gives readers a verbal equivalent of the heavy metal music, loud enough to turn its listeners deaf, likely to call them to suicide. Foster takes readers into the madness of a Plumbum concert, pushing the language until it changes into a babble, a mantra, recalling the experiments of Foster's models: Joyce, Beckett, and Burroughs. After this mayhem and chaos, the novel brakes to a downbeat ending as Jason announces his intention to burn all the money in the world, and the novel indicates he will soon be able to do so. Foster gives us a novel for the apocalypse, for the end of a civilisation. The band's music is art for the end of the world.

A reader is likely to experience this novel as a journey into chaos and confusion—Thelma Forshaw saw it as a novel for devotees of 'heavy rock' as it 'plunges into surreal gibberish to get across rock's smashing of the mind's barriers' (86). The last scenes, in particular, leave the characters behind to describe the ultimate decadence of their stage performances. We can no longer care about them, but can only feel disgust at their extravagant and extreme manifestation of phenomena that we might know through popular rock concerts. Helen Daniel described the novel as 'episodic and disjunctive' and found the Calcutta section particularly 'fragmented' (*Liars* 98–99). Adrian Mitchell found that it 'squandered its imaginative energy' and left the reader with 'a sense of having laboured for our entertainment' (1983:14). When the novel was reissued in 1995, the composer and musician Martin Armiger called it a 'harum-scarum banshee-driven bungee-jump of a novel' (77).

Counter to this reading experience, Narelle Shaw, in the only full-length critical article published on *Plumbum* to date, calls it a 'masterfully orchestrated novel' and details its intricate patterning and range of allusions (1990:92). She argues that its structure is based on the 'biblical archetype of man's fall, redemption, death and rebirth' (80) and finds that it seeks compatibility between Hindu and Christian religions. In an attempt to accommodate *Plumbum* to traditional critical standards of the novel as a formally controlled work of art, she argues that the musical patterning of the novel is that of a classical fugue.

While I share Shaw's admiration for the novel, I believe that she has mistaken its musical model—surely it is that of modern jazz, where brilliance of improvisation is valued over control of form. Foster's art is not an art of control but one of risk. At its most brilliant, the novel conveys a sense of spontaneity and immediacy, so that the reader feels close to the act of writing, aware that the author is extemporising and exploring his art. Foster attempts more than he knows he can do, relying on his own energy and invention to carry the novel forward. The reader must respond like the listener to a live modern jazz concert, applauding the brilliant improvisations and bearing with the occasional tedium, because we are sharing the author's exploration of the possibilities of his material.

Across the length of the novel, he offers us a range of virtuoso effects, from the mimicry of instruments in the opening section to the chaos of the encounter with Calcutta to the extravagant decadence of the Plumbum concert at the end. He gives us a brief overview of Calcutta politics, the politics of international aid, the lyrics of several Plumbum songs, theories on Dutch national character, and a minor digression on the life and fortunes of a small time musician. The novel is replete with information and theories on a massive range of subjects, as well as imaginative extensions of them. Stephen

Knight recognised it as an anatomy rather than a novel: 'That is a hard path to follow, and Foster sometimes stumbles in the hectic imagination and the immaculate control required by this most potent of forms'. It is, as Mitchell notes, a 'medley of events in a medley of styles' (1983).

Yet all these disparate subjects and effects bear on the novel's driving philosophical premise—that our civilisation has come to its end, and our art reflects the total decadence and decline of our values. The only way forward, Foster proposes, is to find a spiritual path that can use our decadence—our greed, hatred, brutality, and lust—to find purity and enlightenment. Any rebirth at the end of the novel will be into a new order and a new religion, one that can direct human weaknesses to spiritual understanding. The spiritualism that Foster found among the materially deprived people of Calcutta and the religious variety of India suggested alternative ways out of the crisis. If we accept that human nature is imperfect and imperfectible, then (rather than preaching perfection) we might seek enlightenment through this imperfection, even through the extremes of human vice. It may be seen as another version of the alchemical journey through the red and black states to a new purity—by descending to the depths of human degradation, enlightenment may come. The novel posits that there may be no connection between morality and spiritual truth; this may be a fallacy of Western Christianity. The band emerges from India with spiritual rather than moral power.

As the novel notes, '[t]he practice of Tantra presupposes a certain level of social decay and moral corruption. Like satire, it can actually debauch the unsophisticated by execrating vices they had no idea existed' (281). Thus satire, the dominant genre of the novel, is aligned with the processes of degradation that the novel describes; it functions as the art form most suited to an age of decadence. Pete serves as the novel's satiric commentator, the author's alter ego, who greets the romantic enthusiasms of Jason with scorn and adopts the spiritual path of sheer hatred.

Pete also emerges as the character driven by intelligence and a materialist morality. Through Pete, the novel takes a profoundly moral stance as it details the descent of the band into abomination. In India, Pete attempts to educate Satya, the poor street boy; then, when Satya dies, he sets himself up as a doctor (on the basis of one year of a medical degree). In no time, he decides that abortion promises the most effective method of solving poverty, and the novel indicates that he is ready to move to killing mothers to solve the population problem. Rational thinking can lead rapidly to this result ('Hitler had the right ideas, only didn't go far enough'). Jason's insight—'It's a mistake to think material well-being is the aim of existence!' (268)—completely undermines Pete's rationality. After all, Pete found Canberra wanting.

We may suspect that most of Pete's opinions are the novelist's, but the novel cannot endorse his extremist rationality. Pete's opinions are modified and challenged by the others, particularly Jason, who voice less rational—even irrational—points of view. A more knowing narrative voice intrudes from time to time to comment on Pete, or to supplement his rants on the state of the world. In the course of the novel, the Western rationality that Pete represents, with its basis in liberal morality, is found wanting, and Pete becomes not only its satirist but also its main comic figure. The satirist is satirised. Jason may be a dreaming fool, but his insistence that material improvement is not the purpose of life surely gains support from the novelist. Perhaps his soft-brained love and understanding have something to offer.

Plumbum asks whether the principles of late Western liberal democracy may be the only way, or even any way, that can survive into the future. It asks: what if the Christian millennium is over, and the decline of Western music signifies a shift to a more pagan age in which conventional morality is inverted? What if the purpose of life is not the material well-being that drives the West? After all, according to the novel, the poor on the streets of Calcutta are visibly happier than the citizens of Canberra. The band's rise carries that possibility with it.

Ultimately *Plumbum* is a moral novel, shocked by the contrast between the comfortable wealth of Australia and the chaotic poverty of India. But it does not offer a clear moral code or program for reform. It suggests that humans are incapable of reform and face a future in which our vices may force us to find a new spiritual way and a new morality. It does not offer such a morality, though it registers the depths of the vice. Through Pete and the success of the band, the novel satirises the popular devotion of our times to celebrity and fame as a sign of decadence. It deplores the elevation of 'sex and noise' over 'love and music' as it follows the band's rise to power. The novel is inventive, excessive, and packed with commentary on the absurdities of our culture.

Yet, somehow, it left most of its reviewers unsatisfied. Many found the novel confused and confusing, or thought it was uncontrolled, or simply unpleasant. In 1985 I wrote that for all its ambition and inventiveness, 'something has gone wrong in *Plumbum*', and I thought it was the novelist's desire both to satirise and celebrate the lunacy of the band (McKernan 3). Now, I think it may be the way that the novel quite deliberately leaves the reader in a state of disgust at the band's behaviour. Reviewers were likely to put the book down with an overall sense of its 'unpleasantness' as Helen Thomas put it (29). Foster was more interested in pursuing his urgent vision of our imminent demise than in pleasing an audience.

Like William Burroughs, the satirist he admired, Foster overwhelms the reader with an inventive energy that culminates in a kind of moral disgust. Foster thinks Burroughs's morality lies in his capacity for self-disgust, in the way his imagination shares this distaste with the reader (*S&N* 76–97). Foster achieves a similar effect, though reviewers were inclined to register the distaste rather more than the ideas and morality.

There is a further possibility that, amidst Foster's lunatic representation of the band's music, readers sense the author's own lack of allegiance to their kind of synthetic popular music. The novel proposes that their sufferings in India give them a spiritual understanding that they are able to convey in their music; Felix finds the 'click-track' of life, Jason understands the order in the random noise of the street, and Sharon writes songs through pure inspiration.

However, the music they produce after this enlightenment appears to be the most superficial, over-produced rock music—Nick continues to intervene in the production, even undermining Felix's percussion. All their suffering does not lead to art; they might have been just as successful going straight from Canberra to a good producer, like Kylie Minogue and Stock, Aitken and Waterman. Even as Jason is about to unleash a mantra that will enlighten the world, Nick is fiddling with the mix. When Pete wanders in search of real music, it is jazz that he finds, and he pushes himself in a jazz duel against his old friend Barney until his hands are bloodied in an effort to prove that he still can create art. Unlike jazz, the heavy metal music mimicked so forcefully in the final section of the novel leaves the author (and his readers) cold.

Literary criticism has difficulties in responding to improvisation. The event of publication suggests that literary art has undergone processes of reflection and editing that efface the act of creation, but Foster's art attempts to retain a direct experience of the creative moment. Critics have objected to its lack of unity or apparent control, though this is part of its improvisatory quality. This quality comes close to the idea of unmediated representation valued by feminist theorists, and termed the 'chora' by Julia Kristeva. It insists on the action behind the art, the experience that lies at the heart of the creation of art. Of course, no art work (no language) can be completely unmediated, but the attempt to write close to experience has a valid artistic tradition.

Most people listening to a live performance of a modern jazz group or watching a dance improvisation appreciate that they are experiencing the moment of creation, with all its risks, rather than a considered and refined kind of art. Foster tries to make literary art that approximates this experience, where the artist's risk-taking is as important as his achievement. In the case of *Plumbum*, excess, disjunction, and a sense of lunacy also form part of its argument about the collapse of Western civilisation and its search for spiritual alternatives. The satirist sacrifices the reader's comfort in an orderly structure, and the reader's pleasure in clear resolution for what he sees as truth.

Several of the other satirical writers of Foster's generation have also explored the decadent nature of contemporary rock music and the cult status of its most successful practitioners. In 1973, Don DeLillo's *Great Jones Street* worried about the commercialisation of art through the amazing popularity of rock music. His rock star, Bucky Wunderlick, withdraws from his band's tour to a warehouse room in New York where he is visited by drug runners and entrepreneurs, and is corrupted by the extraordinary opportunities of the rock world. Bucky knows that his music has reached a point at which it is only noise covered by the screaming audiences at his concerts. Like Foster, DeLillo parodies rock journalism and writes the lyrics for the rock songs (Bucky's songs, like those of *Plumbum*, are modeled on those of Bob Dylan, before they decline into an infantile babble), but he never tries to represent the music nor give us the experience of the band in concert, as Foster does. DeLillo's novels share the sense of a civilisation in decline that we find in Foster's work, and he also worries about the spiritual emptiness in societies devoted to technology. Yet he always appears saner and more detached than Foster, and his humour comes from a strong standard of good sense and morality. Salman Rushdie's narrator in *The Ground Beneath Her Feet* (1999) loves the novel's rock star and celebrates her music in a world of decadence and destruction. Only Foster writes from inside the musician's world, mocking consistently and with a thorough knowledge of the compromises of popular art.

Towards the end of *Plumbum*, Pete wanders alone in the Dutch forest dreaming of the simple life the Blackmans once shared at Knockembandy, well beyond the corruptions and degradations of the rock world. It seems, for all its parochialism and lack of opportunity, 'thousan' miles from nowhere' (1) is a better place to be. Foster would return to the small town in his next novel.

Dog Rock

'I've begun another novel, in a small town setting. Very subdued—I feel rather tired, & somewhat in need of a warm bath after *Plumbum*',

Foster wrote to Dutton in April 1983 (DP 2/17/122). He had returned to his detailed notes on Australian town life, the basis for the Canberra sections of *Plumbum*, and to Pete Blackman's dream of life in the country.

By 1981 Foster had become aware that Bundanoon was about to change forever, with its proximity to Sydney creating an influx of city people, and new technology wiping out its sense of isolation. In an attempt to record every aspect of its ordinariness, he began taking detailed notes on the town while he conducted his postal run (*S&N* 1–18). Notebooks in the ADFA Library show the extensiveness and intensity of Foster's observations of the people, houses, and landscape of Bundanoon. He treated the town as a scientific subject, detailing the building styles, furniture on the verandahs, state of the garden, trees, letterboxes, and the kind of mail for each household. Among his notes are lists of the people who took bowls magazines, *The Reader's Digest*, RSL newsletters, and all the other items denoting a range of hobbies and interests. He collected official letters and guidelines from Australia Post detailing the requirements for examinees for the postal exam. He talked to the town residents and taxi drivers. He found plenitude in the apparent vacuity of a small town in Australia where nothing happens.

In the 'very subdued' novel that emerged, Foster performs in a purer comic mode than in any earlier work. He leaves the big philosophical questions alone for a while to enjoy the possibilities of 'a postal pastoral'. He writes the poetry of rural Australian towns, lovingly recording every detail of life. True to the pastoral form, *Dog Rock: A Postal Pastoral* (1985) is also an exercise in nostalgia, retrieving a kind of rural life that is disappearing as the novel is written. Telecom will soon replace the manual telephone exchange with an automatic system; television already dominates the evenings of the town inhabitants; by chapter 8, the freeway has reduced the distance from the airport to only two hours. Doctors and judges from the city have begun to buy the good land and misuse it. Foster himself may be one of the increasing number of Balthazars in the town, 'distinguished by artistic talent, an obsession with their plight, a sense of their own superiority, a reluctance to work, a gold earring in at least one earlobe and a fondness for soft drugs' (11).

Andrew Riemer sees the influence of Virgil's *Georgics* in the novel's accounts of beekeeping and vegetable growing, and shrewdly recognises that its narrator, D'Arcy D'Oliveres, represents the 'disguised prince' of the Renaissance pastoral romance (*Southerly* 136). Foster claims the literary pastoral tradition for Australia, while Europe represents a world lost to technology. The novel invokes and parodies these traditions at the same time.

Dog Rock also functions as a murder mystery on the English model, in which an eccentric and unlikely detective uncovers crime in an apparently peaceful small town. For once, Foster sets out to entertain his readers. Rather than taking an omniscient (and intrusive) narrative position, he passes the narrative to D'Arcy D'Oliveres, a Pommy postman with claims to the British aristocracy, and D'Arcy's digressions keep readers from any recognition of the criminal. At times, remembering the crime is difficult enough. D'Arcy performs the novel, and it follows a distinctly oral rather than textual pattern. Foster was obviously aware of its potential for performance, as his papers in the ADFA Library include an 'unstaged' play version, commissioned as a monologue for the comic actor Drew Forsythe.

In a further comic conceit, D'Arcy addresses the reader as a confidant and companion, occasionally asking for a hand as he goes about his tasks. The reader proves obliging enough to feed D'Arcy's chooks (chickens) and cats while he is away in England, and we pick him up from the airport on his return in chapter 8. The reader even assists D'Arcy in the final pages by chasing a wombat onto the road, so that he can speed the murderer's demise and save him from the ignominy of detection by the police. Despite his rambling confidences, D'Arcy does not tell us that his prosthetic arm is only a ruse, or of his theory about the identity of the criminal. He has the grace to apologise for this at the end of the novel.

While the surface of the novel appears chaotic, Foster carefully plants or withholds the information that provides a kind of structure. A strange implement posted to the town indicates that a serial killer resides there, and that D'Arcy is suspected. Foster parodies the logic of the detective genre, providing far-fetched motivations, absurd methods, and an abandoned sense of justice. Each of the victims—a Labor MP, a sometime brothelworker and layout artist for an advertising firm, a magician and animal smuggler, a famous radio broadcaster, a judge of the family court, and an organiser of the Women Against Rape in War and Sex with Men in General—provide opportunities for hilarious non-sequiturs, such as the fate of the judge's grand piano:

> that five years ago got away from seven sturdy men, bolted down the drive, rocketed off a ledge, and overshooting completely the house, jungle and pool area of industrialist Sir Watto Urbanski—to the astonishment of the visiting French fencing team barbecuing by the pool—plummeted into a two acre nature reserve at the foot of the scarp, where it cut a swath twenty feet wide through the last remaining stand of red cedar in the whole of Middle arm. (66)

This leads to a description of the competitions between the local Cow Flat fencers and the French team, founded on misunderstanding of the local meaning of fencing.

The detective parody gives Foster an artificial narrative form around which he folds the intricate details of country town life. D'Arcy's gossipy digressions pursue every element of the history, climate, animal keeping, and patterns of work and play in the town, always alert to the ridiculous. D'Arcy explains that this is a 'trivial town, where nothing ever happens which is not essentially trivial', though the events of the novel are '*quadrivial*': 'I shall use the present tense to conceal the thinness of my material' (4). D'Arcy mines this material to account for all the Sunday night activities of the town, including Renee Calvary's return home, the people she wakes, Dion Belvedere's argument with Lisa Goddard and subsequent phone conversation, and the dropping of shutter sixty-three on the exchange. He gives us the nightlong activities of Dudley Semple, the baker, as he prepares the next day's bread while watching a black and white horror movie on television: 'A good baker needs to be aggressive and that's why God, who loves His daily bread, has given Dudley Semple such a rotten life' (26).

By the end of the first chapter we know the layout of the town and the daily activities of everyone in it, the ownership of roosters, the movement of trucks and trains down the railway line. It is a concise celebration of a particular Australian mode of being, in which work is done regardless of profitability because it has always been done. This is a pastoral world, of simple working lives dependent on animals, plants, the railway, and the council roadworks.

It can be no surprise that the particular moment of the novel's account of Dog Rock is the moment before inevitable decline. Like the islanders of Hiphoray in *Moonlite*, the people of Dog Rock and their harmless daily habits will soon be destroyed by the intrusion of the urban, international world, represented by technology and the weekend farmers from the city. As D'Arcy returns from his trip to Britain, he notices the subdivision of good agricultural land into housing estates for the city refugees. We find that the murderer is motivated by anger at these changes, and the way that a dairy farmer works long hours over a lifetime to remain poor, while ignorant professionals from the city can buy up his land and livestock as a hobby. His farm *Labour-in-Vain* has become *Idle-A-While*.

D'Arcy even links the intrusion of city 'pioneers' to Foster's grander theories about the decline of civilisation:

> Rural communities are formed by blood ties over many generations. What we have here is not the birth of something, but the death of something else entirely. I speak as one who's seen it before. This is the metastasis of a cancer, spreading from the arse and the wide-open mouth and hunting out the liver. This is the way civilizations die, read your Gibbons on the Fall of Rome…the last thing I feel like looking at is the future, in the form of tourist Europe. But I've no doubt we'll find there the key to the mystery, or at least, I hope we do. (129)

As in *Plumbum*, the end is nigh. As in *Moonlite*, the small community must be wiped away by the ruthless economic forces of capitalism, and civilisation will die. Civilisation here is a mode of working with nature without regard to profit, and occupying a place in the community connected to other people through family, Church, sport, the RSL, and the bowling club. *Dog Rock* remains, at heart, what Foster called 'a harmless entertainment', but we should note that even in such a wholeheartedly comic mode, Foster does not diverge from his philosophical vision that our civilisation is about to break apart.

About the same time, Foster showed increasing irritation at the use of statistics in the social sciences, and had begun to reflect on the difference between the scientific use of statistics and the creative artist's approach to individuality. In an article published in 1990, called 'Chaos Is Normal', he deplored the way that an individual experience once agglomerated with the experiences of others becomes a statistical law and is used to make causal assumptions. He used as his examples the way that deaths from lung cancer are linked with the statistics on smoking to prove that smoking causes cancer; or that AIDS had been proposed as a risk to heterosexuals on the basis of responses to questionnaires by people likely to lie about their sexual activities. Foster noted that:

> As a novelist, I work through induction, and my work could be seen as attempting to illuminate human behaviour by moving implicitly from the specific to the general by means of largely fictitious case histories. Guesswork, in fact. Such is the eternal nature of the tale. But because of the colligative nature of society, which exhibits (though I cannot understand why) properties I cannot hope to comprehend through examination of my own consciousness, what I put forward remains hypothetical, however passionately I myself believe what I say to be true. (*S&N* 132)

Dog Rock shows Foster's obsession with detailing the particular in opposition to the scientific tendency to generalise. However, paradoxically, as Foster suggests, the very detail of *Dog Rock* leads to generalising. This town may well be Bundanoon down to its neglected mailboxes, but Foster's detailed observation somehow represents every small country town within reach of the city. This is the mystery of the novel, an anti-statistical form that manages to offer us insights into a larger world.

From the detail of lives, buildings, and people's habits, Foster creates a wider picture of a rural society under threat from the city and technology. The novel records for posterity what will be lost. Foster adopts an attention to detail that mimics scientific observation, though he insists that science generalises while art upholds individual unconformity and diversity. The novel celebrates the individual nature of work and life, yet it does see broader patterns. This is Foster, the scientist, observing so closely that he can find worlds within worlds. It is difficult to see that the artist and scientist are far apart.

The Pale Blue Crochet Coathanger Cover, published two years later in 1987, develops this pastoral comic mode with even greater skill. This time, the reader takes the part of the dog, wearing a pale blue crochet coathanger cover around his neck after Captain Hooch is found dead among the fancywork in the Dog Rock African Mission Opportunity Shop. The novel signals that it is the ultimate shaggy dog story, with the reader playing the role of the shaggy dog. After a series of deaths in the town, D'Arcy once again falls under suspicion, while taking upon himself the necessary detective work. Like any postman, D'Arcy hates dogs and takes on the care of Captain Hooch's vegetarian dog only because he holds clues to the crime and proves that he can beat other dogs away on the postal run.

All the victims in this series of 'accidents' work with animals—Captain Hooch the Vietnam vet and owner of the dog, Des Quinsy the vet, Toni the Artificial Inseminator, and Soon Fatt the vet from Vietnam. The reader/dog has participated in some of these accidents and has passed on information from D'Arcy through a transmitter hidden by Purvis the detective. Indeed, D'Arcy reveals himself to have little concern for animal welfare, secretly ringing the pound about the dog, proving negligent of his neighbour's cow, and enjoying the reader/dog's attack on the Jennings' cattle dog. The animals of Dog Rock have begun to take their revenge, particularly on those interfering with their sexual organs through artificial insemination or bodgy pregnancy testing.

As Marilla North has noted, *The Pale Blue Crochet Coathanger Cover* not only parodies the detective story, but it also works as an animal fable (686–696). Foster not only asks the reader to consider the life of a dog through the dog's eyes, but he also imagines a community of animals banding together against the cruelties of humans. Where in *Dog Rock* the hard-working, impoverished dairy farmer takes revenge on city affluence, margarine promoters, wildlife smugglers, and feminists, *The Pale Blue Crochet Coathanger Cover* overturns our attitudes towards animals. Though it is also replete with detail about the changing town, full of jokes and extended comic digressions, it asks us to reconsider human assumptions about the animal world. Behind all the fun and playfulness lies a moral question about our responsibility to domestic animals and our use of the land.

Narelle Shaw argues that the Dog Rock novels celebrate the oral traditions of gossip, and that is the form they take (*Antipodes* 1990). D'Arcy's digressions and bits of information about the town perform as gossip, especially as he exaggerates and even misinforms the reader at times. In the first novel, the reader's role as D'Arcy's confidant reinforces the gossip mode, and the reader is left with the task of spreading the story about D'Arcy's prosthetic arm. Shaw sees gossip as central to the community of the town, and she traces the way in which D'Arcy manipulates the reader into collusion with the gossip network: 'Gossip's ephemerality and Dog Rock's tenuous hold on its identity are creatively linked in Foster's imagination' (32). As D'Arcy asserts, 'Where gossip is perverted into silence or honesty community persists in name only' (*Dog Rock DR* 98).

Shaw sees a further decline in community in *The Pale Blue Crochet Coathanger Cover*, where gossip is not only limited by the demise of the telephone exchange, but overridden by authority—including the city policeman Purvis and the intrusive Post Office by-laws. The infiltration of city habits of language has undermined the remaining sense of community. Shaw argues that in this novel, only the animal population of Dog Rock represents the 'true communal spirit' that has departed as the city encroaches.

If readers found *Plumbum* excessive and out of control, the Dog Rock novels demonstrate that Foster can direct his wit and energy into the intricately manipulated narrative of a comic murder mystery. They are a rare combination of close observation and hilariously exaggerated comic possibilities. Like all Foster's fiction, they are utterly original and overwhelming in their interest in the details of contemporary life. At the same time, they offer a generous spirit of humour and fun.

In D'Arcy D'Oliveres, Foster creates a comic persona full of eccentricity and theories about the world he has observed. His British background gives him a critical perspective on Australian habits, as he insists on reverence to the Queen (he replaces the discarded portrait in the Post Office) and a monarchist loyalty. At the same time, his decline into postal service mocks any aristocratic pretensions he may have. Two hundred years after British settlement, Dog Rock remains an outpost of the British Empire, with its mock-English names and English gardens. Its Australianness appears in its parodic mimicry of things British, and the novels offer a postcolonial satire on Australian domesticity and ignorance of the world. D'Arcy's dreams of Cheltenham and his annual walks on the Cotswold Way mock the Australian longing for another, European, pastoral world, now accessed through Best of Britain Trafalgar tours.

While D'Arcy, the aristocratic Australian postman, may appear a far-fetched fancy, Foster notes that there was at least one other British aristocrat working for Australia Post in the 1980s (in Tasmania). On 11 September 2005, the *Sun Herald* reported that the fourteenth Earl of Loudoun, Michael Hastings, had strong claims to the British throne, though he lived humbly as a rice farmer in the country town of Jerilderie (on the New South Wales side of the border with Victoria). Though not a postman, Lord Hastings married the local telephone switchboard operator and, in interview, jokingly offered himself as Head of State in a republican Australia. Foster's exaggerated creations seem to echo in Australian life.

D'Arcy provided a persona through which Foster could write a more benign and good-natured comedy than his more philosophical and angry satires. D'Arcy's very eccentricity—his obsessions with bees and household mail—allows a steady stream of jokes and comic observation of Australian attitudes and habits. In these novels, the narrator (and the reader) participates in the joke, leaving the author free to indulge his comic talents and demonstrate his technical skills. Later, he would call a more scholarly and philosophical D'Arcy into service for *The Glade Within the Grove*.

Chapter 5

Men's Business: *Testostero* and *Mates of Mars*

Testostero

> The Zeitgeist is a woman or a poof. Red-blooded men are outmoded.
>
> —Noel Horniman in *Testostero* (156)

By the late 1980s, Foster had developed a flamboyant, wide-ranging comic technique. In the Dog Rock novels, D'Arcy D'Oliveres could make vulgar jokes about peas and leeks, or philosophical comments on the decline of civilisation. In these comic novels, Foster leaves no pun unpunned, no gag unexpressed. His skills as a farceur are as evident as those as a satirist. This leaves a problem for some readers and critics: how seriously should we take such a clown?

In his article on the publication of *Testostero*, Andrew Riemer thought that the major obstacle to appreciation of Foster's fiction was this mixed signal about seriousness (*Southerly* 126–144). His philosophical concerns were unavoidable in the exuberant satires of *Plumbum* and *Moonlite*; could they still be found in the more populist humour of *Dog Rock*? *Testostero*, published in the same year as *The Pale Blue Crochet Coathanger Cover*, provided a clearer example of the two strands working together. The novel adopts those stock figures of farce (the separated twins) and pursues a madcap plot in the tradition of Goldoni's *The Venetian Twins* and Shakespeare's *A Comedy of Errors*; it nods towards Commedia dell'Arte and the masked carnival tradition of Venice. Yet it is not only a case of mistaken identities and twisted motives; Foster's twins represent the cultural mismatch between Australia and Europe, and the absurdities of scientific experiments about nurture and nature. Foster intertwines the comic tradition of twins in art, with the experimental use of twins in science. In accordance with tradition, the novel begins and ends in Venice.

In 1984 Foster and Gerda spent a month as the guests of the Commonwealth Writers' studio in Venice. When they arrived, Professor Bernard Hickey, who managed the studio, told Foster that he had never heard of his work, thus inviting his own reincarnation as Professor Perry Patetic in *Testostero*—though the novel was also dedicated to him. Hickey and Gerda (who contributed to Judy Rankenfile) were treated gently compared to Foster's version of himself—Noel Horniman, the vulgar poet from Marrickville. Noel's twin, Leon Hunnybun, the statistical psychologist and aesthete from Contolmondeley (pronounced 'Contumely') College, London, shares Foster's interest in scientific theory and high art, but Noel offers a version of the author as carnival clown, much as Pete Blackman served as the vehicle for his satiric aggression in *Plumbum*.

Noel, like his author, combines the aspiration to high artistic achievement with Australian vulgarity and a degree of barbarism. Walking through the alleyways of Venice, like many Australians abroad, he seeks any indication that his native land exists 'as though he'd been stripped of his identity and asked to reconstruct himself from clues' (2). The titles of his two books of poetry, *Slug Burial* and *Gash Alley*, satirise the masculine hubris and self-importance of much Australian writing (particularly poetry) and clearly refer to

Noel's sexual exploits. Horniman's poems are 'nothing less than the carnal record of one man's spiritual quest. He was born knowing he must find her, whereupon she would provide him with his needs. His tongue and lips, and later on his penis, would be the instruments of his search' (5). No one who has also read *The Fleeing Atalanta* can accuse Foster of preserving himself from mockery.

Venice is full of great, timeless art works depicting man's relationship to God, yet this forty-year-old hooligan (Hooligan is his mother's maiden name) from Marrickville has the gall to call himself an artist. Noel's crude presumption is contrasted with the reverent art appreciation of his twin, Leon. Leon is sexually timid and apparently homosexual; Noel and Leon, with their mirrored names, represent the conventional contrast between crude Australian energy and effete European impotence. Would Noel, if brought up in England, become as sensitive and passive as Leon? Would Leon, raised in Australia, develop the rough energy and gross ego of Noel, expressed in his poetry and womanising? Behind this is the familiar acknowledgment that Australian life, whether small town, suburban, or Canberran, continues beyond the interest of the wider world. On the other hand, everyone goes to Venice.

Venice, too, has its tradition of populist art (the Commedia dell'Arte and the street theatre of the Carnivale), and the novel finds some comfort in exploring this tradition for itself. This allows Foster to rehash the crudest of puns about 'knockers' and 'big cock ups'; he even runs the one about the wombat who 'eats roots and leaves' (18). The novel's Venice contains not only great art works but also gangsters (with connections to Marrickville); Noel, the pubfighting council worker, is more at home here than Leon, the aristocratic art lover. Indeed, Noel ends the novel happily plying his trade as a gondolier and smuggler.

While the novel adopts a Venetian mode for its scenes in Venice, when it moves to London, it offers an 'Intermezzo' of parody kitchen sink drama and drawing room farce. The entire novel between pages 115 and 155 is delivered as a series of play scenes reminiscent of Tom Stoppard's absurdist reworkings of the English tradition. Here the novel satirises the Australian tourist in England, as Noel's Australian family arrives in England with Leon, transformed by his Australian experience into the archetypal yobbo, trailing them. It skips to the aristocratic drawing room of Noel's and Leon's mother, where farcical murder brings Inspector Krishnamurthy to investigate. These scenes demand a strong dramatic imagination from readers so that the visual jokes don't disappear behind the dialogue.

The high point of the novel's mix of modes is Leon's series of letters to Noel after they change places. While Noel takes Leon's job as Head of the psychological research unit in London, Leon travels to Sydney to work for Newtown Council. He finds himself supervising the local swimming pool—though he cannot swim, let alone meet the standards of the bronze medallion ('It's part of our education system' (103)). In one of Foster's brilliant excursions into the poetry of the ordinary, Leon gives a scientifically detailed account of the operations of the filter system of the swimming pool (95–97). He records the banal and ridiculous conversations of his workmates, Horrie, Doug, and Cec, and he reflects on the relationship between statistical method and language in the same terms Foster uses in his 1990 essay, 'Chaos Is Normal' (quoted in chapter 4). Statistical methods, Leon argues, not only cannot be applied to an individual event, but they also have a 'rounding off' tendency (98):

> They undermine our willingness to comprehend the fearful complexity of the real world. As number moves into language, statistical subtlety is lost. I have no doubt that if one expects a certain result one is more likely to get it, for reasons that lie beyond the realms of contemporary psychology, and hence may be said to verge on the 'occult'. We psychologists are constantly pushing the 'unexpected' (the heroic, the saintly) out of human existence. You poets must fight this cynical tendency every inch of the way. (98)

This argument provides the intellectual and philosophical base for Foster's recording of the intricate details of life that usually find no place in art. He chooses art over science because science always looks to general theories, while art attempts to comprehend the 'fearful complexity of the real world'. Nevertheless, the scientific commitment to close observation can provide the basis for art—the very imprecision of verbal language allows for poetry to emerge from scientific description. Leon decides to publish some of his own poetry in Noel's name. On the other side of the world, over Leon's name, Noel is writing scathing reviews of learned scientific articles.

For his part, Noel finds the whole IQ test industry a fraud. Marrickville and the council pool, though, intrude on his poetic response to Venice:

> The sky was that deep plumbago you see over Marrickville at false dawn, from the corner of the Warren View, after a night tomcatting or playing cards. The sea, so green, looked like a C-grade pool in need of a backwash. The contents of a garbage bin were floating on the surface and the water had the heavy appearance of mucus. (42)

Foster writes the poetry of the council pool and the dirty canals of Venice; he maintains the claims of the genres of satire and farce to artistic attention, despite their lowly status in the conventional hierarchy of art. His art of observation and excess counters the tendency to make the world manageable through statistical summary and selection. It seeks the truth and finds complexity, chaos, and the wonderful absurdity of human struggles for control.

The novel also mocks Sir Cyril Surtout-Spoton's attempt to use Noel and Leon for scientific experimentation. Sir Cyril assumes that Leon is the advantaged, and Noel the disadvantaged, twin. The novel suggests, on the contrary, that Australia may offer the advantage in nurture, producing Noel with his pretensions as a poet, bronze medallion, and outdoor job. Leon has a love of art, a sound British education, and a miserable childhood slaving at the manor. In England, Noel's democratic stand against the aristocracy soon disappears when he sees the possibility of a baronetcy, while in Australia lonely Leon looks to benefit from a relationship with Judy and her son, Byron (named after the bay, not the poet). His scientific job has its perks, but Noel is overwhelmed by its demands on his time. Each twin proves so incompetent in the other's role that they lose each other's jobs.

The novel proposes that sexuality is a matter of nurture rather than nature, given the different propensities of the twins. Indeed, sexuality appears a rather arbitrary matter when Cortesana Lottotatz is revealed as the third sibling, a transsexual identical triplet. Given Noel's infatuation with Cortesana, this puts his aggressive heterosexuality in doubt. Noel's declaration that the 'Zeitgeist is a woman or a poof' expresses his sense of exclusion from the world of art and culture in which Leon and Cortesana feel at home. Nevertheless, the novel leaves Noel working contentedly as a gondolier in close contact with Cortesana; their bond is 'as much a tribute to human passion as an indictment of statistical method' (187)—though the implications for their sexuality remain unclear. Leon, now a distinguished Australian art critic happily married to Judy, makes regular visits to his siblings. Does this imply that Australia creates the conditions for heterosexuality?

The third way proves the solution. Venice, not London or Sydney, is the place where art meets life. Noel's working class Italian heritage, combined with the beauties of Venice, leaves him without the need for poetry: 'For to write poetry is commonplace enough and more to be pitied than applauded: but to live in Venice is an achievement to be envied by every sophisticated person' (188). Foster, on the other hand, returned to the Arcadian pastoral world of Bundanoon.

Testostero insists on the importance of daily life to art. It tells us that the Renaissance artists who created the masterpieces of Venice were men, struggling like Noel to maintain their inspiration. So, when he was just twenty years old, Mantegna painted the portrait of Saint Sebastian that thrills Leon's heart; Tintoretto had done all his best work by the age of forty (4). The Venice in which they lived was as riddled by gangsters, dirt, and disease as the modern city, or even a place like Marrickville. The novel laughs at snobbery in art, and in science (where IQ tests link intelligence with wealth and education). As

Martin Johnston commented, the novel shows 'a healthily dismissive approach to anything resembling good taste' (27). *Testostero* is an argument for Foster's own commitment to an art that attempts to encompass the 'fearful complexity of life', including both its vulgarity and refinement, against the tendency to revere 'high art' as separate from the mess of life. True to Foster's insight that Western society is in decline, Venice represents a great civilisation on the way down: 'Venice is falling apart. It's absolutely decrepit. All the plaster is coming off the walls, the houses are collapsing, and no one cares' (6).

Narelle Shaw argues that the novel champions 'the integrity of the comic genre' (1991: 76). She explicates the numerous references and allusions in the novel, from Plautus' *Menaechmi* to Punch and Judy shows, and she notes the structural patterns of drowning and tea drinking across its three locations. She also pursues the novel's references to *Othello* and *Titus Andronicus*, noticing that violence and tragedy lie close beside Venetian vitality and comedy. Shaw finds *Testostero* 'a curiously un-Australian novel in many respects' because of its complex reworking of European traditions, including the 'cruelty and treachery' in Venetian history (76).

On the other hand, some reviewers saw it as a reworking of an Australian genre, the comedy of the barbarian Australian encountering Old World civilisation, probably most familiar in Barry Humphries's Bazza McKenzie cartoons and films (Ralph Elliott). Several reviewers commented on the novel's suitability for adaptation to film, Myfanwy Gollan even invoking Paul Hogan's *Crocodile Dundee* as a comparison (44). When it first appeared, *Testostero* gained more consistent critical approval than any Foster novel since *Moonlite*. Reviewers loved its irreverence and hilarity, and most were ready to forgive the tedium of the central section because of the joyfully tasteless absurdity of the novel's ending. Gollan praised Foster's 'rare and wonderful' talent, and Janet Healey put *Testostero* in the 'ranks of the great comic novels'.

Martin Johnston compared Foster to Pynchon because of the 'atmosphere of anomie, dissolution, entropy and dark ambiguity' pervading the work of both' (27). Just as the Punch and Judy show and the whole carnival tradition encompass both comedy and cruelty, Foster's pessimism about civilisation appeared clearly through the diversions of farce. This pessimism signals the novel's interest in more than a celebration of the comic genre. It insists on a living context of vulgarity and violence for the creation of art.

MATES OF MARS

There are Friends of the Earth and there are Mates of Mars (David Foster's annotation to this heading).

In the context of *Testostero*, Noel's declaration about the Zeitgeist reveals his own egocentric view of the world, but Foster took it up again in his next novels as a matter for further examination. *Mates of Mars* considers what Foster sees as the decline of men as the dominant figures of the Western world, particularly in their role as warriors and aggressors. Its Introduction states its paradoxical premise—that Australians represent both the last gasp of a 'decrepit' Western Christian civilisation, and the barbarian elements in the southernmost reach of the 'Sinic Mahayana Buddhist' civilisation that is bound to overtake it. The novel predicts that Australians of both European and Aboriginal heritage will cede dominance to Asians. This is not a rerun of the 'Yellow Peril' threat perceived by white Australia over most of its history; it is a satirical statement that neither white nor black Australians have done much with the country.

While this may be seen as a political issue, the paradox at the heart of the novel is the premise that a civilisation's survival depends on the savagery of its warriors. It is a subject that Foster had addressed in his discussion of the Arab world of Damascus in *The Adventures of Christian Rosy Cross*, in which the civilisation at its peak contains the elements of its own downfall. From this perspective, the 'softness' of a civilisation in which women and homosexuals could prosper indicates its inevitable decline; but it is in the nature of civilisation that it strives to eliminate its dependence on the violence and brutality that brought it into being.

To address such a millennial concern, Foster looked to his own experience of the martial arts. He claims he first took up Taekwondo in order to beat off his teenage daughters' boyfriends (*boyfriends that have included two Kangaroo International Rugby League footballers, an Australian shearing champion, an Australian bullriding champion and a Northern prawn fishery trawler skipper*) if required, but by the mid-1980s he had gained a black belt, second dan, and was instructing classes in Sydney. Writing about Taekwondo before the 2000 Olympics, he remembered his own initiation into the sport:

> I was crippled, as a child, with polio, limp slightly, and have no flexibility in my right leg. No martial art style could have less suited my physical shortcomings than TKD. But I had the good fortune to meet with an instructor who so inspired me with his brilliant technique I trained, largely to watch him play, so intense was the aesthetic pleasure it gave me. When Francis Seow's suit went into mothballs, Australia lost a great TKD stylist, and a certain Olympic medallist, had it been possible to persuade him to enter a tournament. Which it wasn't. ('Once' 27)

Indeed, Foster deplored the change to tournament sparring that adapted Taekwondo as an Olympic sport—for him, it was an art form.

Mates of Mars relies on Foster's knowledge and experience of Taekwondo, but more significantly on his observations of the varieties of men who made up Australian society at the end of the twentieth century. The martial arts attract men from across the immigrant groups—South Koreans, Chinese Malays, Lebanese Muslims—as well as those with European backgrounds and, of course, Australian Aborigines. For his novel, Foster chose a group of mates to represent this racial and class variety: Steve Overton, the white working class Australian of British/Irish descent; Sven Scrimshaw, the middle class Swedish-British type; Cheng Siong Fai (known as Vincent), the Chinese Malay medical postdoc; Bruce Nonnemacher, the Jewish-Australian professor; and Cyril Jiberan, the Aborigine from the Top End. To represent the rise of women, he included the red-haired Jade

Muldoon, taller and stronger than Bruce. The short, middle-aged Bruce may be recognised as yet another version of Foster—this time, the obsessive intellectual trying to achieve the impossible black belt despite his late start in martial arts.[1] Foster deliberately creates these characters as exaggerated racial stereotypes that give him plenty of opportunity for absurd comedy.

Elements of the band members from *Plumbum* may be detected in these martial arts enthusiasts: Jason in Sven, the womaniser and romantic; Pete in Bruce, the self-absorbed intellectual; Sharon in Jade, the straight-talking feminist; Roland in Steve, the sexually ambivalent virgin; Felix in Cyril, the physically intimidating black man. Wolfgang Coogan, rapist and criminal, makes only a brief appearance in the novel, though he creates some of its action, just as Nick does in the earlier novel.

Foster's commitment to martial arts gave him an intellectual and spiritual structure for the novel, by providing a philosophy that transcended the differing cultural loyalties of his Mates. The novel's discussions of Taekwondo sparring techniques, its disciplines, and its codes make its propositions about the rising Eastern civilisation plausible. Taekwondo requires a spiritual as well as a physical discipline, a process of meditation and reflection as well as action. Its alliance of spiritual progress with physical aggression parallels Foster's continuing search for spiritual enlightenment through a pugnacious writing style. Furthermore, Taekwondo is a warrior code, with origins in the training of men in order to understand and control their own mental and physical power. Its identification of opposing dualities in the yin and yang, and the need to integrate and balance these oppositions, matched Foster's obsession with paradox.

At the same time, the enthusiasm for Taekwondo in Australia makes it a powerful social network, a strong basis for a novel about the social mixture of contemporary Australian society. In the novel, Taekwondo gives Steve Overton—ex-copper and security manager, living on a rundown chicken farm on the edge of Sydney—the opportunity to visit Japan and learn Japanese. It allows Bruce Nonnemacher, the egocentric Chemistry professor, to befriend Vincent (otherwise invisible to him) and to travel to Vincent's home village in Malaysia. It gives Sven Scrimshaw, a male model and failed Chemistry student, the chance to meet Cyril Jiberan, the league footballer imported to help Wests—and a career playing villains in Chinese kung fu movies. Jade finds it the source of self-defence techniques for women, bound to create conflict with Cyril, as martial arts has become secret men's business in the Top End. The martial arts encompass as many classes and races as Australia itself. The novel embraces multicultural Australia, not in the romanticised forms of ethnic food and dancing, but in the shared male interest in aggression and the warrior codes that refine it. Its spiritual dimension offers a way to enlightenment for all men through masculine aggression—just as the Kali Yuga of *Plumbum* sought enlightenment through sensual decadence.

Mates of Mars also confronts the issue that has dominated Australian intellectual discussion since the 1980s: the damage by white settlement to Australia's indigenous peoples. The coach driver on their journey north tells the Mates, '[w]e've tried everything. We've shot them and we've given them everything they wanted. Nothing works' (198). Almost every literary novel published about the time of the Bicentenary of British settlement in 1988 considers the state of Australian Aborigines in some way. Most review the sins of the past—Carey's *Oscar and Lucinda*, David Malouf's *Remembering Babylon*, Kate Grenville's *Joan Makes History*—with only a few, like Thea Astley's *It's Raining in Mango* and Victor Kelleher's *Wintering*, acknowledging the contemporary place of Aborigines in Australian society. Though set in 1988, *Mates of Mars* was not published until 1991, within a few months of Sam Watson's novel of Aboriginal aggression, *The Kadaitcha Sung*.[2] Kim Scott's *True Country*, about a schoolteacher's attempt to understand his Aboriginal heritage by working in the North, was published in 1993, and Andrew McGahan's novel about a young white man going bush to discover the meaning of Australia in the year of the bicentenary, *1988*, did not appear until 1995. These latter novels all try to come to terms with Australia's present and future, rather than only with its past record of race relations. The novels of McGahan,

Watson, and Foster all consider the state of the nation in terms of a masculine crisis.

Foster wrote an unpublished review of Watson's novel, and drew comfort that it was more belligerent than *Mates of Mars*. He found reading it

> a depressing, frequently disgusting and generally infuriating experience...Yet I believe that Watson has got it right, which is what gives the book its undeniable power and unpalatable authenticity. The autochthonous residents of this continent, to use an old-fashioned word that would probably draw a right cross from Tommy—in so many ways the book invites a comparable physical response; 'the old migloo bloody useless in bed' laughs Tommy: 'They got tiny budoo and no heart': how much of this can you cop, gentle reader? My own capacity is limited—were barbarians, uninformed by the religious precepts. (FP 7.2/3)

But he thought that Watson's book would help clear 'away some of the ignorant bullshit around the vexatious subject of race relations in this country', no matter how much it might offend 'migloos' like Foster himself. Foster recognised that the aggression in Watson's novel was aimed at 'migloos', particularly middle-class white readers who thought themselves tolerant.

In 1990 the New Zealand writer Alan Duff published *Once Were Warriors*, criticising the perversion of Maori warrior culture into domestic brutality and street violence. These novels confront the violence in contemporary indigenous communities. Watson's Aboriginal and Duff's Maori heritage did not protect them from criticism from their communities. Foster, as a white man ('in appearance' comments Foster), invited such criticism in describing this violence in his novel, though in *Mates* the violence is not only relieved by a comic and satirical perspective, it is also considerably milder than in Watson's and Duff's books. Much of the violence in Foster's novel occurs off-stage and, for the most part, his fighters play at violence in their martial arts classes; they seem more intent on self-harm than on assaulting their women and children, or any bystanders.

Mates of Mars lavishes attention on the routines and restraints of the *dojang* in Sydney and Singapore, but its climax comes in a brawl between two rival Aboriginal groups, crazy with drunkenness, outside a pub in the North. The Mates observe the fight from the sidelines:

> Staggering under their slabs—a slab being a 24-pack in its cardboard carton—the drunken men from Port Pantscough are caught in the glare from Jacky Nguldul's troopcarrier. They stand dazed, staring into the spotlights. Jumping from the troopcarrier—which again is left in the middle of the road—the newly arrived drunken men set upon the drunken men already present without a moment's hesitation. Slabs are set aside. Weapons are found and hubcaps wrenched off vehicles to serve as extemporaneous shields. The fighting is fierce. Men are flung against verandah posts, bounced off walls, throttled in the dust. Motorcycles are pushed from their stands. The police Landcruiser comes under assault. At one point 3 white men, all wearing blue Jacky Howe singlets, khaki shorts and workboots with no socks, irrupt from the hotel backwards as if afflicted with the backward staggers. In fact, they have been thrown out. Sipping their drinks, which they have jealously guarded, they turn to watch the brawl as if it were a state of origin football match. Two finally venture forth to lift and move the fallen cycles, provided with cover by the third, who screams a volley of racist abuse. But no drunken black man lightly assaults a drunken white man here, or vice versa. (219)

There are many fights over the course of the novel, from attacks on the nightclub doorman to the sparring in the martial arts *dojang*, but the complete pointlessness of this one may leave the reader as shocked as Jade and Bruce, who turn away from the scene.

The interlude, 'Outback Radio', which occurs before the Mates arrive at Neverfuckinlose, challenges the 'from a distance' urban middle-class reverence for Aborigines more directly. As they drive from Alice Springs airport, the Mates tune in to the two-way radio of a passing four-wheel drive. What follows is an eight-page comic exchange between an Aboriginal politician making his way home from Canberra and his contacts in the district: 'D'is mobile people's representative Bravo Yankee Zulu callin store traditional community Delta Echo Neverfuckinlose, from traditional Toyota troopcarrier on Track between Tennant Creek and T'reeways an followin de termite mounds due Nort' (203). This satirises the way in which 'traditional ways' has become a phrase to cover corruption: 'I'd raise it at te next meeting of de tribal Council, cept it's part of de tribal Council's traditional ways it don't never ask or answer questions—make it feel shame' (203). It portrays the Aboriginal politician as a manipulator, using the jargon of Aboriginal rights to organise a range of extravagances—a helicopter to muster the buffalo, new rodeo yards ('Rodeo's part of our traditional ways' (205)), asking the Flying Doctor to bring in the beer supply for the Wet—and bringing home Foster's point about the state of Aborigines: 'You bin destroying our traditional culture for centuries. It's our turn now to destroy it for ourselves, in fact, it's our democratic right' (206).

Foster sustains the humour throughout the passage, but it may raise uncomfortable laughter. Once again, he finds an Australian taboo—the corrupt culture of 'handouts' to Aborigines—and mocks it. Since the novel's publication, many Aboriginal leaders, notably Noel Pearson, have spoken out against this culture. Here Foster's satire risks being dismissed as unacceptably out of line; it stands on its comic inventiveness, on the 'aesthetic' of comedy, and on the grain of truth at its centre.

The novel's movement from Sydney to Arnhem Land raises questions about what Australia means as a nation, and it relates this nationhood to the warrior condition of Australian men. Jeff Doyle has noted that it follows the *Heart of Darkness* structure (also found in McGahan's *1988*), in which men from the cities venture into the outback to test their survival skills. In both Foster's and McGahan's novels, this includes an assessment of their competence as men, and of the meaning of contemporary masculinity.

Peter Schwenger, in trying to establish a model for 'masculinist' writing, has come to the conclusion that this is a typical pattern for consciously masculine writing. Ernest Hemingway and James Dickey in particular write narratives about men encountering a wilderness where their qualities as men can be tested. On the basis of novels by Hemingway, Yukio Mishima, Philip Roth, Dickey, and others, Schwenger proposes that 'masculinist' writing focuses on the physical body, particularly the penis, because the masculine aligns itself with action rather than reflection. Indeed, writing itself may be seen as endangering masculinity by damaging the writer's capacity to act. Schwenger argues that the comic and grotesque are appropriate modes for the encounter with the male body, because the penis may be seen as both comic and grotesque. He claims: 'There is a force behind the grotesque which is inhuman, both stupid and vital at the same time. It is a force strongly bound up with the physical; it is a force that goes to extremes. By virtue of its excesses it deforms proportion and classical contours. In this respect it is allied to caricature' (108).

Certainly, Foster's writing deliberately 'deforms proportion and classical contours'. It bursts with excess, vitality, and stupidity (in the sense of comic absurdity). Foster's claim that the genre of satire belongs to men aligns with Schwenger's analysis, though Schwenger refers to caricature and the grotesque rather than the broader satirical genre of which they form part. *Mates of Mars* demonstrates Schwenger's notion of masculinity in its accounts of physical pain and violence.

The pattern of maiming and destruction of the male body, evident in *Plumbum* (Jason's eyes, Roland's disease), becomes central to *Mates of Mars*. Steve begins the novel as a paraplegic; in its course, he organises the removal of his own legs, suffers a tracheotomy, and is finally killed by a fall in the prawn trawler. Cyril bears the usual wounds of a professional footballer, but dies rapidly, with symptoms of AIDS, after his accidental killing of the totemic kite. A rival Aboriginal tribe captures Sven (already suffering from broken ribs) and cuts open his penis with a rusty razorblade, leaving him with intense pain on urination and eventually HIV infection. Vincent and Bruce, the intellectuals, also suffer bouts of indigestion, asthma, or broken bones. Foster carefully preserves the woman, Jade, from any physical suffering. He proposes that masculinity seeks physical pain and moves towards self-annihilation: 'We all die and fighters often prefer to die in their prime' (118).

By the time he wrote *Mates of Mars*, Foster had become increasingly self-conscious about the 'effeminate' nature of writing compared to the more physical or powerful work of other men. In his chapter in Andrew Sant's *Toads* (1992), a collection of writers' reflections on their working lives, Foster comments on the secretive and perfidious nature of writing, comparing the writer to the Australian prison 'dog' who runs tales to his master—'At least I never molested a child' (*Toads* 73):

> I became aware of my own effeminacy—which is how I would describe an interest in literary culture in the context of my own generation, who grew up before women had assumed their present pre-eminence—before leaving school…Feeling myself an outsider among men, a feeling which persists, I was curious about their world, a world from which the women who raised me had also jealously guarded me. I feel comfortable with women, but they never interested me intellectually. (74–75)

Like his earlier comments about the 'softness' of Australian writing and the way that women readers dominate sales of fiction, this suggests a developing sense that the man who wrote literary fiction had become an anachronism. Foster scorned the effeminacy of the art form he had chosen to follow; once again, he was driven to self-mockery and self-satire. Though any reader of contemporary Australian fiction might notice the pre-eminence of men writers—Carey, Malouf, Moorhouse, Bail, McGahan, Rodney Hall, Brian Castro, and others—Foster deliberately excluded himself from this company. His concern to be 'hard' meant that he could scorn even these writers as 'soft' and effeminate.

In my *Real Relations: The Feminist Politics of Form in Australian Fiction* (2000), I have written about the way that *Mates of Mars* challenges the theory that men's writing forms a mainstream that is disrupted by a more wayward and radical feminist writing (120–130). There I argue that, just as radical feminist writing attempts to mimic the fluid and elusive nature of the female body, *Mates of Mars* (and Foster's notion of satire over a range of novels) mimics the rational irrationality of the male body, the 'comic and grotesque' as Schwenger puts it. Schwenger's proposition about 'masculinist' modes of writing supports the possibility that, while there may be a conventional, normative patriarchal approach to writing (a phallocentric dominant) as suggested by some feminist theories, there is also a more unruly masculinist mode of writing that undermines convention and outrages it. In the writers cited by Schwenger, and in Foster's fiction, this mode is more external and expressive than the more introspective modes promoted as feminist by followers of the theories of Cixous, Irigaray, or Kristeva. Foster, of course, claims the excessive and fearless mode of satire as exclusively masculine territory.

Mates of Mars makes the rational and irrational elements in masculinity a central concern, as well as a literary practice. It lovingly details the structures formed around the martial arts, as if fighting were rational behaviour. It presents Sven, the lover, enshrining his lust in the codes of courtly love. It shows us Bruce, the rational intellectual, indulging himself in irrational outbursts. All sorts of male absurdities are turned over for our amusement—Steve's devotion to his mother, the bonding on the prawn trawler, the rigid pecking order among men in prison. From time to time, Foster shows his exasperation with masculine stupidity; when Jade protests at Sven's dumping of the rubbish overboard, the narrator supports her: 'Laughter all round from the boys on the back deck. Good one, Sven. Laugh as the world chokes through male shortsightedness and avarice' (303).

The novel explores two clashing codes of masculinity in the contemporary world: the irrational code of the warrior and the rational code of the scientist. Martial arts, and the tribal practices of the Aborigines at Neverfuckinlose, pursue an irrational, but highly codified, mode of behaviour. Each pursues spiritual goals through its physical practices. Science, on the other hand, concentrates on reducing the material world to a logical set of structures. Ross Poole has written about the way that in Western culture men aspire to rationality as part of their masculinity, dismissing women as irrational, though this dismissal is itself irrational. In *Mates of Mars*, science and technology are pitted against warrior codes. In tribal culture, men have clear warrior roles in defending their tribe and position within it; in a modern, post-industrial society, they are encouraged instead to pursue the challenge of technology, using their rational abilities. Foster mocks both masculine ideals while lovingly detailing their obsessions.

If 'women and poofs are the Zeitgeist', it comes partly as a result of the triumph of technology—of the rational mind over the strong body. The scientists' successes in developing technology gradually strip away masculine physical privilege, allowing any feeble physical specimen to be as successful as the man who devotes himself to acquiring bodily strength. Once again, Foster has found a paradox at the heart of our civilisation, and at the heart of his own concerns.

When the Mates set out to rescue Sven and Jade from a rival tribe, they encounter a mysterious and intimidating world beyond the rational. Bruce initially declares the pre-eminence of his 'rational mind' over Cyril's spiritual apprehensions, but the prospect of fighting to the death shakes his confidence. After they have eaten the kidney fat of the man they kill, this committed intellectual dives into a crocodile-infested river to retrieve a can of beer—an act of ridiculous male bravado that is, in scientific terms, merely a biological effect of adrenalin and testosterone. Then Cyril's sudden death after spearing the rival spirit-kite disturbs any rational response. While they are all shocked at this, Vincent remains rational enough to makes notes for a scientific paper on the phenomenon.

At Neverfuckinlose, the Mates debate the usefulness of war for population control. Vincent argues from a scientist's point of view: 'Birth rate must be kept high as possible for maximum genetic variation and death rate must be kept higher', while Bruce thinks that only 'the more successful men should mate' (287). But Sven's experience and pain are pushing him towards a more extreme notion of purity: 'Man is a blight on the earth' (287).

Mates of Mars celebrates men in its excessive, lavish observation of their various enthusiasms and idiocies. Indeed, the novel's obsessive accounts of masculine organisations and rituals share in the masculine fascination with detail. There can be little doubt that Foster intended the novel to defend masculine attitudes at a time when feminism held them up to criticism and dismissal. The novel's satirical mode, its focus on violence and aggression, its excess, and even its occasional obscenity might all be seen as part of a rearguard masculinist action against feminism. In the prison section of the novel, Foster notes the 'continuity of tradition' (346) from the convict era in the attitudes of Australian men:

> Indeed, it is possible to recognize, even in a modern gaol, the aetiology of many of the Australian male's most endearing characteristics. Or it was, until Feminists and Multiculturalists convicted the Australian male on both counts. Nowadays, so many men outside are so confused as to who and what they are, even going so far as to berate themselves for crimes they never committed, that a spell in boob would do them all the world of good. The penal system in Australia has long served to reinforce traditional values, and those calling for its abolition should bear this in mind. (347)

Even here, Foster cannot resist the ludicrous—he is advocating locking men up to make them men! (Who is calling for the abolition of the penal system? Certainly not feminists.)

Though the novel lavishes its attention on the enthusiasms of men, clearly masculinity does not hold all the answers. Jade's presence as a sensible counterbalance to the silliness of the men provides some evidence of feminine insight, but the possibilities of the feminine are explored more fully through the experiences of Sven. In 'The Castle of Maidens' section of the novel, Sven performs the role of the heterosexual explorer, treating sexual conquests in a similar way to fighting conquests. He keeps a diary of his observations of women, which he destroys regularly on a 28-day cycle, like the female menstrual cycle. He visits Kathy, a prostitute in the Western suburbs of Sydney, to examine the tattoo on her back—a dragon whose fiery breath becomes a flesh-coloured lotus. This is the work of Idlevice, a tattoo artist versed in Taoism, who sought 'liberation through the flesh' like Sven. Sven's visit serves as an act of veneration of the 'sacred whore'—it is a spirituality based on sexual excess.

In this section of the novel, Sven invites the simple William to share in the 'bunning' of a woman academic from one of the middle-class suburbs of Sydney's North Shore. Foster refrains from commenting on this practice of shared sex with men, who maintain their heterosexuality by placing a woman between them. He recounts this incident in a detached, non-judgmental way, neither relishing it nor condemning it; but it nevertheless conveys a level of misogyny, directed particularly at middle-class, educated women.

Sven's usual partner in 'bunning' was Wolfgang Coogan, who has been killed before the novel begins—probably at the feet of Jade and the Dykes on Bikes. Wolfgang has also organised women 'on the block' for the football or bikie club, and his taped records of these events provide a soundtrack for the rest of the novel, with Sven addicted to listening to them, and Vincent accidentally picking them up. Foster suggests that these practices—shared sex with women—form a bond between men, though he does not explore the implications of vicarious homosexuality. He implies, too, that Steve, living with his mother and rejecting all forms of sex ('[n]ever fucked man, woman or dog in me life…wouldn't be guilty of it…' (286), has good reason to repress his sexuality—he responds to the touch of Sven and Cyril.

Apart from Jade, who disturbs some of the presumptions of the other Mates, the women in the novel play marginal roles: 'real men, Australian working men, had no time for women or God' (88). Steve gives allegiance to his mother, who might have been able to lift the Bedford one-ton truck from his severed legs; Bruce believes 'women constituted a home' (132); Sven regards Kathy as the 'sacred whore'; Black Coral is a seductress. These stereotypes are likely to disturb or offend women readers, and Foster makes no attempt to deplore them. I once asked Foster why the bunning incident was included in the novel—he replied that it is the kind of story that men tell each other. We can read it as part of Foster's evidence about masculine culture—and more recent scandals about the behaviour of football teams on the loose confirm that these practices continue. Foster takes an amoral view, and he doesn't turn away from the perturbing, misogynist, or criminal elements in male attitudes. It is Wyndham Lewis's notion of satire as speaking truth, rather than pleasing.

Through the fate of Sven, the novel finally addresses the masculine refusal to integrate the feminine. Vincent, the master of Tao philosophy, advises Sven that he needs to find the 'yin' in his personality: 'There is room for yang later, but first you have to yield. You have to be a woman' (323). Enduring the pain of his mangled penis, infected by HIV, and suffering intense depression and brutality from the other inmates in prison, Sven meditates until he finds insight. He writes to Jade: 'Jade, I agree with Women's liberation, and have in fact liberated my own internal "woman". I now feel completely sexless' (379). He intends to take orders as a Buddhist monk.

To be a woman is to be 'completely sexless'. Just as the three triplets of *Testostero* represented three sexual options, this suggests that a man has the choice of three sexes (heterosexual man, homosexual man, and woman), and to be a woman is to have no sex at all. Woman, as represented by Judy Rankenfile of *Testostero* and Jade Muldoon in *Mates of Mars*, is of another order to the transsexual Cortesana or the transformed Sven. But these women also become mothers.

If Sven's discovery of his 'internal woman' reads as satire on glib New Age sentiments, it also suggests a serious necessity: Sven has understood that 'man is a blight on the earth' and that personal and universal salvation requires an 'unmanning' of men. Typically, Foster mocks what he proposes seriously. He would take this idea further in *The Glade Within the Grove*, where the three sexual options are presented as man, woman, and eunuch. Somehow, Foster evades any examination of homosexuality.

In the parts of the novel that deal with Sven's sexual quest, Foster leans heavily on satire's dispensation for obscenity and offence in the name of truth-telling, but the saving elements of satire—wit, inventiveness, irresistible humour—are found elsewhere in the novel, in its devotion to detail and its exuberant accounts of masculine logic. In all the scenes where the Mates come together to talk, travel, and fight, Foster's comic originality carries the reader through potential outrage.

More than Foster's other novels, *Mates of Mars* integrates philosophical quest and social observation, and it formally mimics the obsessions of its characters. Its rambling, barely controlled form displays the qualities that it celebrates and criticises. It closely observes important aspects of Australian life that have never found their way into fiction before, and it recognises the historical shift from white Australia to a society that must acknowledge the Aborigines and Asians in its midst.

While Foster's narrator derides multiculturalism, the novel embraces the multicultural nature of Australian contemporary society more than any other novel of its time. Ironically, the comic stereotypes of the novel support Foster's insistence that people are different from each other: men from women, tribal Aborigine from Asian intellectual, individual from individual. The narrator tells us, '[r]ecent genetic studies have shown that human beings are actually apes. There is no missing link' (137–138). But Vincent's experiments with macaque monkeys demonstrate that even monkeys are individuals: 'There was a great range of personality among these macaques and it sometimes troubled Vincent, pooling the results from all these monkey brains as though they were one and the same. Still, if they could do it in human psychology, and they did, all the time' (154). The novel resists the tendency of multiculturalism and popular feminism to simplify differences and treat everyone as if they are the same, confusing the right to equality with an assumption of sameness. It exposes the fallacy behind these generalisations.

The characters in *Mates of Mars* invite greater sympathy from readers than do Foster's earlier creations. This is not to say that they have complex inner lives or developed psychologies—they remain the dispensable figures of satire. But Steve Overton repositioning the light switches, Bruce struggling with his martial arts ambitions, and Vincent wondering about his experimental monkeys are also identifiable, vulnerable human figures. They do not become alien or contemptible creatures like the band members of *Plumbum*. And they are consistently funny and entertaining, particularly in any extended dialogues with Steve. For once, Foster likes them enough to leave us with an image of the four surviving Mates celebrating their friendship each Christmas Eve, sometimes in the company of Vincent's and Jade's 'beautiful kids'. Australia's future, he suggests, lies with the feisty feminist and with the Asian man who knows the place of both yin and yang, both intellectual and physical skills, both spiritual and financial understanding. Perhaps Foster allows himself this rare benign ending because it is signalled as a fantasy for a future beyond the moment of the novel's writing (1991).

Both the subject of *Mates of Mars* and its mode are excessive. Another writer would have published four or five novels from the material that it covers. When it was first published, almost every reviewer baulked at this excess, claiming that it told them more than they wished to know about hard-style martial arts, the trawling industry, Australian prisons and so on. Yet most found a part of the novel that was too insightful to deny—whether its observation of the many paradoxes of masculinity, the comic tour de force of the Outback Radio section, the mystic potential of Aboriginal culture, or Sven's revelation in prison.

This may be deplored as the 'squandering of material', and *Mates of Mars* may have been a more acceptable novel to teachers of literature and award committees, and a more manageable novel for readers, without the 'flashback' to Bruce's work at Darling Harbour, without the detail about the rubber industry in Malaysia, without the 'bunning' incident, or without the adventures on the prawn trawler in the Gulf. But it is a strange thing to demand less of a novel, and excess is essential to Foster's art; his novels, like life itself, offer more than a reader can comprehend.

Foster's insistence on detailing 'the fearful complexity' of life means that *Mates of Mars* marshals as much evidence as Foster can find for the condition of modern Australian men. It also offers something to offend every reader. I have known feminists to enjoy the novel's mockery of male obsession, only to object to its portrayal of the 'bunning' and Black Coral; I have seen enthusiasts for Foster's utterly original accounts of Western suburbs working-class culture lose sympathy when he mocks Aboriginal culture. When Candida Baker asked Foster about the novel's risk of charges of racism, Foster explained that 'the trick is to be equally unfair to all characters' (1991: 5). In fact, he manages to avoid these charges because *Mates of Mars* is not about the failure of Aboriginal culture, any more than it is an attack on feminism (least of all that), or on Japanese depredations in the Pacific, or on corrupt Australian business. These are only passing victims of Foster's satire. Its main thrust is, once again, a spiritual quest to understand the paradoxes of Australia's situation at the end of the millennium. As Helen Daniel noted, the novel combines a 'zany gloom about Australia and perpetual optimism in the quest for the talismanic secret of things' (1991: 8).

This 'gloom' or what Johnston calls 'anomie' gives sharpness to the novel's absurdities. Foster certainly mocks many of the treasured assumptions of contemporary Australian life, and he plays with their comic possibilities. But he is not a reformer, nor a moralist in the sense of proposing a set of values. The problem is too great for that. No matter how men behave, they will remain a 'blight on the earth'. A return to some kind of aboriginal relationship with nature is out of the question, even for Australian Aborigines. The only solution the novel can offer is that of meditation, and recourse to a life of the spirit. In this way the novel performs the most serious function of satire, directing readers to consider the state of their souls.

Mates of Mars is, in my view, Foster's greatest novel, written with unflagging energy and imagination, addressing serious issues about the state of Australia and the future of the planet, and consistently funny in its observation of Australian society. Foster courageously takes on multiculturalism and the continuing concern about the state of Australian Aborigines. He mocks feminism and the ludicrous nature of male self-regard. Perhaps this indicates my preference for Foster as a social observer and humourist, rather than as a spiritual commentator. Yet *Mates of Mars* is as philosophical as *Plumbum* or *Moonlite*. Here, Foster's material seems to match perfectly his philosophical and moral purposes.

Endnotes

1. Among the Foster papers in the ADFA library is a letter to 'Bruce' from 'Vincent' asking when he will meet 'Jade' (MS 160 1/29).
2. I discuss this further in 'The Bicentennial and the Millennium: The Dissident Voices of David Foster and Sam Watson'.

Chapter 6

A Religion for a Philosophy: *The Glade Within the Grove* and *The Ballad of Erinungarah*

The Glade Within the Grove

In an interview with Erica Travers, published in 1992, Foster discussed the need to battle the entropy that threatened to destroy the world, and the difficulty for Australians to accept the necessary discipline for such resistance. Arnold Toynbee's *A Study of History* provided historical examples of the kind of radical change required in human society if we are to stave off the destruction of the natural world, but his evidence suggested to Foster that, while intellectuals could produce a radical ethical philosophy, only a religion could convince people to change their mental and spiritual outlook:

> If one could do anything productive at this point as a Western person or as a citizen of a dying world, which I have no doubt that we are, we can prepare the way. I think that Australia plays an interesting part in the West as it is very much a fringe-dweller. If you see it as essential that a new philosophy with a new system of ethics needs to emerge, it needs to take into account necessary changes. Obviously, I think that the environmental movement is indicative of the kind of ethical changes that have to come about, and won't come about from an examination of Judeo-Christian religion because man is the centre and the being of existence in the book of the Judaic peoples.
>
> The new ethics that will have to come about will be so revolutionary they may discount the value of human life. Perhaps the life of a tree might come to mean more than the life of a man. But, just by propounding the necessity for it you won't change the world. I mean, we've already got the philosophical movements that see the need for change and know what the changes should be, but they won't be able to change people. Only an avatar or a higher religion emerging from the ground up ever changes things. Basically, I feel that only a new higher religion can really change the course of the way we behave. I have some intimations of what kind of changes would be necessary, but it's a fictional task for me. (Travers 74–75)

Foster's conviction that human society was doomed to self-destruction had not diminished over the years, but by the 1990s this prospect had a millennial force. The world needed a new religion and Australia, where no religion had successfully taken root, might be the place for it to begin. Foster set about contributing to the salvation of the world—finding a religion that did not make humans central, and thus might stem the wanton destruction of the natural world that threatened the existence of all living things. There could hardly be a more ambitious assignment for a comic and satiric writer to undertake. Yet no one talking to Foster about this philosophy and about his next novel, *The Glade Within the Grove*, could doubt his sincerity of purpose.

Other factors supported his preparation for a major work. In 1991 the Australian Government awarded Foster a Creative Fellowship, popularly known as a Keating award after the then Prime Minister. He took the award as a commission to produce a significant work, and settled down to the task of reading and researching for his novel. In preparation, he read monumental works such as James Frazer's *The Golden Bough*, Edward Gibbon's *Decline and Fall of the Roman Empire*, and Toynbee's *A Study of History*. He also revised his elementary Latin to read the satires of Juvenal, that other satirist of a civilisation in decline, in their original language. In 1994 the acclaimed novelist Annie Proulx visited Australia to attend the Melbourne Literary Festival. While speaking to her at the Festival, Colin Steele, the Librarian at the ANU, discovered that Proulx had read *Dog Rock* and was keen to learn more about its author. Through Steele, Proulx and Foster made contact, and she generously promoted Foster's work to her own publisher, the prestigious independent London company, Fourth Estate. At about the same time, Random House acquired the Australian rights to Foster's backlist from Penguin and reissued most of Foster's fiction to coincide with the new novel, making his early work accessible to new readers. Fourth Estate agreed to publish Foster's new novel in the United Kingdom on the understanding that Proulx would serve as editor and adviser on it.

The novel that emerged in 1996 encompassed Foster's concerns about the imminent destruction of life on the planet, a lyrical engagement with the natural world, and a comic attitude to his characters. It was accompanied by a poem, *The Ballad of Erinungarah* (published a year later by Random House), which offers both the lyrical and satirical, and the poetic and prosaic sides of Foster's creativity. Foster's 'fictional task' needed to break the bounds of his previous fictions; he would need to address the doomed future of human civilisation through an Australian perspective.

In Frazer he had found an account of the religion of Cybele that celebrated the forest tree and whose extreme exponents castrated themselves in her honour. Cybele was a Phrygian goddess who gradually subsumed the Greek goddess Gaea and the Cretan Rhea. She was the goddess of the earth in its primitive and savage state, and she presided over a group of priests, called the Galli, who worked themselves into a state of frenzy then ritually mutilated themselves in her honour.

A lesser god, Attis, was associated with the Phrygian cult of Cybele, and the Greeks turned him into a young and handsome shepherd, chosen by Cybele to be her priest under a vow of chastity. When he broke his vow, Cybele struck him with a madness that led him to castrate himself, and she eventually changed him into a pine tree. The Galli celebrated Attis in an annual spring festival that lasted five days—a day of mourning, followed by a day of frenzy and wild music, then a day of self-mutilation and castration of novices, a day of joyful dancing to celebrate the resurrection of Attis, and a day of rest. Frazer notes that the Emperor Claudius incorporated the cult of Cybele into the established religion of Rome, though Romans had worshipped this Asiatic god from as early as 204 BCE (457–463).

Clearly, the cult of Attis and Cybele was expressed in a festival of death and rebirth, winter and spring, and was of a kind found everywhere in Europe, translated by Christianity into the Crucifixion of Christ and his Resurrection on the third day at Easter. Foster saw that the Christian Easter followed the pattern of the Attis ritual—death and mourning, followed by the joy of rebirth. He also noted that in Australia, Easter comes in autumn, a reversal of the pattern of natural religion. In the novel, as Calvin Ecks drives south from Sydney towards the Shoalhaven Gorge, the narrator D'Arcy D'Oliveres notes the importance of this disjunction:

> This green is not a true green. There is no annual season in which these leaves change colour and fall. There is no spring explosion of bud, no aureole of venous spring verdure, no panoply of leaf in high summer. There is not even a period in winter when these trees are bereft of leaves. They do not shriek the solstices.
>
> So? No. It is not a question of asking if this matters, but of gauging the extent to which it *does* matter, *has* mattered, by the disconcertion the bush produces in us. (13)

He goes on:

> The cult of Christ in contemporary Australia, commands about the same degree of fervour as the cult of Vespasian did in Antioch, or the cult of Domitian in Ephesus. This I ascribe less to the fact that we started as convicts and Irishmen than that all the festivals of the Christian Church...are celebrated six months out of kilter here, which renders them diabolically inappropriate, an inversion of the natural order being characteristic of satanism, as you'd know if you'd ever celebrated the winter solstice at the summer solstice, or sat down to murder a hot cross bun on some gloomy day in autumn. (14)

He concludes that 'the annual rebirth of an apparently dead tree is a cardinal metaphor to our Northern Faith...and I maintain that without this metaphor Catholic Christianity is sorely tested, even fatally impaired' (15).

So Christianity in Australia has been hampered by its insistence on following northern hemisphere liturgy, thus severing religious practice from the natural world. D'Arcy suggests that white Australia's willingness to destroy the natural world may follow from this religious disconnection with it, particularly the way the eucalyptus tree refuses to share the seasonal moods of Europeans. Foster's novel speculates about other religious possibilities, seeking pre-Christian answers for the Australian condition.

While, after centuries of argument, Catholic Christianity settled on celibacy for its priests, the cult of Attis offered a more extreme devotion—sacrifice by male castration. Foster seized on this practice as a kind of solution to the masculine aggression at the centre of *Mates of Mars*. There, the problems of the world appeared to be a function of masculinity, of its drive to sexual conquest and its self-centred disregard for the future. At the end of *Mates*, Sven Scrimshaw, infected by AIDS and with his penis mangled, achieves a kind of sexlessness and devotes himself to contemplation and prayer as a monk. Sven had castration of a kind forced upon him; what would happen if men voluntarily embraced such a fate? The cult of Cybele and Attis might be the new religion Foster was seeking.

With the support of Frazer, Gibbon, Toynbee, and other sources listed in D'Arcy's dispersal sale at the end of *The Glade*, Foster found evidence for the continuing heritage of Phrygian religion in contemporary Australia—the Christmas tree, the continued wearing of Phrygian caps in various forms, the disputed celibacy of priests, and so on. Furthermore, the rise of savage rock music, the fashion for tattoos and piercing, and the public celebration of homosexuality in the Gay Mardi Gras supported the notion of a residual adherence to the cult of Cybele in Australia. Foster was responding to a longstanding challenge to Australian artists—the need for some spiritual response to the Australian landscape in a society that was utterly secular in its foundations. A whole tradition of landscape painting has arisen from this challenge, and a corresponding range of nature poetry. While some Australian poets and painters have sought inspiration in indigenous cultures—the Jindyworobak poets, for example—Aboriginal religious beliefs have never become part of white Australian custom. Indeed, the colonial nature of European Australia remains most evident in this religious disconnection with the natural world. In addressing this paradox, Foster was participating in a major strand of Australian art tradition, the attempt to reconcile secular white society with some spiritual understanding of the place it inhabited.

The major symbol of such disconnection is, of course, the eucalyptus tree. Evergreen like the pine tree of the Cybele cult and the Christmas fir tree, the eucalypt endures in green (or grey) leaf through the changing seasons. It resists any colonising or classification, and few Australians can identify many of its variations. In this native tree Foster found the central symbol for his proposed religion. In order to save the forests and find a religious relationship with their land, Australians needed to overcome their ambivalence about the eucalypt and love the tree to the extent of metamorphosis. In *The Glade Within the Grove*, several of the male communards castrate themselves in honour of the goddess Brigid. Attis MacAnaspie, found as a baby among the sawdust in a timber mill, proves his superior devotion by becoming a mallee tree—a form particularly despised for its toughness by white settlers.

At the time the novel was published, Foster's focus on the trees in *The Glade Within the Grove* appeared as part of a wider fascination with the cultural place of trees. Also in 1996, Simon Schama published his extended examination of the place of trees (and water) in Western culture, *Landscape and Memory*, confirming Foster's accounts of the history of trees on the continent of Europe. Schama shared Foster's conviction that Christian civilisation was the enemy of the forests, and he argued that the continuing reverence for the tree in the symbols of Christianity marked both its triumph over nature and the loss of a bond with it. In 1997, Murray Bail's *Eucalyptus* also took up the shameful ignorance of Australians about the native tree, as he created European-style fairy stories for each of a range of eucalyptus varieties. Bail's novel followed a tradition of enriching the landscape with European meaning, and his silence about the trees' indigenous meaning reflected a wider absence. We have little knowledge of the religious beliefs of the south-eastern Aboriginal tribes, but trees do not seem to have had the central place in Aboriginal religion that they do in European spiritualism. Obviously, the desert and saltwater people of Australia's north, whose artwork and religious beliefs are best documented, had no experience of the dense forest that lingers in the European imagination. It seems that, for indigenous people, trees were sacred as signs of the creative spirit of the earth, rather than sacred objects in themselves (Berndt et al.).

At about the same time, too, William Robinson painted his magnificent visions of the trees of the Australian rainforest, including the triptych *Creation Landscape: The Ancient Trees*. As I have argued elsewhere, Robinson's tree paintings reflect his Catholicism ('Tree-Dreaming'). His paintings present the trees as natural cathedrals, looking up at them from the root base and exploring each element of their glory[1]. The viewer becomes part of the forest, seeing it from a range of perspectives at once, aware of the roots and leaves of the trees. In keeping with Schama's theories, these paintings express a Christian association of trees with a lost paradise—the rainforest being a particularly endangered part of the Australian environment. Robinson's art expresses a European intimation of nature as the home of God. Notably, his ancient trees are Antarctic beech trees rather than the tough, tenacious, and dominating eucalypts.

The Glade Within the Grove, then, seemed to speak to an intellectual moment for other writers and artists interested in the human relationship to trees and in their spiritual possibilities. As usual, though, Foster pushed his ideas to the point at which they became discomfiting. Through the voice of D'Arcy, he put forward the central ritual of the pagan tree cult—the self-castration of men in their prime—as a practical solution to

> all this overpopulation today, all this degradation of farmland and forest, all these unrealistic demands being made on men, this Greenhouse effect, this salination, these Christian Brothers molesting boys, all these women deacons who want to be ordained, these priests demanding to be married, this body piercing and sexual sadism that goes on, this waxing of shoulders… (xiv)

The comic way in which the list moves from grand generalities to the trivia of shoulder waxing cannot disguise its import—in one way or another, Foster speculates that the life of a tree might be more important than the life (or at least the sexual potency) of a man.

Fiction gave Foster the freedom to expound his philosophies and gather disparate evidence to support them. The novel allowed him to put forward ideas that might seem distasteful, savage, or inhumane, through the layered ironies of a satiric narration. It also gave him the opportunity to reflect on his own generation of Australians, the generation of 1968, and their contribution to changing sensibilities. As I have mentioned in earlier chapters, Foster has lived out some of the hippie ideals of this generation and knows first hand the paradoxes of back-to-nature theories. For this novel, he needed a narrative voice to convey all his learning about ancient history, his observation of the forests of the South East, and his understanding of the follies of a commune transformed into a cult. He decided to sacrifice his Dog Rock narrator, D'Arcy D'Oliveres, to the task.

In the Dog Rock novels, D'Arcy is a garrulous, gossiping busybody, obsessed by householders and devoted to beekeeping and raising chickens. He feasts on information and retains his sense of Britishness and loyalty to the monarch, despite his humble role as postman in a tiny Australian town. In *The Glade Within the Grove*, D'Arcy has become both more learned and scholarly, and more vulgar and lackadaisically Australian in his speech patterns. Retired from Dog Rock and suffering from the effects of cigarette addiction, D'Arcy is progressing towards death by lung cancer—though Foster denied any proven connection between the habit and the disease in his essay on the misuse of statistics, and D'Arcy quotes the same studies. In *Dog Rock*, D'Arcy's attitude toward women had an element of gentlemanly chivalry, his lust limited to the excitement generated by Renee Calvary bucking her car as she reversed out of the post office car park after a shift. In *The Glade*, D'Arcy claims to feel uncomfortable writing about sex: 'I'm no Manichean, but we won't be getting between the sheets with Balthazar and Monica. We knows what goes on, and I never thought it made for compelling reading' (11).

Nevertheless, his imagination extends to details such as the musky smell of Monica Ecks as she pulls on her harem pants after sex with Balthazar, or the single hair growing near Paula Zoshka's nipple as Brian Chegwodden reaches for it with his mouth. D'Arcy dismisses the 'portion of the hindbrain, or limbic system which responds to sexual stimulus' as 'illiterate—as witness the fact it never learns—and irrational—as witness the fact it never wants to' (12), but he clearly feels some of the sexual energy that drives the commune and pushes the men to extreme acts. It appears that he is now a man of considerable sexual experience and, for the purposes of this novel, it is necessary for him to be so. As Attis walks home after his sexual initiation with Diane Zoshka, D'Arcy expounds on his changed circumstances in the voice of a fellow sufferer:

> He cannot now view the World as it is, but has a stake in the World. He must fight for his rights, must maintain his lust, must defend his turf, must protect his child, his child's child. He has

> earned a life lagging. The Book of Wisdom, the philosophical Rose Garden, has effectively slammed shut.
>
> 'Make Love, not War,' says Grainger's guitar sticker, but you can't make love and not make war. Wise up, Grainger.
>
> No one can be hip who is sexually alive! O Feminist, O Christian, O Buddhist, hear this Truth. Stop torturing us. (343)

This sexually anguished D'Arcy has much in common with both the satirical Pete Blackman from *Plumbum* and the womanising Sven Scrimshaw from *Mates of Mars*—men tormented by their lust for women, and trying to reach beyond it towards some spiritual enlightenment. Indeed, *The Glade* brings together two elements of Foster's obsession in earlier novels: the imminent destruction of the environment by Western greed (*Moonlite*) and the energetically creative and destructive nature of male sexuality (*Mates of Mars*). In Foster's view, male sexuality appears to be both the problem and its answer.

D'Arcy's increased self-consciousness as a narrator might be attributed to the written, rather than spoken, nature of this novel. His direct address to the reader created the gossipy tone of his earlier narrations, but *The Glade* has a more ambitious textual goal—D'Arcy tells us that he is undertaking a Saga, 'taking the word in its modern meaning of an epic-like narrative' (xxxiv). He is anxious lest the Saga not be committed to 'the word processor and thus lost' (xxxv); the textual record is of prime importance. As an educated man, D'Arcy feels a duty to compile the written record of events in the Valley, as the residents 'are some of the most amotivational Anglo-Celtic people to be found outside the New South Wales North coast or the Tennessee Appalachians' (xxxv), and outsiders who know about it cannot understand its importance 'or else lack a capacity to put it into legible handwriting, let alone historical perspective' (xxxv). D'Arcy constantly references textual authorities of various kinds—from the classical satires of Juvenal and Horace, to Alan Bloom's *The Closing of the American Mind* and the VW car manual.

But the novel does not conform to the modern understanding of Saga. D'Arcy readily accepts that the 'low, scurrilous, scabrous tone of the satire' (xxxv) may intrude into his high-minded narrative despite his best efforts, and the novel proper begins with Michael Ginnsy's ludicrous appearance at the University of Sydney Union cafeteria in 1968 (3), after forty pages of introductory material. Any pretence that D'Arcy is working from reliable sources disappears immediately as the novel imagines a series of events leading to the Sydney wake for Martin Luther King. D'Arcy has completed a Creative Writing course, and he clearly creates rather than records the scenes and characters he puts before us. D'Arcy takes responsibility for this 'bizarre and unsubstantiable tale' (xiii), insisting on its historical foundation, but making it clear from the beginning that he is driven by his concern that 'everything has gone terribly wrong for this civilisation' (xiii).

The theory offered at the end of the Preamble, that Christ was a eunuch, is presented as D'Arcy's theory, and his digressions on the history of religion, his pursuit of parallels between contemporary Australia and the ancient world, even his intimation of the Passion among the trees, may be read as the obsession or even the madness of a dying man. The novel invites us to sheet home all its failings to D'Arcy's incompetence as he apologises for its uninteresting characters, and for his 'bad blue with narrative pace' (409) that leaves the novel unfinished. We can read this as a calculated disarming of criticism, or as an indication that, for Foster, credible characters and conventional narrative are trivial matters beside the novel's philosophical and religious ambitions.

Readers must cope with frequent shifts from the sublime to the ridiculous. We must endure the tedium of the communards' discussions of Valley practicalities, their dreadful ordinariness, and indistinct personalities—the interchangeable sexiness of Monica Ecks or Paula Zoshka, the nondescript nature of Olaf Abernethy and Grainger (who never speaks), the superficiality of Brian Chegwodden. These are not individuals with rich interior lives, or exciting exterior ones. In general, the Valley communards reveal only the shallow characteristics of their satiric roles; major participants in the sacred passion such as Diane Zoshka (the schoolgirl activist) and Attis MacAnaspie are less articulate than even the characters from *Plumbum* and *Mates of Mars*. D'Arcy draws attention to his failures here: 'Attis…lacks personality in my depiction. But there is a reason for this (Fear. Awe.)' (62).

The communards represent elements of the 1968 rebellion so far as it existed in Australia: Eugene Ecks the American Vietnam deserter, Barbara Byng the emergent politician, Sister Annunciata the lapsed nun, Balthazar Beauregard the hippie, Olaf Abernethy the conscript on the run, and so on. Monica Ecks and Paula Zoshka appear mainly as a focus for the lust of the men, including the narrator. Mehmed Contramundum, who serves as the Greenbrown man, emerges from somewhere in Foster's/D'Arcy's imagination acting for nature as a destroyer of humans. They are joined by Nisi Papadimitriou, the single mother, and the tedious journalist, Brian Chegwodden. As D'Arcy tells us, the Vietnam anti-war movement has created an alliance of 'draft dodgers, dole bludgers, dope dealers, dropouts and deserters, radical nuns, Maoists, Stalinists, anarchists, Trotskyists and Quakers' as well as students (8). Under ordinary circumstances these have 'no business being in the same room, let alone the same committee' (9), but the war and military conscription have drawn them together.

We can laugh at this, but anyone with a memory of 1968 might reflect on the changes that did occur as a result of this zeitgeist of rebellion (if not revolution) among a generation of ordinary people even in Australia. We might also note that this rebellion did little to brake the technological advances and population explosion that have devastated the environment.

The activities of the communards never rise above the comic and banal. None of them has particular insight, knowledge, or wisdom. They are more interested in sex and food than spiritual issues, and they speak in the simple clichés of their generation. They intrude on D'Arcy's digressions (rather than the other way round), but they are the necessary basis for the novel's argument for the possibilities for

Australia—that comfortable place, so apparently irrelevant to world affairs. D'Arcy narrates the novel in at least three distinct modes: his learned digressions on history (particularly classical religions and the possibilities for the future), his extended, lyrical descriptions of the forests, and his comic account of the communards moving to the Valley and the MacAnaspie family living on its ridge. The last of these—the traditional novelistic mode of plot and character—appears least important to the narrator. The three elements rub against each other, as the banalities of the communards' lives provide D'Arcy with opportunities to expound his theories in sometimes wonderful slips from bathos to grandiloquence and back. For example, at the Wozzawunwun flat, Paula Zoshka and her younger sister Diane argue about the importance of university matriculation:

> 'See what I mean, Paula? It's all happening, and all you want to do is talk about examinations, which are just another form of state oppression. Education is not where it's at.'
>
> Herewith Diane, distaff Justinian, closes the Schools and severs the golden chain of the Colonial Platonic succession. 'I declare it in advance,' writes Spengler in 1920. 'This current century will not have passed without having seen the Western Soul outlive its will to win victories for Science. European science is on the road towards a self-annihilation through an over-refinement of the intellect.' And perhaps as well, or we'd be living today, as experts in the '60s predicted for us, in plastic, electronic cottages, interfacing from these with paperless Post Offices, when not taking holidays on the moon.
>
> 'Aw shit, man, where'd you get this honey?' Balthazar, deeply impressed, teaspoon in hand, from the pantry door. He had the munchies. (231)

D'Arcy goes on to support Diane with evidence of the successes of postal telegram boys—all of whom left school at fourteen years ten months—and boasting of the achievements of Australia Post employees: 'Had Australia Snail Mail entered, as a nation, the 1994 Commonwealth Games, we would have placed fifth in the gold medal tally' (231).

In this short passage, D'Arcy uses the most ordinary of conversations between sketchily presented characters to comment on the place of education in terms of Plato, exemplified by the careers of former telegram boys. Every detail contributes to the novel's vision: the failure of science drives Foster's interest in religion; the celebration of Australia Post not only confirms D'Arcy's allegiance to his profession, but also encompasses a range of Australian folk culture and history; even Balthazar's discovery of the honey has bearing on the plans for the commune.

While the communards may resist reader sympathies or interest, the depiction of the MacAnaspie family living at Wonderview above the Valley shows Foster at his comic best. This masculine family represents a popular Australian tradition of comedy, with Horrie MacAnaspie as chief comedian. He speaks with unfailing vernacular wit: 'His intercourse is largely raillery; he will introduce himself at a menswear store with some such remark as, "What are you doin there, you lazy, good-for nothin bastard, goan to serve us here or aren't ya?" The true Aussie wit, that so often expires, during Happy Hour at the Black Stump, in fisticuffs' (64).

Horrie's father Charlie maintains the eccentricities of an older generation, and sons Fergus and Darryl keep up a comic tussle, with developmentally disabled Norman staying at home. Iris, the lone woman in the household, supports her men with an appreciation of their exuberant approach to life, with a soft spot for the more sensitive foundling, Attis. But the MacAnaspie men are as pagan (though nominally Catholic) as any of the communards. Their loyalty is to their country, and they serve in the major campaigns from Gallipoli to Vietnam (where son Barney is fighting at the time of the novel).

They anchor the novel in a recognisable Australian tradition—one that refuses to take seriously any concern about the future. While Foster clearly enjoys them more than his city refugees, he makes their negligence and destructive behaviour clear. They're the loggers of the forest, the men who fight wars, who drive trucks and ride bikes through the wilderness, and who lust after the women in the Valley.

The novel celebrates their individuality and courage, describing their daredevil antics at the bush muster and the Wozzawunwun rodeo, or their feats on motorbikes, admiring even old Charlie's refusal to wear outer clothing. They represent the masculine ideals of old white Australia, and Foster/D'Arcy seems to endorse those ideals by giving them attractive comic energy.

Yet the evidence of their destruction is clear: 'Were there a bob in clearing this country, rest assured it would have been' (xxix). The MacAnaspies are part of a society lacking interest in progress or in spirituality. Attis, the chosen one, apparently devotes himself to the goddess Brigid to the extent of becoming a tree. Fergus, too, joins the new religion—we are told that he becomes abbot of the monastery. Darryl, however, refuses castration and spends his time in the Valley competing with Calvin Ecks for the women. In the end, it seems that Darryl (after a period in prison) reopened the Valley in 1986 by clearing the Gap Road, and he and his family remain there. The other mountain man, Kimberley Moon, offers a counter-image; he is the sensitive horse-riding poet (another traditional Australian figure), who becomes a eunuch during the Autarky (the 'self-sufficiency'). D'Arcy finds him selling Phrygian caps in the Wozzawunwun store and claims him as the source for much of the novel's detail.

The Glade will defeat those readers who believe a novel must offer an entertaining narrative and interesting characters. Here, the novel is a vehicle for philosophical speculation, for information, for comic comment on Australian absurdity, for observation of previously unnoticed aspects of ordinary life, for lyrical descriptions of the forests. It comes closer to the genre of the anatomy, most famously practised in Robert Burton's *Anatomy of Melancholy*, and described by Northrop Frye as the epic variant of Menippean satire (311–312).

It fulfills Foster's own requirements for satire: it is a medley of styles and ideas, full of intricate concrete detail, improvisatory rants, wit, and humour. Foster did not write it in a chronological way; instead, he spent years making additions to its main outline, so that it is an accumulation of wisdom, humour and insight, with sections of brilliant writing laid over a relatively thin frame of narrative.

The novel mocks what Australia has become, and it mocks the Baby Boomer generation that aspired to change the world and failed. It would be possible to select the most brilliant passages of the novel—the description of the seven horsepower Sunshine engine in Horrie MacAnaspie's shed (68–69), the bush muster (141–152), the extraordinary insights such as the speculation about our desire for the human face as evidence 'for the soul's existence and lack of authority' (220–221), the wry commentary on the importance of a water view in Sydney real estate (32), the many beautiful descriptions of the trees and plants in the forest, the hilarious renderings of classic Latin texts—and dismiss the strange and sketchy narrative. But the novel is more than satire; it is also a heartfelt statement about the future of our civilisation.

It is clear that Foster is approaching spiritual mysteries and he must disguise them in comedy and satire, even in ordinariness. By a process of accretion, the novel tells us about Phryx Phringstl's emasculation, Mehmed's attack on Smitty, Attis's metamorphosis, and the way the women and children fail to age so long as the Valley is cut off from the rest of the world. The whole novel tacks and turns to avoid telling the reader precisely what happened in the Valley. D'Arcy hides the only description of the Passion in an endnote comment on the Trotskyite physicist, Derek Frodsham:

> I asked Kimbo how it could be a *bona fide* physicist got sucked into a religious cult. You know what he said? He said 'If you had seen what we seen, mate—if you had watched that writing appear on the trunks of all the trees, if you had seen that creek turn red, as though it were running blood, if you had heard the birds scream, the way they screamed that day, and it wasn't just because of the fire that threatened them—if you had seen the figure of a man you knew as well as we knew Att converted to a tree, with a flow of gum streaming from His groin, and a flow of gum streaming from His knife, and a flow of gum streaming from the cock and balls He held in His hand—a flow of gum flowing like blood and washing away the soil, and every gum tree on that plateau, oozing

> gum in great carbuncles—well you wouldn't be asking that question.' (193)

Such otherworldly moments cannot be conveyed directly. Everything of importance that happens to the communards happens 'off-stage' and at several removes from our narrator. We can only apprehend it by gathering pieces of information from the mass of material presented to us by D'Arcy. In the final versions of the manuscript, Foster even jumbled the numbering of the Acts and Scenes of the novel. We must endure all the various changes of mode and shifts of scene to prove that we are fit to approach the spiritual mystery at its centre. The novel is satire put to a sacred use—rather than any reformist program. Indeed, the civilisation as presented by D'Arcy is beyond reform; our only hope is some apprehension of the wonders of nature hidden in D'Arcy's extended and incantatory descriptions. Foster seems to be demonstrating Robert Elliot's argument that satire has developed from ancient, pre-Christian practices by giving it a sacred role; here it encases the mysteries.

In his writing about the forest, Foster risks everything on his language skills. If we don't respond to his magnificent descriptions of the forest, then the novel will stand as a random collection of odd comic incidents and manic diatribes with 'no heart'. Nicholas Brown has used a passage from the novel as a touchstone for his own examination of the South Coast region of New South Wales because 'Foster offers an extended synthesis of several voices from the South Coast, drawing together a range of inscriptions and allusions to evoke a complex locality' (87). Brown notes that Foster is 'testing the nerves and sinews of language in encompassing a landscape.' To anyone who has walked in the Shoalhaven Gorge, it seems a real landscape, but John Blay objected to the novel's inaccuracies—the shining gum is found only on cold mountains, while red cedar has never been found south of Pigeon House. The name Erinungarah implies that it is based on the Errinundra region of North Eastern Gippsland in Victoria, known for its shining gum and mountain plum pine, as well as the last stand of cool temperate rainforest on mainland Australia. The Victorian/New South Wales border lies only a few kilometres from Delegate, where D'Arcy gets out of his car to walk south towards the Valley—that is, towards the Errinundra National Park. But D'Arcy makes it clear that this is a magical Australian landscape, collecting together an array of native plant life regardless of its usual habitat:

> Lilly pilly and prickly tree fern, native daphne—one of a myriad—muttonwood and mock olive. The rainforest through which we descend evokes a pristine Peloponnese; it is not entirely to be marveled at, we feel so much at ease. Our forefathers loathed the bush of Sydney, admiring the rainforests of Wollongong. Unhappily, the rainforests proved easier to clear as their species, with a few topical exceptions—bolwarra, bastard rosewood, native laurel—won't sucker, after being burned. Of a sudden, a midsummer night's dream of cerris oak and sweet bay. We hear the Embden geese genuflecting on the creek flat, adding their voices to those of the purling creek and discreet bellbirds. A water monitor basks on a rock, invigilating the late light. (xxix–xxx)

Foster finds words to suggest both the habits of the animals in the forest and their connection to human spirituality, as the geese rummage near the creek ('genuflecting') and lizards lie breathing ('invigilating') (xxx). Each of the several hymns to the forest in the novel pushes the language to see how its very detail can indicate spiritual possibilities. The analogies of language suggest a parallel plane, beyond the physical world it describes. The aesthetic achievement of the writing invokes a spiritual world.

The novel also tests its readers, as if they are aspirants to initiation in the mysteries. For those who persevere through its digressions and evasions, it offers some glimpse of the spiritual contact with nature that D'Arcy argues is essential to our future. That is, the novel is not simply declaring that we should embrace a tree religion, but it also tries to convey something of a spiritual apprehension of it through language. To read Foster's (or D'Arcy's) accounts of the forests is to be submerged in a lyrical poetry in which the manifold abundance of words stands in for the wondrous variety of nature. Given the novel's overwhelming atmosphere of lament, this myriad of words offers a kind of consolation for the absence of the forests. If the novel has a climax, it is when we are led with the communards into the Glade to see the stand of ancient trees rising above:

> The Seven Sisters—for so they are yclept—grow touchingly close to each other. No lianas obscure them, no other species grow between. They grow straight up, and their canopy is a hundred and fifty feet above the Valley floor. The trunks measure twenty feet in circumference ten feet off the ground. The only comparable softwoods remaining on the island continent would be the bull kauri at Lake Barrine, on the Atherton Tableland in North Queensland, or maybe one of the twenty-three surviving adult Wollemi pine discovered by a canyoning abseiler in the Blue Mountains as recently as 1994. Check out the big bull kauri, multiply them by two, put them away, last of their kind, in some sacred, secret place; now you understand why the Family join hands and hug each other and weep and scratch deferentially the grey bark to smell the red heartwood, sweet with ancient wisdom. Now they know why they came to this Valley, and are blown away that they came before they knew why they had come. (360)

Of course, the communards can only respond in their inarticulate way:

> 'Shoulda told us about these trees, Ginnsy.'
>
> 'I tried to, man, but words can only do so much.' (360)

This last stand of red cedar, growing through centuries, represents the sacred centre of the novel. The communards stand in wonder, lost for words. Given the importance of words as a means of understanding the sacred in this novel, we may well ask whether the communards could have committed their subsequent sin against nature if they shared D'Arcy's learning and resources of language—'we could go on, we could fill books' (359). They see that the tallest tree is dead and, without compunction, they proceed to cut down the sacred trees to build their dome. Attis, with his experience as a timbergetter, leads this activity under the direction of Darryl. 'Stumps, today, the Seven Sisters, but one stump taller than the rest, and you'll find on it none of the tell-tale teeth marks indicating use of a chainsaw. It was felled by hand' (405).

No wonder the goddess descends on the Valley to demand recompense. This idealistic generation was to cast off all the voracious greed of the past, but they sacrifice these mighty trees—the last of them—to their own, admittedly alternative, technological dream, a geodesic dome. One might remember the islanders of *Moonlite*, who discover the last of the great auks only to destroy them. D'Arcy's awareness of the end—not only in his own death, but also in the destruction of the trees and the ruin of the buildings in the Valley—ensures the prevailing elegiac tone of the novel. It is a lament for lost opportunities and the lost natural world, bound up with the recognition of inevitable human mortality.

The Glade invests in language as a source of understanding and as a consolation for what is lost. If there is a spiritual world, an access to the immortal, then it must be found in the possibilities of language. Foster's detailed lists of native plants generate an incantatory effect. Against the loss of vitality in Australian life and the loss of the 'old growth' forest, he pits a superabundant language. He conjures up word lists of forest plants that insist on a human recognition of the excessive variety of nature. The text is sacred in this sense—though words cannot recreate a lost stand of red cedar in the bush.

With its elements of 'magic realism' and its undermining of the narrator and narrative progression, *The Glade* appears to have some of the elements associated with postmodernist fiction, particularly the fiction of Australian novelists like Murray Bail and Peter Carey. While 'postmodernism' has become an imprecise and mobile term for contemporary art, it is associated with the undermining of representation and a questioning of the authority of language. *The Glade* appears to work in the opposite direction: it explores the possibility of language to convey more than it represents. Foster reaches towards an immanent world, beyond the material one we live in. His words are not simply the representation of material things, but they function as analogies that can lead to the apprehension of an otherwise unknowable universe. The metaphors of alchemy serve this purpose in the poetry of *The Fleeing Atalanta* and amid the slapstick of *The Adventures of Christian Rosy Cross*. In *The Glade*, Foster can turn the listing of the hardware in Horrie MacAnaspie's shed, a succession of specialist terms for familiar instruments, into a delightful kind of prayer that reveals surprising connections between things:

> A pre-war runabout, covered in rust patches and dust, alternatively mud, sits up on a red stringy-bark block, tray covered with thick blond plywood, seams rising. Over this tray, Horrie without so much as looking from his work could let rove the mutilated right hand to come upon a bottle of meths, or a bossing mallet, or a bakelite switch, or a long-throw bucket hoist, or give a touch-up to a kero tin half containing Vaseline, jointing cement and female connectors; or scratch himself with a farrier's pritchel, or stroke a black welder's helmet, or spar with a fretsaw blade or two, or a suction siphon, or pore over a purloined milkcrate, packed with measures, claw hammers and brushes, bristling with wood glue; or prod the fruitbox, stuffed with welding gloves and welding electrodes, while, with the mutilated left hand, actuating the actuator or spreading a pelt on the fleshing beam to take to it with a skiving knife. (68)

This is the poetry of the everyday—comically surprising, but also suggesting a wonderful array of connections between things, through words. This exploration of language possibility—whether through observation of such mundane things as hardware in a toolshed, through extravagant celebration of the forest, or through philosophical meditation (often translating classic work into Australian idiom) is the novel's greatest artistic achievement. It has more in common with James Joyce's modernism than with post-modernism.

Elsewhere, I have compared *The Glade Within the Grove* with Salman Rushdie's *The Satanic Verses* (1988), arguing that both confront the problem of the sacred text (*Current Tensions* 214–220). Rushdie rewrites the Koran, undermining the notion of the inspired text. Foster, of course, writes his own sacred text, claiming inspiration. D'Arcy may be as unreliable as Salman the scribe, but he asks us to believe. The two satirists address the problems of belief in the last years of the twentieth century: Rushdie aware of the dangers to secular society of a fundamentalist belief in texts, Foster deploring the emptiness of a secular society with no beliefs and finding consolation in the text. The two novels provide a host of interesting elements to compare, including their comic excess, their shift from a recognisable present to a mythical past, and their mix of styles. They offer further support that the 'postmodernist' epithet often disguises the strong drive towards satire in the contemporary novel. Rushdie's poet, Baal, declares that his role is 'to name the unnameable, to point at frauds, to take sides, start arguments, shape the world and stop it from going to sleep… And if rivers of blood flow from the cuts his verses inflict then they will nourish him. He is the satirist, Baal' (97) a prediction of the effects of *The Satanic Verses* itself.

By contrast, Foster's satire proposes a religion and offers a kind of text for it. Foster is in no danger of physical attack from determinedly tolerant secular Australians; they are more likely to turn away from his religion in disgust than protest about it. His novel was greeted by silence in some quarters, and rapturous praise in others. It won his first Miles Franklin award, and reviews included British critic Juliet Fleming's declaration that *The Glade* 'tempts us to feel that here the work of the novel is done so well there can be no achievement beyond it' (22).

Others saw only a tenuous connection to what a novel should be. Indeed, the work (including its accompanying poem) sits more easily within Northrop Frye's classification of the novel/anatomy hybrid, an encyclopedic form that combines the narrative of the novel with the digressive, exhaustive learning and intellectual patterning of the anatomy, and may include both poetry and prose (312). *The Glade* even conforms to Frye's notion of the satiric epic, to the extent of its presiding ambivalent female archetype, '[t]o the extent that the encyclopaedic form concerns itself with the cycle of human life, an ambivalent female archetype appears in it, sometimes benevolent, sometimes sinister, but usually presiding over and confirming the cyclical movement' (322). So, Foster's idiosyncratic masterwork recalls a literary tradition that predates the modern novel. It has more in common with *Tristram Shandy*, or Isaac Walton's *The Compleat Angler* (1653), than with the novels of Foster's contemporaries.

The Ballad of Erinungarah

While the novel stands alone for many readers, Foster wanted it to be published together with the ballad found in the postbag by D'Arcy—*The Ballad of Erinungarah.* The novel also serves as a gloss on the poem, and the poem proves baffling without it. D'Arcy tells us in his Preamble to *The Ballad* that *The Glade Within the Grove* 'is a gloss, a supplement to *The Ballad of Erinungarah.* A view from the Mind, to be read in conjunction with a view from the poet's Heart, to effect a stereopsis' (xiii). In the event *The Ballad of Erinungarah* was published a year later in a separate volume with a common introduction.

In form, *The Glade* and *The Ballad* recall Vladimir Nabokov's *Pale Fire*—a novel that includes a poem by one voice and a gloss on that poem by another, a (probably mad) editor. As in *Pale Fire*, the dominating voice of the total work is not the poet but the editor. Nabokov, of course, had translated and edited Pushkin's work and was familiar with the scholarly apparatus and opportunity for eccentricity in the established mode of scholarly editing. *Pale Fire*'s poem is embedded in its editor's interpretations and delusions, while the separate publication of *The Ballad* obscures its relationship to D'Arcy. Detached from its context, Foster's poem challenges reader expectations of poetry; it demands to be read seriously as a series of lyric poems, though it relies on the premise of the commune explored so elaborately in the novel.

While D'Arcy narrates *The Glade*, *The Ballad* is the work of 'Orion', Timothy Papadimitriou, a child of the Valley. At first D'Arcy mistakes the poem for a work from the prison: 'Woe is me, to the refrain of the righteous, rubbing together the fourth fingertip and thumb, as the world's smallest violin orchestra' (Preamble). And even he can see that the poem is written in 'an unselfconscious manner, by a scarcely tutored mind'. Where D'Arcy explained away all the failings of *The Glade* as the results of his own inexperience, the lapses of *The Ballad*—its frequent drops into bathos, its strange mix of vocabularies—may be read as signs of Timothy's youth and lack of education.

Yet, as early as 1987, Foster read some of these poems as his own at a reading (recorded on video) in the library of the Australian Defence Force Academy. At the time, he was seeking his Jewish heritage (he believes that his father was Jewish[2]) and looked to Judaism for 'a religion to anneal my personality'. He read versions of poem 9 and poem 51, clearly written before he had completed *Mates of Mars*, as part of his own spiritual search. The untutored 'Orion' has adopted some of his creator's work.

At this reading, Foster declared that he found most contemporary Australian poetry merely 'cut up prose'. For him, poetry was characterised by its 'source' in inspiration, not by intellectual engagement. He found poetry painful to write because it relied on the poet achieving an intense emotional and mental state that could not come merely from intellectual effort ('Red band'). By comparison, the work of many of his contemporaries (he excluded David Campbell and Les Murray) was no more than 'poesy'. In fact, he thought his novels had more poetry than most of what is published in Australia as poetry.

Foster insists that the *Ballad* follows traditional ballad form, with a four-beat bar throughout, including breaths and spaces. But it plainly does not have the repeated chorus and rhyme elements that most of us accept as traditional ballad form (Leigh Dale identifies it as modeled on the Galliambic meter of Catullus (191)). It is difficult to argue with a jazz drummer, but the *Ballad*'s meter wavers from pentameter to tetrameter and back. This is not verse for memorising, but for contemplation. Like Christopher Brennan's *The Wanderer* poems, these 202 untitled and barely punctuated poems follow the spiritual search of its narrator, occasionally describing recognisable elements of landscape, but often moving to abstraction as they pursue the emotional experience of the solitary narrative voice.

Traditionally, poetry has been regarded as a more spiritual literary genre than the novel with its interest in the social world. In Australia, the legacy of the Romantic poets, especially Coleridge and Wordsworth, has influenced a tradition of nature poetry that seeks spiritual meaning from the native natural world. David Campbell and Les Murray, the poets praised by Foster, are twentieth-century practitioners in a major tradition that can be traced back to Charles Harpur and Henry Kendall and includes John Shaw Neilson, the Jindyworobaks, and Judith Wright. Curiously, though, Foster is also developing an idea proposed by an Australian poet from a more satiric tradition, A. D. Hope, that it is the role of poets to recreate myths of the ancient world to discover their meaning for living people ('Epistle from Holofernes'). Foster's poetry shares some of Hope's cruelty and refusal of sentimentality.

While the passages of nature description in *The Glade* test the possibilities of language to convey the spiritual mysteries, *The Ballad* breaks free even from the conventions of D'Arcy's wayward narrative to explore a more personal response to nature. One hesitates to analyse a poem offered as a gift from some mysterious source—Les Murray makes a similar claim of inspiration for his narrative poem *Fredy Neptune* and declares that 'this book doesn't *like* being talked about in the lofty class-terminology of literary studies' (364). Nevertheless, a critic must make some attempt to understand and respond to these poems.

Sensitive readers find that *The Ballad* does have the mesmeric quality that D'Arcy claims for it. Kerryn Goldsworthy finds that it has a 'hypnotic quality—unlocatable, but it has something to do with the combination of imagery and rhythm' (12). Pat Buckridge thought the Ballad 'dazzling in the sheer beauty and virtuosity of the poetry' and compared it to the poetry of Shaw Neilson, Yeats and Shakespeare (9). Craig Williams wondered whether Foster might be a contemporary Shaw Neilson.

Where the language and imagery of the poems encompass the bird and plant life of the bush they are often beautiful and vivid, but a jarring and deflating element intrudes in many of them. The ballad begins with a direct address to the 'accursed god who does not exist' (1) and the (possibly paranoid) narrator responding to 'misheard' voices. There follows a striking image of the winter sun (2) struggling across the sky while the narrator listens to the sun's questions before it goes 'bleeding into the day/To return bleeding into the night'. Several lyrics about the natural world lead the narrator towards Erinungarah, and gradually references to castration and pagan rites begin to appear. The poetry interweaves its imagery of the Australian bush with increasing obsession with gods and castration.

By poem 15, Gwendolyn, the witch of the Erinungarah Valley, has appeared amid a vibrant bush setting: 'A parrot minstrelsy/And the cream stream of the coachwoods/Tumbling towards the sea'. Gwendolyn refers to Christ as the 'last to be born' of the gods (16) and the murderer of the others, and the poem seeks wisdom from these earlier gods. Gwendolyn (17) questions the right of Christ: 'Who authorized this god who stood and said/No god but me?' and another voice begins to speak—the voice of the severed head, Crom.

In poems 18 to 23, Crom's voice conjures an Irish pre-Christian world in which trees still grew down 'to the strand' but 'a wise man of the oak/With a cross upon his breast', presumably Saint Patrick, offers the people 'a world without war'—'a dream world/And not even a beautiful dream' (21). The deforestation of Ireland is linked with the move to Christianity in these poems (just as Simon Schama claims in *Landscape and Memory*). Crom declares that Christianity offers 'a filthy paradise' (23) in a 'city of gold' rather than the 'wholeness' of pagan life; in his code, 'a holy man' 'Reddens his hand with the rest/But he reddens it with his own gore/Then he wears a woman's dress' (23). Clearly, castration is indicated. When Gwendolyn prays to the 'mother of gods', a Sacred Stone answers her (26–29) explaining the rivalry between Brigid, the goddess of the harvest, and Venus, the goddess of sexual love. Gwendolyn replies that 'We have no gods at all' (30), but she is prepared to die in order to free the old gods.

After reflecting on the loss of the gods, the poem (33–37) describes Phryx slicing off his own genitalia in an accident involving the water pump and a broken wine bottle. By 38 we have returned to Orion's own experiences in the Erinungarah Valley, where he built a house for his wife and child when he was fifteen. But he left the Valley to go to high school and missed the day of the Passion when the goddess arrived and the creek 'temporarily ran red' (41). At the school on the hill, Orion falls in love with a schoolmate and resists a return to the Valley. He is filled with guilt at his unfaithfulness and his submission to Venus (56).

When he returns to the Valley 'on a holiday weekend' (63)—in the novel D'Arcy notes the strange chronology here, as the June holiday weekend comes before the winter solstice—Orion finds an amazing change has come over the communards. They are working happily and diligently, and his wife (Cindy Ecks) explains that a beautiful woman (the goddess Brigid) has visited them. A series of poems follows in which Orion contemplates the ravages of Venus and the imprisonment that comes with man's desire for women, correlating this with images of the bush to the point where the trees become the focus for his desire:

Is this her? Is this my lady?
This gully gum whose many limbs
Extend like the arms of Siva
Invoking cherubim?
Is she this river peppermint
Whose thick belichened bole
Strips to the waist
Then leans to the side
What is her protocol? (83)

Orion imagines the responses of the communards to Brigid's visit—sighing, crying with joy, dancing, and music to the beat of a rhythm 'older than time itself' (91). Brigid singles out Attis and asks him: 'Where is the sacred tree? Where is the book I gave mankind?' (104). She notices that they have cut down the trees to build a shelter and asks why these people cannot see how closely related they are to the trees: 'tell me why your impulses/Destroy the world you love' (112). Clearly, the glade within the grove contained a sacred tree where Brigid 'was sleeping peacefully/Before some man that tree did fall/To build this hall for his family' (117).

Leaving Brigid, Attis moves into a frenzied dance but soon finds that all the other men in the community are also activated by the goddess's visit. They are frantically building mud huts when Mehmed, now transformed into a leaf-bearing Greenbrown man, interrupts to demand their obligations to the Grove by the refusal of sex with women (131). He claims Attis as his son.

The poem then describes Orion's escape from the Valley with the chestnut-haired girl from school (148), and his remorseful decision that he must become the 'scribe that reads the scribbly gum' and recount the story of the Valley (149). Diane and Attis argue about his following of Mehmed, and Mehmed appears again announcing the need for the men to become eunuchs:

'Who is the wisest of we three
Eunuch, woman or man?
One of us went absentee
While two this planet overran
Two through their fecundity
Have fouled the glade within the grove
One flees moribundity
Veneris nimio odio' (159)

When Orion returns to the Valley, he finds the communards gathered in the dome around an empty chair, while Kimberley Moon reads a love poem. Orion answers:

'Love' I exclaimed at the top of my voice
'Is a net that yez fling in the sea
And as often as catchin the fish of your choice
Yez'll capture a creature like me
God help the woman who loves a man!' (173)

But Kimberley pushes him into the empty chair, telling him to take the hand of the goddess to regain his 'sanctity' (174). In the final stanzas, Mehmed seems to have set fire to the Valley while Diane visits the goddess to plead for her husband, but Attis has clearly decided to follow Brigid. In the final stanzas, he attempts to kiss Brigid and so loses his chance to become a god. He is left alone with his 'warm chainsaw' on the yellow track (201). The poem ends with another version of the winter sun poem (2) and Orion's prayer to Attis and Brigid for the strength to become their acolyte (through castration).

What are we to make of this strange poem? A first response may be to ask whether it is a good poem. By Foster's standards, its source in inspiration makes such a question irrelevant. But readers may apply different standards, looking for signs of artistic control, and a sustained command of language registers. Dale suspects it may be a tribute to literary hoaxes, modeled on Ossian, the third century Gaelic bard invented by an eighteenth-century Scots poet. Some will find its subject matter distasteful or eccentric. Given its mix of elements—its wayward meter, its conjunction of simple language, vulgar slang and arcane vocabulary, its layers of speakers and narrators—the astonishing thing is that at times the poems create a trancelike atmosphere. It is possible to extract several individual pieces that work in a traditional way as nature lyrics—for example, poems 11 ('When young although I walked this track'), 43 ('I like this valley during rain'), 47 ('When wind off the snow comes blowing'), or 86 ('She came like a boronia').

Others have the verve and wit of Foster's prose writing: 84 ('I stole a car and drove it drunk') describes Timothy hooning around 'Wallyville' with his girlfriend in a stolen car, and ends with the laconic response of the men watching from the RSL. Number 95 contemplates the mess humans leave on the landscape, with a rhythmic chorus of 'nothing wrong':

Nothing wrong
There is nothing wrong
There is nothing wrong at all

In this unformed road that winds between these hills
Nothing wrong…
…In anything that man has built and done
Provided man himself stands clear
Why even that emptied bottle of beer
Looks smart enough as its sits in the sun
Now that the tattooed arm that flung it has gone

Yet in many of the poems the beautiful imagery of the bush is intermingled with the story of castration, or halted by some clunking word or phrase from an arcane vocabulary; in 7, a series of vivid images of the bush at night ('cuckoos bleat at satellites') leads to images of castration and women's genitals as the 'wound' ('born of that wound/ Only the contrary wound can heal'). Poem 13 ends with 'aril of their lust has stained the brush where the birds/ succuss them' ('aril' means 'a seed-covering'; 'succuss' means 'shake'). 'May abrogate the energumen's spell' ends 52 ('energumen' probably means 'one possessed by a devil' in this case).

In the novel, D'Arcy talks about the need for Courtly Love in approaching the goddess, referring in courtly love terms to the moment when Attis 'defiled' the goddess (292). In the poem, Attis tries it on in the vulgar phrase, 'Give us a kiss ya tart!' (200). Here, the crucial event of castration is a comic accident in the case of Phryx and an offstage assumption as Attis is left holding his 'warm chainsaw' (201). That is, when it approaches the Passion, the novel appears to be more formally poetic and reverential than the poem.

Here in the poem, where the layers of masks give him the opportunity to offer his alternative religion in all solemnity, Foster does not always resist destroying a lyric with a phrase that rips apart its mood. These intrusions on the poem's lyricism must be conscious decisions by such a gifted writer. Though Foster, through D'Arcy and Orion, appears to be offering us a religious alternative for Australians—a return to a primitive natural religion where trees are revered as sacred—he seems to withdraw commitment to it at the last moment. Perhaps he loses his nerve. Perhaps he cannot play it straight. The poem may be another 'Sufic satire', mocking what it presents as truth.

This is to read the poem as a collection of parts, and clearly we are meant to read it as a whole. If, overall, *The Glade* leaves us with a sense of lament, *The Ballad* leaves an aftertaste of nastiness. Here, the narrator's self-disgust is projected onto the other characters, so that there is little respect for their struggles. *The Ballad* seems to propose that we need to love the trees more than our own children ('the life of a tree may be more important than the life of a man'). As he did in *The Fleeing Atalanta*, Foster uses poetry as a medium for a savage reckoning of men's relationships with women. The final effect is misanthropic, especially when compared with the comic forgiveness of the novel.

This misanthropy does not neglect the conventions of misogyny, which are familiar to Christians and pagans alike. Amid the baffling elements of *The Ballad*, readers are unlikely to miss the statement that 'woman was born to the world of the flesh/ As man is born to the spirit' (27) spoken at first by the 'voice of the vanquished' then revised by Mehmed in 135 with a reference to a 'cinerary urn of women's cunts'. Sympathetic women readers, such as Kerryn Goldsworthy and I, struggle to come to terms with this. Others react in straightforward, if predictable, ways: Leigh Dale finds the novel radiates 'anxiety about and hostility towards women and homosexuals' (191) and Anne Summers reads both novel and poem as part of an attempt (with Murray Bail's *Eucalyptus* and Paul Sheehan's *Among the Barbarians*) to 'make the eucalypt emblematic of a world that is both masculine and monocultural'.

Foster's concern about the future of the world, an impending destruction driven by human greed to consume and overpopulate, carries him from Konrad Lorenz's warning about the imminent collapse of society to this self-hating misanthropy. Clearly, fertility and overpopulation are no longer the problem; it is an individual man's need to come to terms with his mortality, and the driving lust that reminds him he must die. Women (and many would protest that they, too, fear death and long for spiritual enlightenment) bear the symbolic weight of that mortality. Yet, *The Ballad* also offers a consoling beauty in its celebration of the natural world. Like all Foster's work, it mixes delight and despair.

'Castration'

A few months after the publication of *The Ballad*, Foster emerged from behind the masks of D'Arcy D'Oliveres and 'Orion' to publish an article in *Heat* magazine on the potential of castration as a means of curbing the sexuality of men and leading them towards spiritual enlightenment. The article offered a brief history of the castration of men and the role of eunuchs in past civilisations. It was replete with the kind of learning behind D'Arcy's theories in *The Glade*. This time, they were David Foster's theories.

The article invites no laughter; it does not in any way frame itself with irony. Foster begins by noting the vulnerability of the male testes to attack, and he surmises that 'the operation that forms the eunuch appears, as it were, condoned by Nature in the very structure of the male genitalia' (121). He provides explicit descriptions of the practice of gelding calves, and notes the evidence for similar practices with men in Roman Britain. While he begins by talking about the guilt that meat-eaters and milk-drinkers must bear for the killing and castration of male domestic animals, it becomes clear that his interest in castration is not really about the expiation of guilt. Foster sees sexuality as the link between the body and soul, as being 'of the same stuff as our spirituality' (123). So castration offers a spiritual answer to the mysteries of male sexual desire, 'the Great Release, for which all men, at some time in their lives, long' (126).

Foster cites Lorenz on the breeding of male domestic animals for 'greed and lust' (119), but this article is not really proposing castration as a solution to overpopulation and the damage it continues to wreak on the planet. One wants to protest that it seems clear by now that the education of women holds a key to population control—wherever women are educated to reasonable literacy, the rate of childbirth drops. But Foster is not really interested in population control, or the role of women; he is driven by the spiritual dilemma of male sexuality. His survey of eunuchs, castrati, transsexuals, and priests proposes that castration offers a way to spiritual enlightenment at the expense of carnal pleasure and paternity. It ends with the proposition that the only other way is offered by the Dark Age Irish: 'a fourth category of eunuch, the saint, who retains both penis and testes' (129).

Among the many issues raised by this extraordinary and sometimes distressing piece of writing, there are some that especially bear on Foster's fiction. The first is the way Foster drops any fictional mask. He tells us that he imagined that Brigid spoke to him and quotes the poems from pages 106, 107, 109, and 110 of *The Ballad* over his own name—they are not presented as the work of Orion or Timothy Papadimetriou.

When Foster quotes Juvenal, 'You hear in the Wilderness voices that cannot be heard in the Bathhouses' (128), he is referring to his own experiences in the Wilderness. Once again, he implies that the *Ballad* is a work of direct inspiration, rather than a poem created through the speaking voice of an invented character. Additionally, much of the essay appears as part of D'Arcy's digression on castration in section 58 of *The Glade*. It is as if Foster is not content to let D'Arcy make his 'few reluctant comments' (398) on the subject, but wants to argue for it in his own voice—considerably less reluctantly. This tends to retrospectively shift the meaning of the novel, from an ironic exploration of the metaphoric possibilities of castration to an argument for it, using D'Arcy as a mouthpiece.

In his essay, Foster takes a judgmental position on contemporary sexual culture and on the life in Australia's cities, specifically Sydney: 'There can be few more classically wicked cities than contemporary Sydney, but then, to celebrate Christmas at a summer solstice is the act of an invert' (127). Clearly, it is Sydney's notoriously tolerant attitude toward homosexuality that is at issue:

> The promiscuity of male homosexuals unrestrained by vestigial female modesty, is medically and socially intolerable...We

> ought not permit transsexuals to misdirect the self-castratory impulse by availing themselves of synthetic oestrogens in a futile effort to become women. Misunderstood and misdirected, the holy impulse becomes a travesty. (123)

This 'we ought not' marks a shift from the exploration of an idea to moral stricture.

At one point in the essay, Foster describes his attempt to visit the hospital where a young Queanbeyan man is recovering from self-castration. He is no longer writing about a fiction of his own inventing, or about his personal struggles with the condition of being a man. Here he encounters the world that readers share with him—an actual world, where young men have been known to attack their own genitals. Foster has become so immersed in his theories about a possible future religion (though, realistically impossible) that he has begun to believe they have some practical possibilities for other people in the present. This looks like ratbaggery.

Foster anticipates the charge of madness and deflects it back at the reader: 'It is surely madness to continue as we do castrated by tolerance, reduced to debauchery' (128). However much we may agree or disagree with this statement, it cannot negate concerns about the author's position. Does this mean that all the beauty and wit of the novel and the poem were simply elaborate covers for a crackpot idea that the world could be saved if men would castrate themselves?

David Matthews reviewed *The Ballad* with 'Castration' and suggested that not only was D'Arcy a 'kind of hyper-Foster' but that Foster had become a 'hyper-Foster' himself (9). He thought the 'novel-ballad-essay complex' demanded to be read politically as well as aesthetically: 'Foster's writing relentlessly pounds out the message that there is an opposition between a corrupt and effete urban culture and a more authentic and natural rural culture'. For Matthews this amounted to 'some dubious primitivist propaganda'. Leigh Dale saw it as part of an attack on human rights by the entrenched elite in Australia who 'play' at being oppressed: 'high Europe ventriloquising for the Moral Majority' (192).

We can read 'Castration' as a kind of excess from Foster's writing of *The Glade* and *The Ballad*, rather than as an integral part of the project. As far as I know, he did not see it this way until after the essay's publication. In effect, his demand that it be read with the novel and poem ensured that it would undermine any success with *The Glade*. All the readers who responded to the marvellous language of the novel and poem might now feel that they had endorsed the propaganda of an eccentric, homophobic eco-fascist. This pattern of self-sabotage has become a feature of Foster's career, evident within his writing and in some of his public appearances. As we shall see in the following discussion of Foster's essays, his emergence into the public world through attendance at conferences or writing for newspapers and journals has turned him into a polemicist, a controversialist of a different kind to the novelist.

ENDNOTES

1. Reproductions of these paintings may be seen in Lynne Seear (ed), *Darkness & Light: The Art of William Robinson.*
2. *His father, during their one meeting, would neither confirm nor deny this. One of Foster's colleagues on Marrickville Council, Jack Fagin, a member of the working-class Newtown synagogue, told Foster it was 'common knowledge' that George Foster was Jewish. Foster (and his half-sister Kim) surmise that George's mother buried the family's Jewish identity. As Foster puts it, 'only through show-biz could someone be conceived who was both part-Jewish and part-Aboriginal, with no proof of either. My mother, never short of male admirers, had an exotic beauty in her youth that clearly appealed to my womanizing father's taste, at least for a time'* (annotation by David Foster).

Chapter 7

Back to the Holy Isle

When Foster first began to attend the writers' festivals, conferences, and public readings that are part of the promotional round for contemporary novelists, he appeared a diffident, quietly spoken figure, uncomfortable with public performance. Indeed, at the Adelaide Writers' Festival of 1976, he did not perform at all—he went to his assigned session only to decide that the other writers were more interesting, so he declined to speak (12 Apr 1976 DP 2/13/93). After the publication of *Dog Rock*, he decided to embrace the task of performance and began to transform himself into D'Arcy D'Oliveres for public readings. At the Association for the Study of Australian Literature (ASAL) conference in Launceston in July 1987, he took to the stage dressed in his postman's uniform of blue shirt and trousers and he delivered, from memory, a chapter of *Dog Rock* in the persona of D'Arcy to a surprised and delighted audience. At the 1996 ASAL conference in Brisbane, he performed from memory the prologue to *The Glade Within the Grove* and some of *The Ballad* as D'Arcy, rolling his own cigarette and wearing D'Arcy's bush hat. This performance was low-key compared to his participation in a panel on the Literary

Canon with other writers at the conference; here, he recited about 100 lines of Juvenal in Latin, to demonstrate the virtues of a close knowledge of one writer, as opposed to the 'promiscuous' reading of many.

Appearances of this kind allowed Foster to perform the role of satirist, interacting with (and sometimes irritating) particular audiences. Usually, he adapted his material to rouse what he perceived as the sensitivities of his audience. So, in a 1991 reading at the women's bar in Canberra, Tilley Devine's, he began by observing that he was refused entry on a previous visit; Steven Conte has commented that his delivery was 'uncompromising, almost hostile' (2), though it should be noted that Foster was defensive rather than aggressive, possibly because of nervousness (av 1991). In 1995 he gave a paper at the Australian Defence Force Academy which gave a detailed account of the relationship between martial and literary arts and argued, in passing, against women in the military and the bush fire brigades (av 1995). In March 2001, he appeared on a panel to discuss Aboriginal Reconciliation at the Queenscliff Writers' Festival with the Aboriginal activist, Marcia Langton, and the political commentator, Robert Manne, and created a disturbance with 'A Plea on Behalf of Eros', a paper that argued that the 'transcendence of race must occur within an individual heart' (21) and that assimilation, through miscegenation, offered hope for the future.

Studs and Nogs

Unlike many other writers on the circuit, Foster carefully prepares a paper whenever he is invited to talk to an audience. These talks are always original, and written with the wit that marks his fiction. *Studs and Nogs*, published in 1999, collects some of these talks about writing and art, as well as several essays on a wider range of topics, originally published as journalism in the *Independent Monthly* and the *Sydney Morning Herald*. I have referred to several of them in writing this book because they give insight into Foster's contrary personality, his working methods, and his quirky logic. But the essays deserve attention as literary works, as well.

Of all the essays on literary subjects, 'Satire' (first published in *Phoenix Review* in 1987 after Foster's residency at ANU) remains a brilliant demonstration and argument about the satirist's art, rare in its address of contemporary satirical fiction in terms of Roman satire. 'Naughty Novelists', first delivered in 1987 at the ASAL Launceston conference, laments the proliferation of writers and the self- promotion necessary to find readers, with the perceptive observation that novelists increasingly write about novelists: 'Self-referentialism is a diagnostic feature of a dying art' (*S&N* 172). 'Classics and Canon', the 1996 ASAL talk, cuts through all the academic cant about the 'canon' to argue that, while a canon is merely a list of recommended books, no work written in English has yet lasted long enough to be called a 'classic'.

Foster's novels are full of information and observations about the world beyond writing, and some of his essays demonstrate the background to them: 'Taming the Tiger' recounts his experiences on a prawn trawler that informed a section of *Mates of Mars*; 'Creating One's Hometown' describes his preparation for *Plumbum* and *Dog Rock*; 'The Quandary of an India Addict' recalls the writing of the Indian section of *Plumbum*; 'Gallipoli' and 'The Deforestation of Ireland' consider the history of the trees and overlap in places with D'Arcy's digressions in *The Glade Within the Grove*.

Indeed, these essays support the view that a major purpose of his novels is to serve as a vehicle for Foster's talent as a witty commentator on aspects of the world otherwise neglected by fiction. Where the novels lack developed characters or narrative, they are rich in such commentary. We may recall Wyndham Lewis's comment that the satirist often has a scientific approach to his material. Here we find Foster providing the close observation of a scientist in the literary form of the essay, though the scientist's pose of rationality will be discarded along the way. Foster often intrudes as a character here, earnestly enquiring about his subject—he is the man riding a bicycle on the wet roads of Ireland, the interrogator of the Australian tourists at Gallipoli, the middle-aged man struggling to keep up on the prawn trawler.

When Michael Duffy edited the *Independent Monthly*, he commissioned Foster to write pieces on the Northern Territory and other subjects of interest. This produced 'Bloody Justice', his account of the white legal system handing a Warlpiri man over to his tribe for payback, and his amusing reflections on 'Barra' fishing with his son in the Territory. The *Sydney Morning Herald* published his views on Aboriginal Reconciliation after he won the Miles Franklin award, as well as his 'Fire Storm', a heartfelt account of frontline experience in the Bundanoon bushfire brigade.

The quality of these essays may make the reader wonder that Foster hasn't been a regular contributor to Australia's few journals of comment. Yet he says in his Introductory Note to *Studs and Nogs* that 'paradoxically, I do not always feel "close" to the narrative voice in these essays' (xi). He also draws attention to one of the problems of the essay as opposed to the novel—the author of an essay can be held accountable for the opinions expressed. Foster's claim that 'as a writer of comic novels, in the main, I am not in the business of affirmative diction' (xi) suggests that he is aware that an essayist does not have the same privilege to offend as the satirical novelist.

For example, 'Towards Aboriginal Reconciliation' was published in the *Sydney Morning Herald* as an opinion piece with the heading: 'Race Debate Is Skin Deep'. In June 1997 it appeared to be an intervention in the debate about the Stolen Generation, instigated a few months before by the *Bringing Them Home* report to Federal Parliament on the practice of separating Aboriginal children from their parents. The report was full of distressing accounts of the experiences of children barred from any relationship with their natural parents, in the name of integration into the white community. Foster's main argument took little account of this: he argued that mixed race Australians should not be denied their white heritage: 'Let us regard any person born in Australia as Australian, pure and simple excepting only those initiated few who retain a tribal culture' (*S&N* 148). Foster claimed to understand the rural white Australians, whose ill-will had become obvious towards people of 'little Aboriginal blood, ostensibly socially undisadvantaged, but encouraged to regard themselves as Aboriginal' (*S&N* 147). It was a typical Foster approach to a subject, informed by the knowledge that his own mixed race grandsons would be classified as Aboriginal rather than white Australians.

Foster offended liberal-minded readers in his denial of disadvantage among mixed race people, and in his use of the term 'mating' for the relations between black women and white men. He has published a further essay on this subject in *Quadrant*, insisting that all those with both Aboriginal and European or Asian heritages be accepted as simply 'Australian'—distinguishing them from the tribal people who still live in an Aboriginal culture (23–31). During his Blaiklock lecture at the 2004 ASAL conference, the novelist Kim Scott, who has struggled personally with such identity questions, lamented, 'David Foster, you're not helping!'[1]

As Pat Buckridge has suggested, readers may prefer to see Foster's novels and poetry as artistic achievements wrought on the basis of eccentric and unpalatable theories, like Yeats's later poetry. His essays offer opinions and arguments that demand some attention, but they too are literary creations in which language leads the thought. At their best they are elegant and learned, carefully applying traditional rhetorical skills to explore their subjects.

For example, 'On the Dual Pursuit of Literary and Martial Art' draws together a wide range of information in rhythmic prose that follows classical patterns. He begins with a reference to the anthology of poetry edited by Field Marshal Wavell, making an aside about Wavell's reputation among Australian troops in the Second World War, then turning the language over to make a decisive point: 'whatever his demerits as a commander, he was given a field to marshal, and the side he was on won the war' (29). Foster brings his range of learning about the history of the martial arts to a reflective discussion of literature and fighting which adopts classical rhetorical balances: 'whether or not we are natural poets, we all must use the language, and whether or not we are natural fighters, we all may be called upon, in time of war, to fight' (*S&N* 22).

The essay meditates on writers and fighters, from Julius Caesar to Mishima, with a sidekick at Salman Rushdie's 'cowardice'. It provides an account of Oriental martial arts and their history, while deploring their reduction to 'sport'. The extensive list, so often a feature of Foster's novels, here changes our perspective on history:

> The sudden, unexpected loss of a vigorous career, as when Xenophon is cashiered, or Josephus taken prisoner, or Polybius deported or Thucydides sent into exile, has led to the creation of some of the world's most enduring literary works. Such authors have the advantage over the majority of merely literary authors, in that they have something compelling to say; and when a man of action seeks, *in extremis* to express himself, he will choose words for his means of expression, because literary art is the art to which all men have access, if they can read and write. (25)

Foster shifts ground immediately to note the eagerness of prisoners to write poetry 'the minute those iron doors slam shut' (26).

Yet all of this information and surprising insight, presented in rhythmical cadences of language, feeds Foster's thinking about spiritual enlightenment and the decadence of our 'feminised' society. The participation of women in martial arts competitions and the bush fire brigades demonstrates this tendency, though typically, Foster follows the idea through: 'I am not arguing that women should not learn to defend themselves, or explore their masculinity, but let them see it as women's business. I'm all for homosexual battalions, too, but let there be no intermixing' (38). He ends by describing the psychic crisis triggered by his own commitment to Taekwondo 'after which I could no longer effectively speak' (40). It can be little surprise to readers of *Mates of Mars* and *The Glade Within the Grove* that he concludes that the pursuit of the 'Dual Path' requires celibacy.

This essay meanders through its material, picking up ideas from an astonishing range of sources, before Foster brings it back to the topic of the current state of Australia and his own state as a writer and fighter. It is not so much an argument for the practice of martial arts, or against women in the military/fire brigade, as an inquiry into the possibilities of language and the ideas that follow from it. The result is an original and exhilarating exploration of the subject, no matter whether or not the reader accepts its conclusions.

In most of these essays, Foster shows that he's more interested in pursuing the potential of ideas than winning arguments. 'A Personal View of Literature and Science, *fin de siecle*' (*S&N* 56–75) revives the 1960s debate between C. P. Snow and F. R. Leavis to consider the current overpopulation of the world and Foster's view that technology has failed to improve our spiritual state. It offers a survey of the Ancients versus Moderns debate, an insightful understanding of the current practices of literature and science, and a reference back to his own world, in which young men suffer such spiritual despair that they commit suicide. Foster's essays refuse to stay on one plane of argument but move freely among scholarship, observation, and opinion—like his novels. His love of language is as apparent in these pieces as in his fiction, or poetry, and we sense that his interest in analogy and the rhythms of language is more important than the logic of argument. This quality ensures that they are surprising and often funny, while they are unlikely to win supporters to a cause.

A more conventional piece of journalism, such as 'Kennel Mates' which is about his namesake, the world champion woodchopper, demonstrates the novelist's observational skills, while reflecting on the peculiar position of the 'axe man' in Australia: 'if all Tasmanian trees had to fear was a man with an axe in his hand, there would be little cause for concern on anyone's part' (*S&N* 184). The four pages of 'Fire Storm' convey the shock that Foster experienced in helping a burnt fellow firefighter onto a helicopter after a 1998 bushfire in his district. The piece begins with a walk in the bush the next day, where his wife draws attention to a hairy fanflower, given its Latin name (*scaevola ramosissima*) by Baron Mueller because of its supposed resemblance to a man's hand burnt in the flames of a fire. This brings Foster back to his own observation of the man's burnt hands and his account of the fire. But the piece ends with a call for firefighting to return to 'men's business' because of the inefficiencies that follow women's presence on the field: 'Why not confer on young men some pride and purpose and pay?' (*S&N* 210) In its initial deflection of the horror of the fire, its careful detail about the bush and the process of firefighting, while reflecting on the suffering of the burnt man, this short piece has the understatement of a Henry Lawson story, such as 'The Union Buries Its Dead'. It is typical that Foster not only draws out of it a sensible argument about paying firefighters, but also ensures that he will lose supporters by excluding women.

It is not difficult to see the relationship between these essays and Foster's fiction—even when they do not bear directly on it. Foster has the satirist's interest in ideas, rather than in characters or narrative, and the essay form gives him the opportunity to pursue this interest speaking in his own voice. In this respect, it is worth noting that other satirists, including the 'cowardly' Salman Rushdie, also have found the essay a congenial outlet for their ideas and opinions. George Orwell's satires extend the speculations of his essays, and the eighteenth-century masters of the form, Jonathan Swift and Alexander Pope, wrote brilliant essays. It seems possible to speculate that the satirist may turn to fiction when the essay no longer allows the full development of an idea's potential—that satire may be an extension of the essay. In Foster's case, the essays sometimes extend the ideas presented in fiction, though his comments about his lack of engagement with the voice suggest that he is more comfortable with fiction. Certainly, these essays warrant consideration alongside his best fiction.

In the New Country

The same year that he published *Studs and Nogs*, Foster produced another comic novel, *In the New Country* (1999), his second to be published by Fourth Estate in Britain—and, he says, written to appeal to a British audience in the wake of *The Glade*. It marks a return to the comic entertainment of the Dog Rock novels, and it has none of the grand themes of *The Glade* or *Mates of Mars*. With D'Arcy's death at the end of *The Glade*, Foster returned to a third person narrative and gave his attention to a rural area to the west of Bundanoon—part of the western slopes district of New South Wales, stretching from Mudgee to Boorowa. From its beginning, the tone of this novel is more farcical than *The Glade* or *Mates of Mars*, and its intention of mocking the current state of Australia is evident from its opening—a hilariously detailed account of the Sydney City to Surf running race: 'Gorillas, as is well known, run the City to Surf in groups of three' (1).

Foster takes us to the impoverished country towns on the western slopes, where local industries, such as the abattoirs, have closed, leaving most of the men unemployed. The Asian economic crash of 1998 and the appearance of Ovine Johnes Disease in the sheep threaten demand for Australian products and thus the viability of these towns. This is the New Country of the Catholic Irish who settled the area in the mid-nineteenth century and flourished sufficiently to build the imposing churches and convents found in most country towns of any size. Now, Foster suggests, it faces the same fate as the Old Country, where tourism has turned Ireland into a place of quaint and amusing encounters, rather than a living, spiritually vigorous culture.

Much of this novel is written in dialogue, with the voice of Adam Hock (Ad Hoc), stock and station agent and Deputy Mayor of the Shire, providing a comic commentary on the state of Australia as the Olympics (and the millennium) approach. While most of the New Country inhabitants look to the past (the MacPeatrick brothers are in their nineties), Ad is full of energy and ideas for the future. He wants to rebuild the tiny Fane of St Fiacre at Crooked Corner for the Japanese wedding industry, and plans the St Pats old boys' reunion in an attempt to lure the district's one National Treasure, Dud Leahey (Dud Lay), back home to finance the revival of the district fortunes. At the same time, he is resisting the law that would have all sheep likely to be infected by Ovine Johnes Disease destroyed.

A dead body is found by chapter five—that of Ad's cousin, Mike Hock, possibly one of the men in gorilla suits who ran the City to Surf. But the detective genre is cast aside as the novel seeks the ancestry of the town's occupants and their relationship to the local 'sacred site', the Hole. By the end of the novel, the dead body of a police detective and the 'Gucci' kangaroo that collided with his motorbike are left soaking in ice-filled bathtubs, forgotten by the rest of the characters. Mike Hock's death allows Foster to indulge the schoolboy pleasure of writing an obscene funeral oration for Father Carney to deliver: 'There was never a morning, since I made his acquaintance, I didn't wake feeling for Mike Hock [my cock]... Though never the biggest of fellows, he carried himself erect. I recall him throbbing with vitality, in those days it positively oozed from him' (57).

For Jarvey Foley, the Irishman given the task of restoring the Fane of St Fiacre, Australia is a Fairyland, an upturned image of his homeland. The narrative voice (for Foster can't help intruding from time to time) sees Ireland as the land of the White Dreaming where 'each Hibernian geologic feature has one or more attached myths' (80). But, according to Jarvey, Ireland is ruined: 'The trees are gone. Most all the oak and birches. Only the rhododendrons and fuschias [sic] remain and they're not even Irish. And Ireland is all full of tourists ...Well, a few tourists is all right. But they are after takin over the whole country' (95).

The old St Pats boys have Irish Catholic backgrounds, but the records kept in the Fane reveal that the MacEwes (MacYews and MacHughs) are descended from Carmel O'Roy of the Hole, described as 'a Woman of the Kamilaroi' (Carmel O'Roy)—that is, they can claim to be Aborigines. In no time, they are hooning around in their Haitch Ar (HR Holden car), drinking beer from longneck bottles, and addressing everyone else as 'Gub'. Where Shorn MacEwe had worried about 'some bunch of abos forcing me off the place' (64), he now has 'Great Expectations of Native Title' (105). Ad Hock mouths some of the platitudes of white liberal response to native title claims—and a commercial solution:

> They're all Kooris, but they didn't even know that until a week ago. We robbed them of their birthright. It's not enough we stole the country, under the bogus premise of 'Terra Nullius'. It's one long story of conquest and deceit, and what can a Gub do to make amends? All I can think of is to somehow raise their self-esteem, in acknowledging their true identity. I'd like to see them givin didge lessons to Japs, I think that's what's needed here. (122)

Here Foster's concerns about the erasure of the white heritage of mixed race people becomes a trigger for satire. The novel is dedicated to his part-Aboriginal grandsons, 'in the hope that Australians may learn to see them, so that they may be permitted to see themselves, as Australians, rather than as aboriginal Australians'. At about this time, too, Foster discovered that his elderly mother had been fostered, and had no birth certificate or adoption papers. He surmises, on the basis of her physical appearance alone, that she may be one of the 'Stolen Generation' of part-Aboriginal people taken from their parents.[2] While his grandsons might be classified as Aborigines, thus denying their heritage from white grandparents, his mother had no wish to be considered a member of the 'Stolen Generation'. Foster asserts their right to be called Australians, no more or less, regardless of their racial heritage.

In the novel, the Aboriginal claimants are called the 'very dark, dark Irish' and the Hole, the centre of claims for native title, is the focus for cattle-stealing and bushfire-lighting. Old Pat McPeatrick tells Adam, '[a]nd there was very dark Irish indeed here once, but I suspect they're gone. They was as black as the ground where a non-crownin firestorm has come through, but we knew they was Irish 'cause they drank like Irishmen. Blacks, as you know, don't drink' (130).

As Andrew Riemer notes, the novel works as a classic pastoral comedy, with its simple locals plotting and planning, and resisting the laws and assumptions of a more sophisticated urban society (1999). Ad Hock, who aspires to sophistication, provides a means to mock the Australian self-promotion of National Living Treasures, or the Olympics, or even Australian pride in overseas 'successes' like Rupert Murdoch or Peter Allen (Foster's own school contemporary and model for Dud Leahey). In the tradition of Shakespearean comedy, the novel culminates at a party, the St Pats School Reunion, and concludes with the wedding plans of Billy Minogue and Jarvey Foley. This also parodies the Shakespearean (and Furphean) device of the heroine disguised as a man (Billy reverses her plan to change sex). At the same time, the novel has an edge of savagery that recalls the bleak rural comedy of Steele Rudd's 'Dad and Dave' stories.

Foster packs it with Australian jokes of all kinds (some circulating as 'urban myths'), relating to car names, kangaroos, koalas, bushfire brigades, as well as topical matters such as the Olympics, sex-change operations, native title, and the economic crisis of the late 1990s. Yet it is driven by his serious obsessions about the state of masculinity, the treachery of eating the animals we raise, the need for a spiritually meaningful relationship with the natural world, the 'choice' between adultery and celibacy for men, and even the decline of Australia to a three-day Japanese tourist stop. It asks questions about the meaning of heritage in Australia, both in terms of white history—where a dead country town has more appeal than a dying one—and the claims of those with Aboriginal ancestors. The town of Knocklofty has a present so lacking prospects for a future that the past must be conjured up, even if artificially by Ad Hock's tourist plans, in the hope that people from somewhere else—Japan or the United States—might invest it with meaning.

Behind this chaotic but gloomy comedy, we can discern Foster's increasing sense of detachment from Australia.[3] He now appears defeated by the postcolonial malaise of Australia, satirised so energetically in *Moonlite*, *Mates of Mars*, and *Dog Rock*. For most of the novel, Ad Hock maintains an enthusiasm for the task of boosting Australia as an interesting place, and the novel commits itself to finding amusement, at least, in the eccentrics of the local bushfire brigade. Yet the humour seems a little forced. If the Eucalypt Dreaming of Australia cannot make room for white men, then the Oak Dreaming of Ireland might offer some spiritual hope. But Jarvey Foley assures Australians that Ireland can no longer provide this hope; it has been reduced to a tourist construction to please Americans.

So, on the surface, *In the New Country* claims Australia and tries to invest it with a mysticism borrowed from Ireland, mixed with that of Aboriginal Australia. In this way, it continues some of the obsessions of *The Glade Within the Grove*. It can only offer such claims as a joke, though. And the effort begins to show as the novel breaks down into a tedious dialogue between the main characters at the end.

When Adam Hock visits Dud Leahey in America, he finds that Dud refers to Australia as 'Dim Dim' (145). By the end of the novel, Ad, too, declares that he is 'over Australia': 'I'm over the New Country. I think I'm over Australia. I've put the boot in, I've deplored it bein put in by others, and I've copped it myself' (203).

He may be speaking for the author, who seems to lose interest in his novel as it comes to its close. For all its inventiveness and humour, the novel leaves us with a sense of defeat; the absurdities of Australia's white and black past cannot make up for the prospect of a future reliant on the phony needs of global tourism. It is as if the voracious capitalism that cleared the Scottish highlands and pushed out the Australian Aborigines in *Moonlite* has returned in a more virulent form to destroy rural white Australia and its one remaining force of resistance: anarchic energy.

In a sense, *In the New Country* parodies the obsessions of *The Glade Within the Grove*. There, D'Arcy (for all his self-parody) seems to believe in the possibilities of a new religion that would save the planet, and must emerge from the Australian experience. *In the New Country* can offer only the joke Catholicism of Father Carney and Jarvey Foley, spurious claims by the local 'Aborigines' to the land they have lost, and a mocking version of the sacred place—the Glade has become the Hole.

The Land Where Stories End

Foster's interest in the Irish was reinvigorated by the trip he made to Ireland in 1996 as a result of winning the James Joyce Suspended Sentence award. In the course of this visit he suffered 'an intense alchemical episode' that lasted two weeks during which he did not sleep or 'intermingle' ('Red band'). During this time, he took a boat trip to Skellig Michael, an imposing cliff-faced island in the Atlantic southwest of Kerry. The island is remarkably like St Kilda, the model for Hiphoray in *Moonlite*, with a partner island and gannetry. But Skellig Michael was settled in the seventh century by Irish monks who built stone stairways up the cliff face and subsisted there in meditation and prayer. For Foster, this Holy Isle was a revelation: 'I suddenly realised why, sixteen years before, I had felt such a compelling need to write the novel *Moonlite*, and I was also presented with a fable...entitled *The Land Where Stories End*' (9).

The Land Where Stories End was published in 2001 by the small publisher, Duffy and Snellgrove (Michael Duffy and Alex Snellgrove), rather than Fourth Estate or Random House. It is a carefully produced hardback with a full-colour reproduction of Filippo Lippi's 'Madonna con Bambino e due angeli' on the cover, and its title page claims that it is narrated by one of the angels in this painting. It also has images from Mattheus Merian's *Atalanta Fugiens* as section headings. No casual bookshop browser would know that it is the work of David Foster. His name appears only on the imprint page—the last page of the book, rather than the conventional verso of the title page. Foster says this was a deliberate ploy to circumvent the closed world of publishing and reviewing—once again, he seems to have set out to defeat his readers.

While the pictures on the cover of the Australian edition and title pages reference Foster's preoccupation with Christianity and alchemy, his other major allegiance—Australia and its vernacular life and language—appears nowhere in this book. After all the years of struggle with Australia and its spiritual emptiness, Foster returns to the place of his 'oak-dreaming,' Ireland. Perhaps, like Adam Hock, he was 'over Australia.' The novel was later published in Ireland by Brandon Books, with a stunning photograph of Skellig Michael on the cover, and it received appreciative reviews from Irish critics.

Ostensibly, *The Land Where Stories End* is a fairytale: the story of a woodcutter who seeks the hand in marriage of the king's daughter. Despite the claim that the cheeky angel in the foreground of Lippi's painting is narrator, its narrative voice makes no reference to the Italian setting of that painting. The narrator is not a child, though his mostly simple language and explanatory style imply that he addresses a child of the modern world—except, of course, that the fairytale encompasses 'dirty' things and sexual matters. For the most part, the narrator maintains the fairytale pose, offering occasional knowing comments on the events he relates. The simplicity of the writing contrasts ironically with the themes of the story: the desire for a spiritual existence beyond the physical limits of human life, with its 'wees and poos' and 'dirty things'.

The Land Where Stories End may disappoint readers who enjoy Foster's satirical observations of contemporary Australian life. Nevertheless, it does mark a revisitation of the interests of the first part of *Moonlite*, this time with a firmer sense of Foster's own spiritual struggle. If *The Glade* suggests that the dying D'Arcy is renouncing the world of the flesh, *The Land Where Stories End* confirms Foster as a full-blown Manichean. The Promised Land, where the woodcutter lives, is the World of the Flesh; the Land he seeks (Where Stories End) is the Spirit World.

The woodcutter, like Foster, has married two wives and fathered many children. He has also cut down many trees and eaten many animals. Yet he sets off to see if he can release the princess from her tower and win her hand. Along the way, he meets witches, ogres, and a saint, and he is imprisoned in a barrel by the King. After several adventures, though, he is able to lead the saint to the mystic Land—a tiny island invisible to most humans—but because of his continued desire to be married, he falls to the bottom of the cliff. He is now married to the Virgin Mary, 'his own pure soul' (204).

Here, Foster's concerns about the imminent destruction of the world as a result of human exploitation of its resources have contracted to the state of an individual man's soul. The woodcutter is a sinner, but only in the sense that every carnal human must be—he likes to eat and drink, and to have sex with women. He cuts down trees for a living and 'enslaves and loves' (88) animals that he later eats. He is a buffoon character, simple in his desires and needs. The monsters of the forest challenge him with these carnal desires, and he suffers physical tortures, ludicrous in their extremity: 'What say I reach up your bum with my eagle claw here and pull out your liver and lights?' (90).

When the king orders him to be nailed into a barrique and cast into a dungeon, the woodcutter endures the prospect of drowning in his own excreta ('wees and poos') until he begins to embrace death as a spiritual release. When the king finally opens the barrique, the woodcutter loses a sense of ecstasy and bliss promised by the complete breakdown of his body. It is this physical body that binds him to the Promised Land when he longs for the Land Where Stories End.

Is this a longing for death or for immortality? Foster seems to propose that living itself constitutes a sin when eating, drinking, urinating, defecating, and fucking pollute the world in one way or another. Women, of course, tempt the woodcutter to 'dirty things,' but his whole means of subsistence depends on cutting down trees and killing domestic animals. The tempting witches and savage men-women who torment him in the forest represent a fearful aspect of women, but the woodcutter's affection for his wife and the comfort she gives him alleviate any sense of misogyny. The Manichean must reject women because they bind him to the flesh, not only to sexual desire but also the maintenance of children. The woodcutter has already established these bonds, so his hunger for a spiritual world is proportionately difficult, if not to say impossible.

All this may seem like a fable of Original Sin with its penalty of death for the crime of living. Yet the Christianity of the story is imbued with paganism and the creatures that accompany it in European fairytales—ogres, witches, and leprechauns. The monks who enter the story following Saint Finn give it a context of early Celtic Christianity—a Christianity largely independent of Rome and adapted to local pagan practices. After Finn stands in the river all night, communing with God, he emerges to announce the Lord's Word—the celebration of Easter out of kilter with Rome, the wearing of the Celtic rather than Roman tonsure, the drinking of beer rather than wine as 'the blood of our Saviour.' Foster's comic point has historical basis—the first two of these led to conflict with Rome and the defeat of Celtic monasticism at the Synod of Whitby in 664.

This is a Celtic, Druidic version of Christianity, with an emphasis on physical suffering and celibacy. It is Christianity as 'Men's Business' (120), as Foster claimed in his 'Castration' essay. At the end of that essay, he cited the Dark Age Irish ('with their Druidic reverence for Nature and "great hatred of Venus" ') as the source of a fourth category of eunuch, 'the saint, who retains both penis and testes' (129). So, for all its peculiarities, *The Land Where Stories End* follows logically from Foster's obsessions in *The Glade Within the Grove*.

Like *The Empathy Experiment*, *The Land Where Stories End* might have been dismissed as another exercise in eccentricity, if not for the discipline and consistency of its style. It has a lightness and simplicity of narration suited to its fairytale form. The formality of the fairytale allows Foster to distance himself from his material, to subdue his imaginative excesses and his anger. He is no longer performing as the misanthropic satirist, but as a restrained storyteller who shares the dreams and curiosities of his audience.[4] This restraint contrasts with the excessive and extravagant language of Foster's 'big' novels, *The Glade Within the Grove*, *Mates of Mars*, *Plumbum*, and *Moonlite*. Though the fairytale is full of humour and wit, the language is so spare that it mimics the self-discipline that the story proposes as a source of enlightenment.

While it is certainly not without mockery and brutality, the story offers a benign attitude to the failings of the woodcutter and his family. His physical predicament is common to us all, as we go about consuming and polluting the natural world, and the trials of the woodcutter are narrated with a comic relish. The final scene, when the woodcutter puts the saint on his shoulders so they can climb up the Holy Isle (which the woodcutter cannot see and the saint cannot feel) conveys a sense of magical revelation: 'This was the most beautiful place ever he had seen, if only he could see it. Sharp-eyed Bran, who had climbed to the highest peak on the white island, saw two male figures, one atop the other roaming around in the sky above the sea' (202).

Of course, the fable and fairytale have become part of the repertoire of international postmodernism—and not simply in the mixed forms sometimes called 'magic realism.' *The Land Where Stories End* recalls Angela Carter's collections of fairytales, with their examination of women's desire. Lorna Sage writes about Carter's fairy tales as working by 'narrative levitation—abstraction, patterning, getting above yourself' (2001, 224). This, of course, is the way that *The Land Where Stories End* works, quite literally in the final levitation of the woodcutter and the saint. Salman Rushdie, too, has found that the fairytale offers a kind of formal control that subdues the satiric voice apparent in his more realistic novels. Yet, one senses that Foster has little interest in these international developments. His fairytale came to him as part of his own experience in Ireland, in particular the vision of Skellig Michael.

The Land Where Stories End offers us a sophisticated contemplation of the paradox of human existence and desire for spiritual understanding, in an apparently simple form. This form accommodates Foster's pursuit of philosophy and abstraction, rather than the irritations of the complex social world that dominate his other novels. No matter how unpalatable we may find its Manichean view of the battle between the Flesh and the Spirit, or its insistence on the spiritual pre-eminence of men over women, its pushing away of triviality to seek the philosophical basis of a theology moves towards a consolation for the impossibility of human perfection.

A Year of Slow Food

After these books, no Foster reader would have been surprised to hear that he had entered a monastery and abandoned the domestic life of Bundanoon. But with typical contradiction, Foster's next book celebrated domestic married life, amid the cycle of seasons in the southern highlands of New South Wales. *A Year of Slow Food: Four Seasons of Growing and Enjoying Food in the Australian Countryside* presents an account of the Fosters' life on their small holding in Bundanoon. Written with Gerda, the book gives a description of their activities through each season of the year, with a recipe for every week. Beautiful photographs by Peter Solness contribute to an idyllic picture of Australian country life in harmony with nature.

The book directly addresses the popular books by Peter Mayle, Frances Mayes, and Christopher Stewart about country living in Southern Europe, and insists that 'you don't have to expatriate yourself' to experience some of this life and good 'slow food'. Entries by David concentrate on his husbandry of animals—chickens, pigs, cows, and bees—with some reflection on both the pain of sacrificing their lives for food and the pleasure of eating fresh meat. Gerda writes mainly about the garden and gives a practical approach to nutrition, including reference to her work with prisoners in nearby jails. She makes several wry asides about living with the antisocial novelist: 'We have an understanding in this family: we only hold parties when David is away. It suits all of us' (56).

In some ways, Gerda and David Foster are working through the process of European settlement of Australia for themselves, insisting that the European pastoral dream, normally associated with Tuscany or Provence, can be achieved here—at least in part. David writes, 'Australia, for its faults, is where we now belong. Let us make the most of it' (3).

ENDNOTES

1. Herbert Blaiklock memorial lecture (unpublished) ASAL conference, Sydney, July 2004; Kim Scott has confirmed my memory of his lecture. See also, Kim Scott, 'Australia's Continuing Neurosis: Identity, Race and History', Alfred Deakin Lectures, 15 May 2001. <http://www.abc.net.au/rn/deakin/stories/s291485.htm>
2. *His daughter's partner, the Rugby League footballer Craig Wing, who played his early football with the mixed-bloods of South Sydney Juniors, picked Zöe's grandmother as a mixed-blood woman on sight—without prompting. Foster's first wife, Robin, is of the same opinion—after years of work among Northern Territory aboriginals* (David Foster's annotation).
3. *It received favourable reviews in its intended target, the UK.* Time Out *thought it 'sad, touching and very, very funny', while the* Guardian *described Foster as 'a worthy successor to Flann O'Brien'* (David Foster's annotation).
4. In a letter to the author on 15 November 2003, Foster declared that satire is 'a young man's form, appropriate to the attitudes of youth, and I would no more attempt it now that I would consider re-entering the ring as a Karate fighter'.

Conclusion: Surviving as a Writer

When David Foster began writing fiction, he was part of a generation of newly educated young people who wanted to bring Australia into the modern cultural world. The prosperity experienced during the years following World War Two gave his generation freedoms that had been denied their parents, as well as a determination to move on from the conservative artistic attitudes they saw as endemic to Australia. These writers (in the early 1970s, few of them women) began as experimenters across a range of literary genres from poetry (for example, John Tranter, Michael Dransfield, and John Forbes) to drama (David Williamson, John Romeril, and Jack Hibberd) to prose fiction (Peter Carey, Murray Bail, Frank Moorhouse). Foster has remained faithful to the idea of experiment and risk as essential to art.

In the 1970s, and even up to the 1990s, critics were inclined to align radical forms of art with radical politics, ascribing a political dimension to experimental forms that now might seem only superficially radical. Foster has always claimed that he is not political. He sees himself as a philosopher and a modernist, and the ideological legacy of modernism appears to be individualist rather than committed to any community politics. He has developed as a satirist as part of this pursuit of individualism, not as the result of a political or moral program.

Science taught Foster that the securities of rational positivist thinking had disappeared. By the time he became a science student, Heisenberg's Uncertainty Principle, the laws of thermodynamics, and developments in particle physics had already revealed the weakness at the centre of the most fundamental belief of the Enlightenment—that the universe was orderly, rational, and comprehensible. Indeed, the world appeared to be moving towards disorder rather than future improvement. Foster could see that the concept of history as progress was a flawed one, and that fictional structures also impose a false order on reality. His choice of fiction over science, though, gave him the opportunity to range more widely over the questions that confront civilisation. His fiction explores the kind of answers that art can give when science has reached its limit. Foster found his way, through science, to the paradoxes that have preoccupied so many postmodernist artists. All kinds of belief structures and grand narratives have come into question in the past thirty years; Foster has found his own original way to participate in this discourse.

As I have argued in this book, Foster's satire is not the product of his dismay at finding that the society in which he lives fails to meet some moral standard held by the satirist. Rather, he is overwhelmed by the complexity of the universe and the multiple possibilities for understanding it. Satire emerges from an attempt to hold disparate things together, and from a refusal to accept a unitary solution to the meaning of the universe. He sees the absurdities inherent in such complexity, especially the need to hold contradictory beliefs at the same time. The struggle with contradiction leads to a comic and ironic art.

A fundamental pessimism, too, arises from Foster's perception that the universe is moving towards disorder and that our civilisation is on the point of collapse. His fiction recognises that the destruction of the natural world and refusal to acknowledge the differences between people and their cultures diminish the variety and potential of life. This pessimism appears to be reinforced by Foster's temperament; his philosophical despair meets an energetic, mocking, and often angry creative impulse. If satire can be seen as a mode of writing that inhabits a text, then Foster can be seen as performing satire through a range of personae, including one called 'David Foster' who sometimes writes essays or speaks at literary festivals and conferences.

The novels find plenty of decadence and stupidity in Australian and Western society. Yet the failures of society clearly are not external to the satirist. He shares the absurdity and contradiction that he finds around him, and the spiritual obsessions of the fiction follow from his awareness of his own failings. These are inescapable consequences from the condition of being human, and of being a human male in particular. Foster's preoccupation with masculine dilemmas may appear superficially 'masculinist', but his insistent critical approach to all issues forces him to struggle with the implications of male aggression, selfishness, and greed. He is a modernist individualist, seeking within himself and finding a spiritual condition that reverberates for our civilisation. As Sven Scrimshaw declares in *Mates of Mars*, '[m]an is a blight on the earth' (287).

While Foster's art is individualist and, at times, eccentric, the tenacity and toughness of his examination of his own condition leads his fiction to reflect on issues that embrace not only the state of Australia but also the history of civilisations. From his position as an individual reflecting on his own spiritual state, he finds that Western civilisation is in decline—that Christianity has nurtured the conditions that encourage the voracious destruction of the earth and the ultimate demise not only of humanity but also of the natural world that supports us. Foster looks to large, millennial issues rather than to the contemporary politics and social issues that usually occupy the social satirist.

In considering Foster's career as a whole, though, it is plain that in the 1970s he shared some of the concerns of his generation—the desire to wake Australia out of its complacency and comfort, an exasperation with the mimic nature of Australian culture and its cringing attitude to Britain and America, and an interest in American experimental writing. In retrospect, his work appears part of a nationalist project, shared with many others of his generation, determined to seek out Australian vernacular speech and attitudes and bring them into fictions that move beyond the limitations of realist literary forms. The anti-colonial impulse of this writing might be seen as a development of an earlier left nationalism. Its aesthetic, though, is modernist.

Foster's early writing was particularly concerned with Australia's colonial status and its cultural failure. The narrator of 'North South West' struggles with his sense of belonging to a secondhand, mediocre culture. *Moonlite* explores the legacy of British colonialism, determinedly unveiling the belief systems behind the destruction of indigenous ways of life. While the novel acknowledges the repeated colonial pattern of damage to indigenous people, its main concern is the postcolonial condition of white Australians, forced from their sacred places in Europe, and bound to the materialist values of a secular democracy. In keeping with Australian sentiments of the 1970s, though, the novel expresses clear resentment of the English—'the ideal society would contain no English gentlemen' (139).

The Dog Rock novels return to a consideration of Australia as a colonial mirror of Britain. D'Arcy D'Oliveres speaks as a British exile in an Australian country town, disinherited from his rights as an aristocrat (though the locals suspect that he may inherit a peerage, after all). D'Arcy's allegiances to the Old Country, to the Queen and the rituals of the Post Office, suggest a more benign attitude to Britain, the source of so many of the names, habits, and plants of the Australian country town. The danger to a nostalgically British village life in Dog Rock comes from the expansion of Australian cities and the loss of meaningful work in the country. Like the Scottish islanders of *Moonlite*, these rural Australians face the demise of their way of life as a result of the relentless development of technology and the financial dominance of the professional urban class. Yet their situation is comic; immersed in the trivia ('quadrivia' as D'Arcy sees it) of country life, the protests of people (and animals) against change are in vain.

By the end of the 1980s, Foster's fiction was registering the shift in Australian intellectual sympathies from an anti-colonial nationalism to acknowledgment of liberation movements—gay liberation and feminism—and to a multiculturalism that accepted non-British elements in Australian society. *Mates of Mars* embraces the mix of races and nationalities in contemporary Australia through the martial arts enthusiasm of its group of central characters. Typically, Foster takes the idea beyond the immediate preoccupations of a benign multicultural policy to envision Australia in terms of its place at the edge of both Western and Asian civilisations. These civilisations are at the point of turnover, with Western civilisation, as always in Foster's perspective, about to collapse. Both European and Aboriginal societies have failed to make Australia a vigorous society; the Malaysian/Singaporean Chinese, represented by Vincent, offer an intellectual and philosophical way forward—but those Japanese hitting golf balls from ships off the coast suggest a further threat to the environment from Asians.

Foster's comic extravagances in *Mates of Mars* canvass a range of Australian concerns at the end of the millennium—from the state of Aborigines in the North, to the threat of feminism to masculine activities. What emerges from its digressive adventures is a preoccupation with the condition of Australian manhood (regardless of heritage) and the paradox of masculinity. Sven Scrimshaw's revelation in prison—that he must find his inner woman for spiritual enlightenment—is not only a joke, but it also offers serious hope for the future of Australia and the planet. On the one hand, Foster is fighting on behalf of white Australian men against the challenges to their position in society. On the other, he can see that they are a major problem for the future survival of the earth.

So Foster may seem to belong to the Baby Boomer group determined to hold on to their pre-eminence in Australian society, like those criticised in Mark Davis's *Gangland: Cultural Elites and the New Generationalism* for refusing to make room for younger artists. He may even seem to share David Williamson's view that feminism and multiculturalism threaten the defining nationalist place of the white Australian man, evident in Williamson's play *Dead White Males* (1995). But *Mates of Mars* cheerfully mocks this kind of Australian man—he is most readily found in prison—and probes further into his spiritual possibilities. In several of his novels,

Foster diagnoses the decline of male aggression, with the rise of homosexuals and women to positions of power, as a sign of the imminent decline of a civilisation. By *Mates of Mars*, he seems ready to embrace that decline as necessary for spiritual enlightenment and human survival. Such paradoxes drive Foster to explore an exhilarating range of ideas.

The Glade Within the Grove takes even further the idea of the unmanning of men as a necessary condition for spiritual enlightenment. The failure of white Australians to establish any spiritual relationship with the natural world can only be remedied by drastic means—the emergence of a new cult of tree worship and emasculation. Despairing of Christianity, Foster looks to the pre-Christian myths of ancient Greek civilisation as the foundation for a new religion of nature. In my discussion of the novel and its accompanying poem, I have commented on some of the complexity of ideas that the novel explores. Here I wish to note the postcolonial crisis that informs the novel—the sacred places of white civilisation are not here, in Australia, and a capitalist secular democracy encourages the destruction of those places (such as the Glade) that might hold the potential for the sacred. The extreme solution offered by D'Arcy D'Oliveres—turning men into trees by castration—is posed in all seriousness, and also undermined by a sense of hopelessness.

In the New Country suggests a degree of envy for those of Aboriginal heritage who can claim some spiritual connection to the geographical landmarks of Australia, and for the Irish who continue to live on their own sacred island. At the same time, the novel mocks the tenuous nature of such claims from people long disconnected with Aboriginal culture and religion, and it declares that Ireland has also lost its sacred connections in the superficialities of tourism. There appears to be nowhere to turn for a white Australian seeking some spiritual relationship to the physical world in which he lives. The New Country belongs to Aboriginal claimants, the Old Country to tourists.

Foster addresses these physical limits to spirituality once more in *The Land Where Stories End*, in which the fairytale form allows him to leave Australia and its spiritual failings for a parallel world, very like seventh century Ireland. His woodcutter must endure the consequences of his physical appetites and the mortality of his body, but is granted a kind of enlightenment as he climbs blindly above the sea with the saint on his shoulders. Here Foster appears to be claiming Ireland as his sacred place, with the real island of Skellig Michael as inspiration. The malaise of the white settler society is a spiritual condition, exacerbated by the industrial, technological, and economic development that drives colonialism. But a return to the place of origin and a reversion in time is impossible—modern Ireland is not *The Land Where Stories End.*

So while Foster may be classified with other Australian white men of his generation, defending masculine privilege against challenges from feminism, multiculturalism, and even some forms of postmodernist thinking, he also delineates the postcolonial crisis of such white men—though he continues to refer to Australia as a British colony and to himself as a 'colonial mongrel' ('Aboriginality' 30). Over the course of his novels he explores the spiritual barrenness of a modern secular democracy that has no bond with the natural world which might curb its voracious commitment to technology. It may seem a variation on a longstanding concern of Australian artists—what Patrick White called the Great Australian Emptiness beneath the extroverted cheerfulness of Australian life. In this sense, Foster can be seen to continue White's battle to invest Australian life with spiritual meaning.

Nevertheless, Foster's most recent publications have been in *Quadrant*, the magazine founded in the years of the Cold War to fight leftist ideologies in Australia. In recent years, it has flown the standard against revisionist history, particularly in the debate about the history of white treatment of Aborigines. Foster's two most recent articles—both on the relationship of white society and Aboriginality—appear in a context of a critique of left politics ('Aboriginality,' 'A Plea'). His essays are not out of place here—if anything, they are more polemic than the standard *Quadrant* fare. His article 'Aboriginality and the Hope of Art' was published alongside a poem by Les Murray claiming that the Australian urban intelligentsia sees the rural community as 'scum' (31) and, like Murray, Foster sometimes claims to speak for a disenfranchised rural minority in Australia. Here he positions himself against a 'politically correct majoritarian position' (31), proposing the contradiction of a majority concerned about minority rights, and ignoring the contemporary alignment of political, financial, and social power in Australia. While Foster presents himself as a 'rural maverick', he offers a mix of attitudes familiar (though rarely expressed in such complex language) to any Australian who has ventured out of doors—in city or country.

Over the years, then, Foster has developed from an artistic experimenter, a radical of sorts, to a voice of reaction. His angry resentment of colonialism has not diminished, but where it once led to a critique of Australian conservatism and mimicry of the British, in his recent essays it can sound like a white man's grievance at challenges to his position of privilege. Foster sees these challenges as part of a global culture seeking to diminish the particular nature of Australian experience, to soften the complexity and particularity of art into an acceptable international culture. He sees it as a new kind of colonialism.

Reviewing *The Glade Within the Grove* for the student newspaper *On Dit*, Paul Bradley responded: 'It's a beaut, this book...Why isn't this bloke as famous as Peter Carey?' Part of the answer to this question, of course, is that Peter Carey's career has been extraordinary as he has managed to access that global culture that Foster finds so lacking in authenticity, and his writing is certainly more accessible to readers. Foster's novels insist on an Australian peculiarity and particularity; they belong to a ratbag tradition harking back to Xavier Herbert, Miles Franklin, and Joseph Furphy. Foster demands a lot from his readers, rarely giving them help in understanding his various shifts of pace and language. His ideas are presented through layers of irony and comedy, sometimes with deliberately offensive polemic. While the novels celebrate Australian vernacular language and humour, they are also replete with the sophisticated and obscure language of high culture, and they never imply an uneducated readership—certainly not those rural people Foster claims to defend.

My survey of reviews of his fiction suggests that, in Australia, his work has received consistently positive reviews from literary intellectuals and from those who specialise in the particular subject area of his novels (alchemy, rock music, martial arts). Reviewers with no previous experience of his work and little background in literary criticism tend to find them incomprehensible or elitist. Even in Britain, where Juliet Fleming expressed the highest praise for *The Glade Within the Grove*, many reviewers found it self-indulgent and irritating. When setting courses, teachers of literature must consider their students' abilities, and Foster's novels present a significant challenge, even to tertiary students. Some literary award committees have been reluctant to acknowledge the extraordinary achievement of Foster's novels. As I have found, they are difficult novels to write about, demanding persistence and a degree of intellectual courage.

Australian writers often suffer critical neglect, and the exponential increase in the publishing of new fiction over the past thirty years makes it difficult for any writer to claim public attention for long. The publication of *The Glade Within the Grove* by Fourth Estate and its award of the Miles Franklin prize marked a high point in David Foster's career, but led to no lasting readership or sustained attention. Fourth Estate also published *In the New Country*, but it appears that a Man-Booker Prize (or, at least, a short-listing) is now the criterion for a writer's international reputation, and for renewed interest from Australians. Despite the commitment of a range of publishers, editors, writers, and critics to Foster's work, he has never achieved even regular notice as one of Australia's leading contemporary novelists.

An intellectual reader coming across Foster's work for the first time might find a string of astonishing novels, acclaimed by a few discerning critics, spurned by those who can't understand them. *Moonlite*, *Plumbum*, and the Dog Rock novels, in their different ways, explore the limits of our society and its possibilities. They are aesthetic achievements of a high order, full of poetry and wit. In my view, *Mates of Mars* stands as the most significant novel about contemporary Australia published in the last generation. *The Glade Within the Grove* is revelatory. *The Land Where Stories End* pushes to the limits of metaphysical understanding through language. These novels are important, and should be read by anyone interested in Australian fiction and in the state of Australia at the beginning of the twenty-first century.

My aim in this book has been to help readers understand Foster's work as a whole, so that they may increase their pleasure in individual novels and enjoy them as part of a digressive exploration of ideas. I hope that my elucidation of some of the ideas in the novels, and some approaches to reading them, will initiate a wider discussion of Foster's work. At the very least, I hope that the possibilities for reading the novels in terms of satire, modernism, and a postcolonial perspective are apparent.

Isolated in Bundanoon, and caring for his demented elderly mother for the past five years, Foster feels 'ostracised' by the literary community. On April 1, 2003, he wrote to me: 'I have lost my taste for satire. I want to write books that are strange and beautiful, as I believe The Land is.' Later that year, he declared: 'Quite frankly, I'm "over" literature' (letter to author 15 Nov 2003). Since then he has begun another novel in the fable mode of *The Land Where Stories End*. This novel, provisionally titled *Shahrazad*, plays with the frame story of the *One Thousand and One Nights*. It also allows the author to further explore his interest in the eighth and ninth centuries and 'the somewhat Islamic combination of sexuality and mysticism, my twin obsessions' (letter to author 22 Oct 2006). This critical study cannot be the last word.

Works Cited

ABC Radio. Typescript of unattributed review. 18 Dec 1977. FP MS 160, Series 9, Folder 1.

Abraham, Lyndy. *A Dictionary of Alchemical Imagery*. Cambridge: Cambridge University Press, 1998.

Armiger, Martin. 'Crazier than the Average Band.' *Independent Monthly* 7.4 (Oct 1995): 77.

Baker, Candida. 'The Bard from Bundanoon.' *Age* 14 Aug 1991: Tempo 5.

——. *Yacker: Australian Writers Talk about Their Work*. Sydney: Pan/Picador, 1986.

Bawden, Nina. 'Recent Fiction'. London *Daily Telegraph* 9 Feb 1978 [FP MS 160 Series 9].

Bennett, Bruce. *Australian Short Fiction: A History*. St Lucia, Qld: University of Queensland Press, 2002.

Berndt, Ronald. *A Profile of Good and Bad in Australian Aboriginal Religion*. Repr. from *Colloquium*. Melbourne: Journal of the ANZ Society for Theological Studies, 1979.

——. *The Speaking Land: Myth and Story in Aboriginal Australia*. Rochester, Vermont: Inner Traditions International, 1994.

Berndt, Ronald, and Catherine H. Berndt. *The World of the First Australians: Aboriginal Traditional Life: Past and Present*. Canberra: Aboriginal Studies Press, 1988.

Berndt, Ronald, and John Stanton. *A World That Was: The Yaraldi of the Murray River and the Lakes, South Australia*. Carlton, Vic: Miegunyah Press/ Melbourne University Press, 1993.

Blaxland, Wendy. 'Style, and a Suppressed Rage'. *Sydney Morning Herald* 14 Jan 1978: 17.

Blay, John. 'Place Yourself in Foster Care'. *The Republican* 4 Sep 1997: 17.

Bradley, Paul. 'A Phrygian Good Read'. *On Dit* 24 Feb 1997 [FP MS 160 Series 9].

Brennan, Christopher. *Poems [1913]*. 1914. Sydney: Sydney University Press, 1972.

Broderick, Damien. 'Science Fables'. *24 Hours* 3 (Feb 1978): 62–63.

Brown, Nicholas. 'Everyone Who Has Ever Done a Tree Sit Always Says That the Tree Talks to You'. *Words for Country: Landscape and Language in Australia.* Ed. Tim Bonyhady and Tom Griffiths. Sydney: University of New South Wales Press, 2002. 85–101.

Buckridge, Pat. 'Poetry, Prophecy and Exhilaration'. *Courier-Mail* 7 June 1997: Weekend 9.

Burns, D. R. 'The Coming of the "Contained Account" *Moonlite*, David Foster's Landmark Novel'. *Overland* 129 (1992): 62–67.

——. '"Visionary Monsters" versus "Contained Accounts": Self Contradiction in Australian Fiction since 1960'. *Southerly* 53.2 (1993): 146–153.

Carey, Peter. *Bliss*. St Lucia, Qld: University of Queensland Press, 1981.

——. *Collected Stories*. St Lucia, Qld: University of Queensland Press, 1994.

Connery, Brian, and Kirk Combe. 'Theorizing Satire: A Retrospective and Introduction' in their *Theorizing Satire: Essays in Literary Criticism*. New York: St Martins Press, 1995. 1–15.

Conte, Steven. *Gordian Satire: The Novels of David Foster*. MA thesis. University of New South Wales, Canberra: ADFA Library, 1994.

Corris, Peter. 'Misfits and Depressives in the Raw'. *Australian Weekend Magazine* 5 Nov 1977: 12.

——. Untitled. *Good Reading Guide*. Ed. Helen Daniel. Melbourne: McPhee Gribble, 1989. 76.

Dale, Leigh. Untitled. *Journal of Australian Studies* 56 (1998): 189–192.

Daniel, Helen. *Liars: Australian New Novelists*. Melbourne: Penguin, 1988.

——. 'Matters Male, Martial and Mystical'. *Age* 10 Aug 1991: Saturday Extra 8.

——. 'Pastiche and Parody Run Amok'. *Age* 14 Feb 1987: 16.

Davis, Mark. *Gangland: Cultural Elites and the New Generationalism*. St Leonards: Allen & Unwin, 1997.

DeLillo, Don. *Great Jones Street*. Boston: Houghton Mifflin, 1973.

Doyle, Jeff. 'Heart of Australian Darkness'. *Canberra Times* 24 Aug 1991.

Dutton Papers (DP). David Foster's correspondence with Geoffrey Dutton is held in the Geoffrey Dutton papers, National Library of Australia, MS 7285, Series 2, Boxes 11–15.

Dutton, Geoffrey. *The Australian Collection: Australia's Greatest Books*. North Ryde, New South Wales: Angus & Robertson, 1985.

——. 'David Foster: The Early Years'. *Southerly* 65.1 (1996): 23–48.

Elliott, Ralph. 'A Further Comedy of Twinhood'. *Canberra Times* 25 April 1987: B3.

Elliott, Robert C. *The Power of Satire: Magic, Ritual, Art*. Princeton, NJ: Princeton University Press, 1960.

Field, Andrew. 'Our Literary Lions'. *The Courier-Mail* 30 May 1998: 5, 10.

Fern, Lynn. *William Robinson*. Roseville, NSW: Craftsman House, 1995.

Fleming, Juliet. 'The Origins of Oz'. *Times Literary Supplement* 16 Aug 1996: 22.

Forshaw, Thelma. 'Penetrating Heavy Metal'. *Quadrant* 28.6 (June 1984): 86–87.

Foster Papers (FP). David Foster's notebooks, correspondence, review clippings, and manuscript drafts are held in the Library of the Australian Defence Force Academy. MS 160.

Foster, David. 'Aboriginality and the Hope of Art: Explaining Australia in Arkansas'. *Quadrant* 49.11 (Nov 2005): 22–31.

——. *The Adventures of Christian Rosy Cross*. Melbourne: Penguin, 1985.

——. 'Aggression in Sleepy Hollow'. *Australian Book Review* 65 (Oct 1984): 9–10.

——. *The Ballad of Erinungarah*. Sydney: Random House, 1997.

——. 'Books in My Life'. Unpublished address to Friends of the ANU Library, 1999.

——. *Dog Rock: A Postal Pastoral*. Melbourne: Penguin, 1985.

——. 'The Elixir Operon'. *Strange Attractors: Original Australian Speculative Fiction*. Ed. Damien Broderick. Sydney: Hale & Iremonger, 1985. 132–150.

——. *Escape to Reality*. Melbourne: Macmillan, 1977.

——. *The Fleeing Atalanta*. Adelaide: Maximus, 1975.

——. *The Glade Within the Grove*. London: Fourth Estate, 1996; Sydney: Random House, 1996.

——. *In the New Country*. London: Fourth Estate, 1999.

——. *The Land Where Stories End as Narrated by the Angel Depicted in 'Madonna con Bambino e due angeli' by Filippo Lippi*. Sydney: Duffy and Snellgrove, 2001.

——. 'Like Spinoza the Philosopher'. *Toads: Australian Writers: Other Work, Other Lives*. Ed. Andrew Sant. Sydney: Allen & Unwin, 1992. 72–84.

——. *Mates of Mars.* Melbourne: Penguin, 1991.

——. *Moonlite.* Melbourne: Macmillan, 1981.

——. *North South West: Three Novellas*. Melbourne: Macmillan, 1973.

——. *The Pale Blue Crochet Coathanger Cover*. Melbourne: Penguin, 1988.

——. *Plumbum.* Melbourne: Penguin, 1983.

——. 'Once Were Artists'. *Weekend Australian* 5–6 June 1999: 27.

——. 'A Plea on Behalf of Eros'. *Quadrant* 49.10 (Oct 2005): 20–21.

——. (av 1987) 'A Poetry and Prose Reading by David Foster at the Australian Defence Force Academy Library'. Canberra: ADFA Library, 1987.

——. *The Pure Land.* Melbourne: Macmillan, 1974.

——. 'Quod Potero Sedulo'. *The Best Australian Essays 2002.* Ed. Peter Craven. Melbourne: Black Inc, 2002. 300–304.

——. 'Statement'. *Australian Literary Studies* 8.2 (1977):196–197.

——. (av 1991) 'Reading of Important Writers at Tilley Devine's'. (12 Sept 1991) Canberra: ADFA Library, 1991.

——. (*S&N*) *Studs and Nogs: Essays and Polemics 1987–98*. Sydney: Random House, 1999.

——. 'Red Band Adventures'. *Australian Author* 31.2 (Aug 1999): 8–9.

——. *Testostero: A Comic Novel.* Melbourne: Penguin, 1987.

——, and D. K. Lyall. *The Empathy Experiment.* Sydney: Wild & Woolley, 1977.

Frazer, Sir James George. *The Golden Bough: A Study in Magic and Religion*, Abridged edition. London: Macmillan, 1922.

Frost, Annabel, comp. 'David Foster'. *Australian Country Style* (Mar 1996): 18, 20.

Frye, Northrop. *Anatomy of Criticism: Four Essays*. 1957. Princeton, NJ: Princeton University Press, 1971.

Furphy, Joseph. *Such Is Life*. Sydney: Bulletin, 1903.

Gelder, Ken. 'The "Self-Contradictory" Fiction of David Foster'. *Aspects of Australian Fiction*. Ed. Alan Brissenden. Perth: University of Western Australia Press, 1990. 149–159.

Goldsworthy, Kerryn. 'The Leader of the Opposition'. *Australian's Review of Books* 2.5 (June 1997): 10–12.

Gollan, Myfanwy. 'Verbal Acrobatics'. *Sydney Morning Herald* 7 Feb 1987: 44.

Grant, Jamie. Unpublished typescript of review. *Books and Writing*. ABC Radio National [1978?] [FP MS 160 Series 9].

Hamilton, Andy. 'The Art of Improvisation and the Aesthetics of Imperfection'. *British Journal of Aesthetics* 40.1 (2000): 168–185.

Harris, Stephen. 'David Foster's *Moonlite*: Re-viewing History as Satirical Fable—Towards a Post-colonial Past'. *Westerly* 42.1 (1997): 71–88.

Hassall, Anthony. *Dancing on Hot Macadam: Peter Carey's Fiction*. St Lucia: University of Queensland Press, 1994.

Healey, Janet. Unpublished typescript of review. *Books and Writing*. ABC Radio National [1987?] [FP MS 160 Series 9].

Hope, A. D. 'An Epistle from Holofernes'. *Collected Poems: 1930–1970*. Sydney: Angus & Robertson, 1972. 58–62.

Johnston, Martin. 'Expect Entrancing Double Trouble from the Twins in Surreal Venice'. *Times on Sunday* 8 Feb 1987: 27. Repr. *Martin Johnston: Selected Poems and Prose*. Ed. Martin Johnston and John Tranter. St. Lucia: University of Queensland Press, 1993. 226–228.

Kent, Jacqueline. *Out of the Bakelite Box: The Heyday of Australian Radio*. Sydney: Angus & Robertson, 1983.

Kiernan, Brian. 'Introduction'. *The Most Beautiful Lies: A Collection of Stories by Major Contemporary Fiction Writers*. Ed. Brian Kiernan. Sydney: Angus & Robertson, 1977.

Knight, Stephen. 'Compulsive or Repulsive—It Depends on Taste'. *Sydney Morning Herald* 14 Apr 1984: 41.

Lacey, Stephen. 'Two of Us: David & Gerda Foster'. *Sydney Morning Herald Good Weekend* 6 July 2002: 14.

Leonard, Sue. 'The Latest in Paperbacks'. *Courier Mail* 13 July 1985: 31.

Lever, Susan. 'The Bicentennial and the Millennium: The Dissident Voices of David Foster and Sam Watson'. *'And What Books Do You Read?' New Studies in Australian Literature*. Ed. Martin Duwell and Irmtraud Petersson. St Lucia: University of Queensland Press, 1996. 101–111.

——. 'The Colonizer's Gift of Cursing: Satire in David Foster's *Moonlite*'. *Cheeky Fictions: Laughter and the Postcolonial*. Ed. Susanne Reichl and Mark Stein. Amsterdam: Rodopi, 2005. 107–116.

——. 'David Foster'. *Dictionary of Literary Biography: vol 289, Australian Writers, 1950–1975*. Ed. Selina Samuels. Detroit: Gale Research, 2004. 78–86.

——. 'David Foster's "Decline and Fall"'. *Southerly* 55.1 (Autumn 1996): 41–48.

——. *Real Relations: The Feminist Politics of Form in Australian Fiction*. Sydney: Halstead, 2000. 120–130.

——. 'Postmodernism, History and Satire: David Foster and Salman Rushdie'. *Current Tensions: Proceedings of the 18th Annual Conference of ASAL 6–11 July 1996*. Brisbane: Queensland University of Technology, 1997. 214–220.

——. 'The Question of Literary Independence: *Quadrant* and Australian writing'. *Outside the Book: Contemporary Essays on Literary Periodicals*. Ed. David Carter. Sydney: Local Consumption, 1991.165–176.

——. 'Tree-Dreaming: David Foster's *The Glade Within the Grove* and William Robinson's *Ancient Trees*'. *Australian Studies* 18.2 (2003): 35–50.

Lewis, Wyndham. 'The Greatest Satire Is Nonmoral'. *Satire: Modern Essays in Criticism*. Ed. R. Paulson. Englewood Cliffs, NJ: Prentice-Hall, 1971. 66–79.

Lorenz, Konrad. *Civilized Man's Eight Deadly Sins*. Trans. Marjorie Latzke. London: Methuen, 1973.

McHale, Brian. *Postmodernist Fiction*. New York: Methuen, 1987.

McKernan (Lever), Susan. 'It's All Done with Mirrors: Satire, Slapstick and an Old Comic Plot'. *Australian Book Review* 89 (April 1987): 23–24.

——. 'Surpassing Lunacy: The novels of David Foster'. *Age Monthly Review* 4.11 (April 1985): 3–4.

Matthews, David. 'What Is Going on Here?' *Australian Weekend Review* 5–6 July: 9.

Mitchell, Adrian. 'Disjunctive Worlds That Never Really Make a Point'. *Australian* 24–25 Dec 1983: 14.

——. 'Satiric Portrait of Our Travellers'. *Weekend Australian* 28 Feb–1 Mar 1987: 15.

Mole, John. 'Blow, Man, Blow!' Rev. of *Fascinating Rhythm: Reading Jazz in American Writing*, by David Yaffe. *Times Literary Supplement* 14 April 2006: 27.

Murray, Les. 'How Fred and I Wrote Fredy Neptune'. *The Best Australian Essays.* Ed. Peter Craven. Melbourne: Bookman, 1999. 364–373.

——. *New Oxford Book of Australian Verse*. Melbourne: Oxford University Press, 1991.

Nabokov, Vladimir. *Novels 1969–1974: Ada, Transparent Things, Look at the Harlequins!* New York: Library of America, 1996.

——. *Pale Fire*. 1962. New York: Vintage, 1989.

North, Marilla. 'Postman's Knock: Is David Foster a Clever Dick—or What?' *Meanjin* 56.3/4 (1997): 686–696.

Paulin, Tom. 'Guilty Dreams'. *New Statesman* 10 Feb 1978: 193–194.

Poole, Ross. 'Modernity, Rationality and "the Masculine"'. *Feminine and Masculine Representation.* Ed. Terry Threadgold and Anne Cranny-Francis. North Sydney: Allen & Unwin, 1990. 48–61.

Redmond, John. 'Troublesome Times and People'. *Glasgow Herald* 9 Feb 1978 [FP MS 160 Series 9].

Riemer, Andrew. 'Bare Breech'd Brethren; The Novels of David Foster'. *Southerly* 47.2 (June 1987): 126–144.

——. 'A Cultural Dilemma'. *Voices* 6.2 (1996): 107–112.

——. 'An Exhilarating Ramble Round the Collapse of Rural Life'. *Sydney Morning Herald* 10 Apr 1999: Spectrum 9.

——. 'Introduction'. *A Slab of Foster's*. Ed. David Foster. Sydney: The Yellow Press, 1994. 1–10.

Rogers, Tom. 'Slice of Comic Oz Abroad without Crocodile'. *Melbourne Times* 18 March 1987: 18.

Rushdie, Salman. *The Ground Beneath Her Feet*. New York: Henry Holt, 1999.

——. *Midnight's Children*. London: Cape, 1981.

——. *The Satanic Verses*. New York: Viking, 1988.

Sage, Lorna. *Moments of Truth: Twelve Twentieth-Century Women Writers*. London: Fourth Estate, 2001. 221–248.

——. 'Domestic Warfare'. *London Observer* 26 Feb 1978 [FP MS 160 Series 9].

Said, Edward. *Culture and Imperialism*. London: Chatto & Windus, 1993.

Schwenger, Peter. 'The Masculine Mode'. *Speaking of Gender*. Ed. Elaine Showalter. New York: Routledge, Chapman and Hall, 1989. 101–112.

Scott, Kim. 'Australia's Continuing Neurosis: Identity, Race and History'. Alfred Deakin Lectures. 15 May 2001. <http://www.abc.net.au/rn/deakin/stories/s291485.htm>

Seear, Lynne, ed. *Darkness & Light: The Art of William Robinson*. Brisbane: Queensland Art Gallery, 2001.

Shaw, Narelle. 'Boundary Crossing: The Novels of David Foster'. *Australian Literary Studies* 16.1 (1993): 38–49.

——. 'Experiencing a Wilderness and Cultivating a Garden: The Literary Environmentalism of David Foster and David Malouf'. *Antipodes* 16.1 (2002): 46–52.

——. 'The Fellowship of Light and Darkness: David Foster's *Moonlite*'. *Westerly* 37.3 (1992): 55–63.

——. 'It's a Small Martial Arts World: *Mates of Mars* and the Foster Novels'. *LiNQ* 21.2 (Oct 1994): 63–70.

——. ' "Nothing Is Random": David Foster's *Plumbum*'. *Southerly* 50.1 (1990): 80–92.

——. 'The Passion of D'Arcy D'Oliveres: David Foster's "Dog Rock" Novels'. *Antipodes* 4.1 (1990): 29–34.

——. 'The Poetics of David Foster's Fiction'. *Southerly* 56.1 (1996): 31–40.

——. 'The Postman's Grand Narrative: Postmodernism and David Foster's *The Glade Within the Grove*'. *Journal of Commonwealth Literature* 34.1 (1999): 45–64.

——. '*Testostero*: David Foster's Comic Novel'. *Journal of Commonwealth Literature* 26.1 (1991): 65–78.

Sheehan, Paul. *Among the Barbarians*. Milsons Point: Random House, 1998.

Stow, Randolph. 'Suffocation in Sydney'. *Times Literary Supplement* 4 Aug 1978 [FP MS 160, Series 9].

Summers, Anne. 'Leaving Women Up a Gum Tree'. *Sydney Morning Herald* 6 July 1997: 9; also published as 'A Gum Tree by Any Other Name'. *Courier Mail* 8 July 1998: 21.

Thom, Catherine. *The Ascetical Theology and Praxis of Sixth to Eighth Century Irish Monasticism as a Radical Response to the Evangelium*. PhD Thesis.

Australian Catholic University, 2002. <http://dlibrary.acu.edu.au/digitaltheses/public/adt-acuvp26.29082005/index.html>.

Thomas, Helen. 'Rock, Manipulation and Greed'. *National Times* 23 Dec 1983: 29.

Tranter, John. *The New Australian Poetry.* St Lucia: Makar Press, 1979.

Travers, Erica. 'On the Philosophical: Interview with David Foster'. *Westerly* 37.1 (1992): 71–78.

Watson, Don. *Caledonia Australis: Scottish Highlanders on the Frontier of Australia.* Sydney: Collins, 1984.

Weisenburger, Steven. *Fables of Subversion: Satire and the American Novel, 1930–1980*. Athens, GA & London: University of Georgia Press, 1995.

West, Nathanael. *Miss Lonelyhearts, and a Cool Million*. 1957. Harmondsworth, UK: Penguin, 1961.

White, Patrick. 'The Prodigal Son'. *Australian Letters.* 1958. Repr. *Oxford Anthology of Australian Literature*. Melbourne: Oxford University Press, 1985. 337.

Williams, Craig. 'Ballads, Bards and Bollocks'. *Overland* 148 (1997): 86–88.

Williamson, David. *Dead White Males*. Sydney: Currency, 1995.

Wootten, Hal. 'No Room for Racist Sneers'. *Sydney Morning Herald* 3 July 1997: 25.

Bibliography

1 Works of David Foster

Short Stories and Novellas

'The Elixir Operon'. *Strange Attractors: Original Australian Speculative Fiction.* Ed. Damien Broderick. Sydney: Hale & Iremonger, 1985. 132–150.

Escape to Reality. Melbourne: Macmillan, 1977.

Hitting the Wall: Two Novellas. Melbourne: Penguin, 1989. Comprises 'Eye of the Bull' and reprint of 'The Job' from *Escape to Reality.*

North South West: Three Novellas. Melbourne: Macmillan, 1973.

Novels

The Adventures of Christian Rosy Cross. Melbourne: Penguin, 1985.

Dog Rock: A Postal Pastoral. Melbourne: Penguin, 1985. Rep. with *The Pale Blue Crochet Coathanger Cover* as *Dog Rock.* Sydney: Random House, 1996.

Foster, David, and D. K. Lyall. *The Empathy Experiment.* Sydney: Wild & Woolley, 1977.

The Glade Within the Grove. London: Fourth Estate, 1996; Sydney: Random House, 1996.

In the New Country. London: Fourth Estate, 1999.

The Land Where Stories End as Narrated by the Angel Depicted in 'Madonna con Bambino e due angeli' by Filippo Lippi. Sydney: Duffy and Snellgrove, 2001.

Mates of Mars. Melbourne: Penguin, 1991.

Moonlite. Melbourne: Macmillan, 1981.

The Pale Blue Crochet Coathanger Cover. Melbourne: Penguin, 1988. Rep. with *Dog Rock: A Postal Pastoral* as *Dog Rock.* Sydney: Random House, 1996.

Plumbum. Melbourne: Penguin, 1983.

The Pure Land. Melbourne: Macmillan, 1974.

Testostero: A Comic Novel. Melbourne: Penguin, 1987.

Poetry

The Ballad of Erinungarah. Sydney: Random House, 1997.

The Fleeing Atalanta. Adelaide: Maximus, 1975.

'Klimt: For Rita'. *Weekend Australian Magazine* 16–17 Jan 1988: 12.

'Moon and Sea'. *Australian Literary Quarterly* (3–4 Oct 1987): 3.

'Rebis'. 'Voices of the Heart'. 'Wailing Wall'. 'Yom Kippur'. *Scripsi* 5.1 (June 1988): 138–140.

Essays

'Statement'. *Australian Literary Studies* 8.2 (1977): 196–197.

'Aggression in Sleepy Hollow'. *Australian Book Review* 65 (Oct 1984): 9–10.

'Satire'. *Phoenix Review* 2 (1987/1988): 63–79; rep. in *Studs and Nogs: Essays and Polemics 1987–98*. 76–97.

'Chaos Is Normal'. *Australian Book Review* 119 (Apr 1990): 24–28; rep. as 'On Being Normal' in *Studs and Nogs: Essays and Polemics 1987–98*. 130–144.

'An Unfashionable Talent'. *Independent Monthly* 3.2 (Aug 1991): 40–42.

'The Writer Reader Feedback Cycle…or Naughty Novelists'. *Island* 16 (1991): 30–31; rep. as 'Naughty Novelists' in *Studs and Nogs: Essays and Polemics 1987–98*. 159–173.

'Like Spinoza the Philosopher'. *Toads: Australian Writers: Other Work, Other Lives*. Ed. Andrew Sant. Sydney: Allen & Unwin, 1992. 72–84.

'Writing Fiction in Our Lingua Franca'. *The Great Literacy Debate: English in Contemporary Australia*. Ed. David Myers. Kew, Victoria: Australian Scholarly Publishing, 1992. 125–130.

'My Blue Heaven.' *The Independent Monthly* (Dec 1993–Jan 1994) 66–70; rep. as 'Gallipoli' in *Studs and Nogs: Essays and Polemics 1987–98*. 98–107.

'Bloody Justice'. *Independent Monthly* May 1994: 30–36; rep. in *Studs and Nogs: Essays and Polemics 1987–98*. 185–197.

'A Gathering of Hunters'. *Independent Monthly* (Dec 1995–Jan 1996) 80–83; rep. as 'Barra' in *Studs and Nogs: Essays and Polemics 1987–98*. 198–206.

'On the Dual Pursuit of Literary and Martial Art'. *Southerly* 6.1 (1996): 6–22; rep. in *Studs and Nogs: Essays and Polemics 1987–98*. 19–41.

'Race Debate Is Skin Deep'. *Sydney Morning Herald* 26 Jun 1997: 17; rep. as 'Towards Aboriginal Reconciliation' in *Studs and Nogs: Essays and Polemics 1987–98*. 145–148.

'On Castration'. *Heat* 4 (1997): 7–19; rep. as 'Castration' in *Studs and Nogs: Essays and Polemics 1987–9*. 117–129.

'Classics and Canon'. *Southerly* 57.3 (1997): 222–225; rep. in *Studs and Nogs: Essays and Polemics 1987–98*. 42–45.

'Suspended Sentence'. *Ulitarra* 11 (1997): 98–101; rep. in *Studs and Nogs: Essays and Polemics 1987–98*. 174–178.

'A Walk in the Southern Blue Mountains'. *Crossing the Blue Mountains: Journeys through Two Centuries from Naturalist Charles Darwin to Novelist David Foster*. Potts Point, NSW: Duffy and Snellgrove, 1997. 189–213.

'Banana Republic'. *Sydney Morning Herald* 1 Jan 1998: 23; rep. as 'Taming the Tiger' in *Studs and Nogs: Essays and Polemics 1987–98*. 108–116.

'Lightning Turns the Bush into Friend and Foe'. *Sydney Morning Herald* 13 Jan 1998: 13; rep. as 'Fire Storm' in *Studs and Nogs: Essays and Polemics 1987–98*. 207–210.

'Salzburg Semiotics'. *Sydney Morning Herald* 16 May 1998: 9s; rep. as 'Salzburg Seminar' in *Studs and Nogs: Essays and Polemics 1987–98*. 211–218.

'Nature Morte'. Rev. of *Wormholes*, by John Fowles. *Australian's Review of Books* 3.8 (Nov 1998): 3–4.

Studs and Nogs: Essays and Polemics 1987–98. Sydney: Random House, 1999.

'Red Band Adventures'. *Australian Author* 31.2 (Aug 1999): 8–9.

'Once Were Artists'. *Weekend Australian* (5–6 Jun 1999): 27.

'Hot Air vs the Novel'. *Courier-Mail* 16 Sep 2000: 5.

'Writers on Reading: Too Much Is Not Enough'. *Australian's Review of Books* (9 Oct 2000) 28.

'Festival of Night'. *Australian Author* 32.3 (Nov 2000): 25.

'An Ill Wind'. *Bulletin* 120 (17 Dec 2002–14 Jan 2003): 100–101.

'Quod Potero Sedulo'. *The Best Australian Essays 2002*. Ed. Peter Craven. Melbourne: Black Inc, 2002. 300–304.

'A Plea on Behalf of Eros'. *Quadrant* 49.10 (Oct 2005): 20–21.

'Aboriginality and the Hope of Art: Explaining Australia in Arkansas'. *Quadrant* 49.11 (Nov 2005): 22–31.

'David Foster Talks about *The Land Where Stories End*'. 19 Jun 2007. <http/ www.duffyandsnellgrove.com.au/extracts/Foster_article.htm>.

Produced Radio Plays

Water on the Brain. Prod. Andrew McLennan. ABC FM 31 Dec 1979. ABC Radio 2 19 Jan 1983. ABC FM 2 Sep 1997.

The Elixir Operon. Prod. Andrew McLennan. ABC FM 25 Nov 1980. ABC Radio 2 17 May 1981, 31 May 1982. ABC Regional 13 Jan 1990. ABC FM 9 Sep 1991. ABC RN 15 Sep 1991.

As It Was. Prod. Andrew McLennan. ABC FM 14 Jun 1981, 27 Nov 1981, 27 Jul 1988. ABC Radio 2 28 Nov 1982, 13 Jan 1987. ABC RN 9 Sep 1997.

Knight's Move. Prod. Andrew McLennan. ABC Radio 2 31 Oct 1983. ABC FM 3 May 1983. 29 Sep 1987, 24 Jan 1995, 16 Sep 1997. ABC RN 24 Oct 1984, 21 Jan 1990.

The Adventures of Christian Rosy Cross: An Alchemical Radio Saga in Four Parts. Prod. Rodney Wetherell. ABC FM 1, 8, 15, 22 Sep 1987.

Bananas. Prod. Andrew McLennan. ABC FM 11 Jun 1990, 18 Aug 1991, 5 Jan 1992, 14 Jan 1997.

Hugo's Turkish Travel Pack. Prod. Andrew McLennan. ABC FM 13 Feb 1996, 23 Sep 1997.

The Land Where Stories End. Prod. Andrew McLennan. ABC FM 16 Jun 1997, 12 Jul 1999.

Manuscripts

David Foster papers. Foster's notebooks, correspondence, review clippings and manuscript drafts are held in the Library of the Australian Defence Force Academy. MS 160.

Geoffrey Dutton papers. David Foster's correspondence with Geoffrey Dutton is held in the Geoffrey Dutton papers, National Library of Australia, MS 7285, Series 2, Boxes 11–15.

Other

Foster, David, ed. *Self Portraits.* Canberra: National Library of Australia, 1991.

——. *A Slab of Foster's*. Darlinghurst: The Yellow Press, 1994. This reprints excerpts from *Moonlite*, *Plumbum*, and *Mates of Mars*.

——. 'Books in My Life'. Unpublished address to Friends of ANU Library, July 1999.

Foster, David, and Gerda. *A Year of Slow Food: Four Seasons of Growing and Making Your Own Food in the Australian Countryside*. Sydney: Duffy and Snellgrove, 2001.

2 Works about David Foster

Bibliography

The Austlit Gateway provides a full bibliography of works published in Australian newspapers and literary journals (from 1980) by and about David Foster at <www.austlit.edu.au>.

British, Irish, and American published reviews, and Australian reviews before 1980, are held in clippings files in the David Foster papers, Australian Defence Force Academy Library, MS 160, Series 9.

Biography

Broinowski, Alison. 'Foster at Forty Plus'. *Australian Literary Quarterly* (6–7 Jun 1987): 10.

Dutton, Geoffrey. 'David Foster: The Early Years'. *Southerly* 65.1 (1996): 23–48.

Frost, Annabel, comp. 'David Foster'. *Australian Country Style* (Mar 1996): 18, 20.

'Family Ties: David Foster'. *Australian Good Taste* (Jul 1999): 24–25.

Lacey, Stephen. 'Two of Us: David & Gerda Foster'. *Sydney Morning Herald Good Weekend* 6 Jul 2002: 14.

Wyndham, Susan. 'Foster's grove of Proulx praise'. *Sydney Morning Herald* 8 Mar 1996: Arts 13.

Interviews

Baker, Candida. 'David Foster'. *Yacker: Australian Writers Talk about Their Work*. Sydney: Pan/Picador, 1986. 104–126.

Baker, Candida. 'The Bard from Bundanoon'. *Age* 14 Aug 1991: Tempo 5.

Barker, Karen, and Priya Kalnins. 'A Conversation with David Foster'. *Antithesis* 8.2 (1997): 307–314.

Braun-Bau, Susanne. 'Susanne Braun-Bau in Conversation with David Foster'. *Westerly* 42.1 (1997): 109–128.

Galligan, Anne. 'An Interview with David Foster, ASAL 1996, QUT'. *Notes & Furphies* 37 (1996): 14–17.

Hawley, Janet. 'Plumbing Rock Culture'. *Age* Saturday Extra 10 Dec 1983: 42.

Sorensen, Rosemary. 'Foster vs the World (and Me)'. *Australian Book Review* 133 (Aug 1991): 13–14.

Travers, Erica. 'On the Philosophical: Interview with David Foster'. *Westerly* 37.1 (1992): 71–78.

Waldren, Murray. 'The Loneliness of the Long-Distance Satirist'. *Dining Out with Mr Lunch*. St Lucia: University of Queensland Press, 1999. 118–124.

——. 'The Master of Martial Farce....'. *Weekend Australian* 10–11 Aug 1991: Review 4.

White, Judith. 'The Confucius of Bundanoon'. *Sun Herald* 4 Aug 1991: 105.

Videorecordings

'A Poetry and Prose Reading by David Foster Australian Defence Force Academy Library'. Canberra: ADFA Library, 1987.

'Reading of Important Writers at Tilley Devine's'. Canberra: ADFA Library, 12 Sep 1991.

'David Foster Reads on the Topic of "The Literary and Martial Arts" at the Australian Defence Force Academy on 21 September 1995'. Canberra: ADFA Library.

'David Foster Reads at the Australian Defence Force Academy Library on 26 June 1997'. Canberra: ADFA Library.

Criticism

General Articles and Theses

Brown, Nicholas. 'Everyone Who Has Ever Done a Tree Sit Always Says That the Tree Talks to You'. *Words for Country: Landscape and Language in Australia*. Ed. Tim Bonyhady and Tom Griffiths. Sydney: University of New South Wales Press, 2002. 85–101.

Burns, D.R. 'The Coming of the "Contained Account" *Moonlite*, David Foster's Landmark Novel'. *Overland* 129 (1992): 62–67.

——. '"Visionary Monsters" versus "Contained Accounts": Self Contradiction in Australian Fiction since 1960'. *Southerly* 53.2 (1993): 146–153.

Conte, Steven. *Gordian Satire: The Novels of David Foster*. MA thesis. University of New South Wales. Canberra: ADFA Library, 1994.

Daniel, Helen. 'The Alchemy of the Lie: David Foster'. *Liars: Australian New Novelists*. Melbourne: Penguin, 1988. 77–104.

Field, Andrew. 'Our Literary Lions'. *The Courier-Mail* 30 May 1998: 5, 10.

Gelder, Ken. 'The "Self-Contradictory" Fiction of David Foster'. *Aspects of Australian Fiction*. Ed. Alan Brissenden. Perth: University of Western Australia Press, 1990. 149–159.

Goldsworthy, Kerryn. 'The Leader of the Opposition'. *Australian's Review of Books* 2.5 (Jun 1997): 10–12.

Harris, Stephen. 'David Foster's *Moonlite*: Re-viewing History as Satirical Fable—Towards a Post-colonial Past'. *Westerly* 42.1 (1997): 71–88.

Lever, Susan. 'The Bicentennial and the Millennium: The Dissident Voices of David Foster and Sam Watson'. *'And What Books Do You Read?' New Studies in Australian Literature*. Ed. Martin Duwell and Irmtraud Petersson. St Lucia: University of Queensland Press, 1996. 101–111.

——. 'David Foster's "Decline and Fall"'. *Southerly* 65.1 (1996): 41–48.

——. 'Postmodernism, History and Satire: David Foster and Salman Rushdie'. *Current Tensions: Proceedings of the 18th Annual Conference of ASAL 6–11 July 1996*. Ed. Sharyn Pearce. Brisbane: Queensland University Technology, 1997. 214–220.

——. 'A Masculine Crisis: David Foster's *Mates of Mars*'. *Real Relations: The Feminist Politics of Form in Australian Fiction*. Sydney: Halstead, 2000. 120–130.

——. 'Tree-Dreaming: David Foster's *The Glade Within the Grove* and William Robinson's *Ancient Trees*'. *Australian Studies* 18.2 (2003): 35–50.

—— 'David Foster'. *Dictionary of Literary Biography: vol 289, Australian Writers, 1950–1975.* Ed. Selina Samuels. Detroit: Gale Research, 2004. 78–86.

——. 'The Colonizer's Gift of Cursing: Satire in David Foster's *Moonlite*'. *Cheeky Fictions: Laughter and the Postcolonial*. Ed. Susanne Reichl and Mark Stein. Amsterdam: Rodopi, 2005.107–116.

Martin, Susan. 'The Wood from the Trees: Taxonomy and the Eucalypt as the New National Hero in Recent Australian Writing'. *JASAL* 3 (2004): 81–94. <http://www.nla.gov.au/openpublish/index.php/jasal/article/view/35/44 >.

McKernan (Lever), Susan. 'Surpassing Lunacy: The Novels of David Foster'. *Age Monthly Review* 4.11 (Apr 1985): 3–4.

North, Marilla. 'Postman's Knock: Is David Foster a Clever Dick—or What?' *Meanjin* 56.3/4 (1997): 686–696.

Riemer, Andrew. 'Bare Breech'd Brethren; The Novels of David Foster'. *Southerly* 47.2 (Jun 1987): 126–144.

——. 'Introduction'. David Foster. *A Slab of Foster's*. Sydney: The Yellow Press, 1994. 1–10.

——. 'A Cultural Dilemma'. *Voices* 6.2 (1996): 107–112.

Shaw, Narelle. '"Nothing Is Random": David Foster's *Plumbum*'. *Southerly* 50.1 (1990): 80–92.

——. 'The Passion of D'Arcy D'Oliveres: David Foster's "Dog Rock" Novels'. *Antipodes* 4.1 (1990): 29–34.

——. '*Testostero*: David Foster's Comic Novel'. *Journal of Commonwealth Literature* 26.1 (1991): 65–78.

——. 'The Fellowship of Light and Darkness: David Foster's *Moonlite*'. *Westerly* 37.3 (1992): 55–63.

——. 'Boundary Crossing: The Novels of David Foster'. *Australian Literary Studies* 16.1 (1993): 38–49.

——. 'It's a Small Martial Arts World: *Mates of Mars* and the Foster Novels'. *LiNQ* 21.2 (Oct 1994): 63–70.

——. 'The Poetics of David Foster's Fiction'. *Southerly* 56.1 (1996): 31–40.

——. 'The Postman's Grand Narrative: Postmodernism and David Foster's *The Glade Within the Grove*'. *Journal of Commonwealth Literature* 34.1 (1999): 45–64.

——. 'Experiencing a Wilderness and Cultivating a Garden: The Literary Environmentalism of David Foster and David Malouf'. *Antipodes* 16.1 (2002): 46–52.

Sheehan, Paul. 'White Dreaming'. *Among the Barbarians*. Milsons Point: Random House, 1998. 279–293.

Selected Reviews

The Pure Land

Barnes, Julian. 'The Call of the Bush'. *Times Literary Supplement* 23 May 1975: 577.

Harrison-Ford, Carl. Untitled. *Good Reading Guide*. Ed. Helen Daniel. Melbourne: McPhee Gribble, 1989. 76.

Kepert, L. V. 'Recent Paperback Fiction'. *Sun Herald* 21 Jul 1985: 98.

Leonard, Sue. 'The Latest in Paperbacks'. *Courier Mail* 13 Jul 1985: 31.

The Fleeing Atalanta

Lee, S. E. '"Mystification and Outrage" or "Who Did Steal the Tarts?": Obscurity and Violence in Contemporary Australian Poetry'. *Southerly* 36.3 (1976): 331–336.

Thorne, Tim. Untitled. *Australian* 14 Feb 1976: 28.

The Empathy Experiment

Barwell, Graham. 'What Happened to Little Green Men?' *LiNQ* 6.3 (1978): 116–118.

Broderick, Damien. 'Science Fables'. *24 Hours* (Feb 1978): 62–63.

Lindsay, Elaine. 'A Nightmarish Fantasy of Diverting Deviates'. *Australian Weekend Magazine* 22 Apr 1978: 9.

Mackenzie, Jim. 'An Oddity Too Much'. *Nation Review* 16–22 1978: 13.

Miles, John. 'Humanity's Mad Maze'. *Adelaide Advertiser* 5 Apr 1978 [FP MS 160, Series 9].

Noonan, William. 'Pruning the Brain'. *Sydney Morning Herald* 12 Aug 1978: 19.

Ryan, Yoni. 'Anxieties of University Life'. *Launceston Examiner* 11 Feb 1978: 8.

Writers' Program, ABC Radio (18 Dec 1977) [FP Ms 160].

Escape to Reality

Bawden, Nina. 'Recent Fiction'. London *Daily Telegraph* 9 Feb 1978 [FP MS 160, Series 9].

Blaxland, Wendy. 'Style, and a Suppressed Rage'. *Sydney Morning Herald* 14 Jan 1978: 17.

Corris, Peter. 'Misfits and Depressives in the Raw'. *Australian Weekend Magazine* 5 Nov 1977: 12.

——. Untitled. *Good Reading Guide*. Ed. Helen Daniel. Melbourne: McPhee Gribble, 1989. 76.

Grant, Jamie. *Books and Writing*, ABC Radio [1978?] [FP MS 160].

Paulin, Tom. 'Guilty Dreams'. *New Statesman* 10 Feb 1978: 193–194.

Redmond, John. 'Troublesome Times and People'. *Glasgow Herald* 9 Feb 1978 [FP MS 160, Series 9].

Sage, Lorna. 'Domestic Warfare'. *London Observer* 26 Feb 1978 [FP MS 160, Series 9].

Stow, Randolph. 'Suffocation in Sydney'. *Times Literary Supplement* 4 Aug 1978 [FP MS 160, Series 9].

Vale, Adrian. 'Recent Short Stories'. *Irish Times* 9 May 1978 [FP MS 160, Series 9].

Moonlite

Barnes, Rory. 'A Most Engaging Lunatic Called Finbar'. *National Times* 24–30 May 1981: 52.

Brady, Veronica. 'The Absurdity of Necessity'. *Australian Book Review* 33 (Aug 1981): 1. Repr. 200 (May 1998): 18.

Clark, Manning. 'Entertaining and a Poser of Big Questions'. *Bulletin* 23 Jun 1981: 87, 89.

Cotter, Michael. 'The Experimenters'. *Overland* 88 (1982): 62–65.

Daniel, Helen. 'Bizarre Travels of a Larrikin Prophet'. *Age* 13 Jun 1981: 25.

Fitzgerald, Ross. Untitled. *Good Reading Guide*. Ed. Helen Daniel. Melbourne: McPhee Gribble, 1989. 76–77.

Gelder, Ken. Untitled. *Good Reading Guide*. Ed. Helen Daniel. Melbourne: McPhee Gribble, 1989. 77.

Keesing, Nancy. 'Moonliting Is Fun'. *Sydney Morning Herald* 6 Jun 1981: 46.

McKernan, Susan. Untitled. *Good Reading Guide*. Ed. Helen Daniel. Melbourne: McPhee Gribble, 1989. 77.

Oughton, Louise. 'Black, but Light Humour'. *Empire Times* 1987: 22 [FP MS 160, Series 9].

Pierce, Peter. 'Finding Their Range: Some Recent Australian Novels'. *Meanjin* 40.4 (1981): 522–528.

Rolls, Eric, Helen Frizell, and Elizabeth Harrower. 'Extracts from the Judges' Report for the NBC $10,000 Awards for Australian Literature 1981'. *Australian Book Review* 35 (Oct 1981): 1–4.

Thorne, Tim. Untitled. *Good Reading Guide*. Ed. Helen Daniel. Melbourne: McPhee Gribble, 1989. 77–78.

Plumbum

Armiger, Martin. 'Crazier than the Average Band'. *Independent Monthly* 7.4 (Oct 1995): 77.

Clancy, Laurie. 'Novelist Intoxicated by Language and Rock'n'Roll'. *Age* 28 Jan 1984: 13.

Daniel, Helen. 'Rocking to the Rhythms of Comic Chaos'. *Australian Book Review* 60 (May 1984): 18–19.

Dutton, Geoffrey. 'An Original and Some Vivid Variety'. *Bulletin* 20 Dec 1983: 62.

——. Untitled. *Good Reading Guide*. Ed. Helen Daniel. Melbourne: McPhee Gribble, 1989. 78.

Forshaw, Thelma. 'Penetrating Heavy Metal'. *Quadrant* 28.6 (Jun 1984): 86–87.

Fraser, Andrew. 'Cohesion Wanting'. *Canberra Times* 14 Apr 1984: 18.

Kepert, L. V. 'Feast of Local Fiction'. *Sun Herald* 13 Dec 1983.

Knight, Stephen. 'Compulsive or Repulsive—It Depends on Taste'. *Sydney Morning Herald* 14 Apr 1984: 41.

Mitchell, Adrian. 'Disjunctive Worlds That Never Really Make a Point'. *Australian* 24–25 Dec 1983: 14.

Ray, Mark. 'The Ups and Downs of Rock'n'Roll'. *Launceston Examiner* 17 Mar 1984 [FP MS 160, Series 9].

Taylor, Greg. 'Plumbum: David Foster Puts the Oz Rock Novel on the Map'. *Rock Australia Magazine* 20 Jan 1984 [FP MS 160, Series 9].

Thomas, Helen. 'Rock, Manipulation and Greed'. *National Times* 23 Dec 1983: 29.

Thorne, Tim. Untitled. *Good Reading Guide*. Ed. Helen Daniel. Melbourne: McPhee Gribble, 1989. 78.

Dog Rock

Anderson, Don. 'Dogged Pursuit of Rural Follies'. *National Times* 4–10 Jan 1985: 34.

Baranay, Inez. 'Characters Fantastic Populate Home-grown Trilogy'. *Sydney Morning Herald* 26 Jan 1985: 36.

Daniel, Helen. 'Monologue of a Postman a Comic Collage'. *Age* 26 Jan 1985: 12.

Dutton, Geoffrey. 'A Lethal Spider Under Dog Rock'. *Bulletin* 26 Feb 1985: 84–85.

——. Untitled. *Good Reading Guide*. Ed. Helen Daniel. Melbourne: McPhee Gribble, 1989. 78–79.

England, Katharine. 'Stumbling into Dog Rock, Cow Flat and Foggy Hollow'. *Advertiser* 23 Mar 1985: 6.

Goldsworthy, Kerryn. 'Community Notices'. *Australian Book Review* 71 (June 1985): 20.

Kepert, L. V. 'Foster's Dog: Comedy in All Directions'. *Sun Herald* 13 Jan 1985: 102.

Mitchell, Adrian. 'Surprise Touch of Nostalgia'. *Australian Weekend Magazine* 19–20 Jan 1985: 12.

Peek, Andrew. Untitled. *Good Reading Guide*. Ed. Helen Daniel. Melbourne: McPhee Gribble, 1989. 79.

Sen, Veronica. 'Promise Undelivered'. *Canberra Times* 9 Mar 1985: 20.

The Adventures of Christian Rosy Cross

Baker, Candida. 'A Not-So-Rosy Legend'. *Time* 15 Sep 1986: 71.

Cotter, Jane. 'Your Authentic Picaro: Perpetually Tumescent and Not Well-Off'. *Australian Book Review* 86 (Nov 1986): 7–8.

Daniel, Helen. 'Novel Treatment of Historic Hoax'. *Age* 23 Aug 1986: Saturday Extra 12.

England, Katharine. 'A Fantasy of Poor Christian's Upbringing'. *Advertiser* Aug 1986: 20.

Hanrahan, John. 'Heretic'. *National Times on Sunday* 7 Sep 1986: 38.

McKernan, Susan. 'Looking to Comedy for Some Pointers'. *Bulletin* 21 Oct 1986: 100.

McQueen, Humphrey. 'Humour's Alchemy of Light'. *Sydney Morning Herald* 30 Aug 1986: 42.

Mitchell, Adrian. 'An Alchemy of Words'. *Australian Weekend Magazine* 16–17 Aug 1986: 15.

Riemer, Andrew. Untitled. *Good Reading Guide*. Ed. Helen Daniel. Melbourne: McPhee Gribble, 1989. 79.

Thomas, Mark. 'Modern Concerns and Medieval Garb'. *Canberra Times* 29 Nov 1986: B3.

Testostero

Cromwell, Alexandra. 'Twins Embody Polarities in a Fictional Romp'. *Antipodes* 2.1 (1988): 60.

Daniel, Helen. 'Pastiche and Parody Run Amok'. *Age* 14 Feb 1987: 16.

Elliott, Ralph. 'A Further Comedy of Twinhood'. *Canberra Times* 25 Apr 87: B3.

Gollan, Myfanwy. 'Verbal Acrobatics'. *Sydney Morning Herald* 7 Feb 1987: 44.

Healey, Janet. *Books and Writing*, ABC [1987?] [FP MS 160].

Johnston, Martin. 'Expect Entrancing Double Trouble from the Twins in Surreal Venice'. *Times on Sunday* 8 Feb 1987: 27. Repr. *Martin Johnston: Selected*

Poems and Prose. Ed. Martin Johnston and John Tranter. St Lucia: University of Queensland Press, 1993. 226–228.

McKernan (Lever), Susan. 'It's All Done with Mirrors: Satire, Slapstick and an Old Comic Plot'. *Australian Book Review* 89 (Apr 1987): 23–24.

Mitchell, Adrian. 'Satiric Portrait of Our Travellers'. *Weekend Australian* 28 Feb–1 Mar 1987: 15.

Riemer, Andrew. Untitled. *Good Reading Guide*. Ed. Helen Daniel. Melbourne: McPhee Gribble, 1989. 79–80.

Rogers, Tom. 'Slice of Comic Oz Abroad without Crocodiles'. *Melbourne Times* 18 Mar 1987: 18.

Pale Blue Crochet Coathanger Cover

Box, John. 'Murder in Dog Rock'. *Sydney Morning Herald* 5 Aug 1988.

Condon, Matt. 'Adventures of a Postman Sleuth Make Sequel a "Coathanger"'. *Sun Herald* 7 Aug 1988: 92.

Daniel, Helen. 'Another Bite at Dog Rock'. *Age* 30 Jul 1988: Saturday Extra 14.

Doyle, Jeff. 'From the Outrageous to the Densely Funny'. *Canberra Times* 21 Jan 1981: B4.

Marshall, Jennifer. Untitled. *Empire Times* Sep 1988: 38 [FP MS 160, Series 9].

McKernan (Lever), Susan. 'Dog Rock Day'. *Bulletin* 23 Aug 1988: 116–117.

Peek, Andrew. 'Inventive Fiction Probes Social Changes'. *Antipodes* 3.1 (1989): 62.

——. Untitled. *Good Reading Guide*. Ed. Helen Daniel. Melbourne: McPhee Gribble, 1989. 80.

Porter, Dorothy. 'Sleuth Sorts Out the Mail of the Species'. *Weekend Australian* 30–31 Jul 1988: 15.

Riemer, Andrew. 'Respectable, but They Fail to Shine'. *Sydney Morning Herald* 30 Jul 1988: 77.

Scullen, Edward D. Untitled. *Washington Book Review* (Sept 1985): 19 [FP MS 160, Series 9].

Hitting the Wall

Atkinson, Tim. 'A Modern Fanatic in a Study of Extremes'. *West Australian* 18 Mar 1989 [FP MS 160, Series 9].

Birskys, Betty. Untitled. *Span* 29 (1989): 115–116.

Brissenden, R. F. 'Walls That Do a Prison Make'. *Australian Weekend Magazine* 11–12 Mar 1989: 10.

De Bono, Christopher. 'Quirky, on Purpose'. *Melbourne Herald* 24 Feb 1989 [FP MS 160, Series 9].

England, Katharine. 'Light Relief from Serious Foster'. *Advertiser* 11 Feb 1989: 11.

Fitzgerald, Ross. Untitled. *Good Reading Guide*. Ed. Helen Daniel. Melbourne: McPhee Gribble, 1989. 80.

Goldsworthy, Kerryn. 'Breaking the Angst Barrier'. *Age* 4 Mar 1989: Saturday Extra 11.

Hugo, Giles. 'Fun Filler for Those Education Gaps'. *Saturday Mercury* 18 Feb 1989: 20.

Mann, Charles W. 'Novellas Focus on Jogging and Thieving'. *Antipodes* 4.1 (1990): 66.

Pons, Xavier. 'Unsettled Heroes: David Foster's *Hitting the Wall*.' *AFRAM newsletter* 30 (Dec 1989): 61.

Roberts, Mark. 'The Pathetic Jogger'. *Australian Book Review* 109 (Apr 1989): 34–35.

Thomas, Mark. 'Writing That Proves You Can Make a Joke Out of Anything'. *Canberra Times* 11 Mar 1989: B4.

Mates of Mars

Daniel, Helen. 'Matters Male, Martial and Mystical'. *Age* 10 Aug 1991: Saturday Extra 8.

Dowling, Terry. 'Yen for Yin Among Macho Mates'. *Weekend Australian* 17–18 Aug 1991: Rev 5.

Doyle, Jeff. 'Heart of Australian Darkness'. *Canberra Times* 24 Aug 1991: C9.

Hertzberg, Andrew. 'Mates of Mars'. *Overland* 125 (1991): 95–96.

Johnson, Rob. 'Tensions in Mateship Away from Tourists'. *Advertiser* 28 Sep 1991: 14.

Morgan, Peter. 'Savagely Funny but Satire Lacks Plot'. *West Australian* 12 Oct 1991 [FP MS 160, Series 9].

Peek, Andrew. 'Foster's Do—or How to Kick Your Way to Peace'. *Australian Book Review* 133 (Aug 1991): 12–13.

Sorensen, Rosemary. 'It's Not Nice out There Among the Boofheads'. *Sydney Morning Herald* (3 Aug 1991): 42.

——. 'Foster vs the World (and Me)'. *Australian Book Review* 133 (Aug 1991): 13–14.

Waldren, Murray. 'The Master of Martial Farce'. *Weekend Australian* 10–11 Aug 1991: Rev 4.

The Glade Within the Grove

Adair, Tom. 'Kaleidoscope of Weird Scenes in the Outback'. *Scotland on Sunday* 11 Aug 1996 [FP MS 160, Series 9].

Ahmet, Keri. 'The Glade Within the Grove'. *Southern Highland News* 1 May 1996: 10.

Barnacle, Hugo. 'Taking the Kombi to the Wonga Vine'. London *Independent Weekend* 17 Aug 1996 [FP MS 160, Series 9].

Blay, John. 'Place Yourself in Foster care'. *Republican* 4 Sep 1997: 17.

Bowers, Tim. 'Living in Terrible Times'. *LiNQ* 24.1 (May 1997): 83–84.

Bradley, Paul. 'A Phrygian Good Read'. *On Dit* 24 Feb 1997 [FP MS 160, Series 9].

Butwell, Murray. 'Reader Lost in Words'. *Launceston Examiner* 2 Aug 1997 [FP MS 160, Series 9].

Clancy, Laurie. 'D'Arcy Shares a Gippsland Gospel'. *Sunday Age* 3 Aug 1997: Agenda 7.

Colston, Leo. '*The Glade Within the Grove*'. *Time Out* (UK) 7 Aug 1996: 56.

Daniel, Helen. 'Down in the Glades'. *Age* 2 Mar 1996: Saturday Extra 8.

Dutton, Geoffrey. 'Saga and Ballad in the Valley'. *Australian Book Review* 178 (Feb–Mar 1996): 41–42.

Elliott, Ralph. 'David Foster's Masterpiece'. *Canberra Times* 14 Jun 1997: C11.

Fleming, Juliet. 'The Origins of Oz'. *Times Literary Supplement* 16 Aug 1996: 22.

Gale, Patrick. 'Moral Extremity in the Antipodes'. *Daily Telegraph* (UK) 14 Sep 1996 [FP MS 160, Series 9].

Greenwood, Gillian. 'The Wonderful Baron of Oz'. *Times* (UK) 22 Aug 1996 [FP MS 160, Series 9].

Lofthouse, Jacqui. 'Too Clever for the Job of Telling a Story'. *Literary Review* (Aug 1996): 45–6.

MacDougall, Carl. 'A Struggle to Impress'. *Glasgow Herald* 31 Aug 1996: W15.

Melmoth, John. 'Fruits of the Forest'. *Sunday Times* (UK) 11 Aug 1996 [FP MS 160, Series 9].

Scott-Moncrieff, Michael. 'New Age Down Under'. *Tablet* 11 Jan 1997: 47.

Padel, Ruth. '*The Glade Within the Grove*'. *Mail on Sunday* (UK) 27 Jul 1997: Night & Day 2.

Pender, Anne. 'Satire Is Savage, Yet Serious'. *Antipodes* 11.1 (Jun 1997): 48–49.

Pierce, Peter. 'Trapped in a '60s Dreamworld'. *Bulletin* 19 Mar 1996: 81.

Riemer, Andrew. 'Strange Rites in the Valley of No-return'. *Sydney Morning Herald* 1 Dec 1996.

——. 'After Demidenko'. *Voices* 7.2 (1997): 104–113.

Sharkey, Michael. 'Postman's Knock'. *Weekend Australian* 24–25 Feb 1996: Review 17.

The Ballad of Erinungarah

Buckridge, Pat. 'Poetry, Prophecy and Exhilaration'. *Courier-Mail* 7 Jun 1997: Weekend 9.

Bradley, Paul. 'No Gag Heading, Just Literary Genius x 2'. *On Dit* Aug 1997: 40.

Dale, Leigh. Untitled. *Journal of Australian Studies* 56 (1998): 189–192.

Dutton, Geoffrey. 'The Ballad That Is Part of the Novel'. *Australian Book Review* 192 (Jul 1997): 30–31.

Lever, Susan. Untitled. ABC Radio National, Book program (Jun 1997).

Matthews, David. 'What Is Going on Here?' *Australian Weekend Review* 5–6 Jul 1997: 9.

Riemer, Andrew. 'A Fertile Imagination'. *Sydney Morning Herald* 7 Jun 1997: Spectrum 9s.

Williams, Craig. 'Ballads, Bards and Bollocks'. *Overland* 148 (1997): 86–88.

In the New Country

'Hilarious Look at Aussie Moribund Wool Country'. *Irish News* (Belfast) 22 Feb 1999: 13.

Bantick, Christopher. 'Rollicking Rural Yarn with an Original Edge'. *Canberra Times* 30 May 1999: Sunday Times 18.

Condon, Matt. 'Back to the Bush'. *Sun Herald* 25 Apr 1999: Sunday life 28.

Daniel, Helen. 'A Demon Satirist Turns Resistance Fighter'. *Age* 10 Apr 1999: 6.

Davis, Brian. 'In the New Country'. *Time Out* (UK) 17–24 Mar 1999: 57.

Deevy, Patricia. 'Two Tales of the Irish in Oz'. *Image* Mar 1999 [FP MS 160, Series 9].

England, Katharine. 'Foster's Comic Return to the Glade'. *Advertiser* 26 Jun 1999: Weekend 19.

Fitzgerald, Michael. 'Making Fun'. *Time* 26 Apr 1999: 64–66.

Hunt, Kathy. 'Land Locked'. *Australian's Review of Books* 4.3 (Apr 1999): 21–22.

Lever, Susan. 'Foster's Satire'. *Australian Book Review* 210 (May 1999): 21–22.

Northover, Kylie. 'Staying In'. *TNT magazine* (London) 31 Jan 2000 [FP MS 160, Series 9].

Riemer, Andrew. 'An Exhilarating Ramble Round the Collapse of Rural Life'. *Sydney Morning Herald* 10 Apr 1999: Spectrum 9.

Sharkey, Michael. 'Dud and Dave Go to Vegas'. *Weekend Australian* 24–25 Apr 1999: Review 13.

Shone, Caroline. 'Echoes of Dylan Thomas'. *Bulletin* 27 Apr 1999: 120.

Sorensen, Rosemary. 'Crunch Go the Taboos'. *Courier-Mail* 3 Apr 1999: Weekend 7.

Studs and Nogs: Essays, 1987–98

(usually reviewed with *In the New Country*, above)

Tankard, Paul. 'The Stud Within the Nog'. *Quadrant* 43.7/8 (Jul–Aug 1999): 113–115.

Thomas, Mark. 'Beguiling Blend of Pugnacity, Acuity'. *Canberra Times* 17 Apr 1999: Panorama 23.

The Land Where Stories End

Chifley, Ephraem. 'Strangely Consoling'. *Adelaide Review* 213 (Jun 2001): 38.

Griffin, Michelle. 'Foster's Fairytale to Scare the Inner Child'. *Age* 5 May 2001: Saturday Extra 9.

Hunt, Kathy. 'Bonfire of the Inanities'. *Bulletin* 19 Jun 2001: 72.

Richardson, Owen. 'Foster's Fantasy for the Age'. *Australian Book Review* 230 (May 2001): 36–37.

Riemer, Andrew. 'One Hell of an Angel'. *Sydney Morning Herald* 7 Apr 2001: Spectrum 11.

Sharkey, Michael. 'Land of Hope and Story'. *Weekend Australian* 12–13 May 2001: Review 15.

Thomas, Mark. 'Tales of a Cheeky Angel'. *Canberra Times* 28 Apr 2001: Panorama 17.

The Year of Slow Food

Klugman, Matthew. 'Pastoral Dreams'. *Eureka Street* (Mar 2003): 42–43.

Index

www.ingramcontent.com/pod-product-compliance
Lightning Source LLC
Chambersburg PA
CBHW020947310726
48980CB00001B/84
* 9 7 8 1 9 3 4 0 4 3 9 8 1 *